THE PSYCHOLOGY OF SPORT AND PERFORMANCE INJURY

The use of psychological interventions and counselling strategies has become a central part of injury prevention, rehabilitation, and return to participation process. *The Psychology of Sport and Performance Injury: An Interprofessional Case-Based Approach* is the first book to offer students, academic scholars, and practitioners case studies that are grounded in psychological theory and empirical evidence, with a specific focus on addressing psychological aspects of sport and performance injuries in an interprofessional manner.

This book presents nine "real-life inspired" fictional sport and performance injury cases. It demonstrates the viability and effectiveness of adopting an interprofessional, person-centered approach to injury, rehabilitation, and return to participation process. Each case is focused on a particular phase of rehabilitation, with specific attention placed on relevant biopsychosocial concerns. Within each chapter, a theoretical, conceptual, and empirical analysis of the case is presented followed by detailed accounts on how a range of professionals and significant others can work alongside each other to provide a holistic care for the injured performer within their own competencies.

The Psychology of Sport and Performance Injury: An Interprofessional Case-Based Approach emphasizes the importance of holistic, interprofessional approach to sport and performance injury rehabilitation. This book is a vital resource for upper-level students, academic scholars, and applied practitioners from a range of sport and performance related disciplines such as athletic training, kinesiology, occupational therapy, physical therapy, sport psychology, sports therapy, and strength and conditioning. It offers a valuable reading for a range of individuals and professionals who are involved in sport and performance injury prevention, rehabilitation, and return to participation process.

Monna Arvinen-Barrow is a British Psychological Society chartered psychologist working as Associate Professor in sport and performance psychology at the University of Wisconsin-Milwaukee, USA, and as an online contributing faculty at the University of St Augustine for Health Sciences, USA. She is the co-editor of the 2013 book *The Psychology of Sport Injury and Rehabilitation* and has an interest and expertise in biopsychosocial aspects of sport and performance injury occurrence, rehabilitation, and return to participation process. In 2016, Monna received the Dorothy V. Harris award from the Association for Applied Sport Psychology for her distinguished contributions in the field of sport and exercise psychology as a scholar/practitioner.

Damien Clement is Assistant Dean in the Honors College and Associate Professor at West Virginia University, Morgantown, West Virginia, USA. Damien is a certified athletic trainer (ATC) and a national certified counselor (NCC) as well as an Association for Applied Sport Psychology certified mental performance consultant (CMPC). His research interests span both sport and exercise psychology and athletic training. In 2014, Damien was the recipient of the Dorothy V. Harris award by the Association for Applied Sport Psychology for his distinguished contributions in the field of sport and exercise psychology as a scholar/practitioner.

THE PSYCHOLOGY OF SPORT AND PERFORMANCE INJURY

An Interprofessional Case-Based Approach

Edited by Monna Arvinen-Barrow and Damien Clement

LONDON AND NEW YORK

First published 2019
by Routledge
2 Park Square, Milton Park, Abingdon, Oxon OX14 4RN

and by Routledge
52 Vanderbilt Avenue, New York, NY 10017

Routledge is an imprint of the Taylor & Francis Group, an informa business

British Library Cataloguing in Publication Data
A catalogue record for this book is available from the British Library

Library of Congress Cataloging-in-Publication Data
Names: Arvinen-Barrow, Monna, editor. | Clement, Damien, editor.
Title: The psychology of sport and performance injury : an interprofessional case-based approach / Edited by Monna Arvinen-Barrow and Damien Clement.
Description: Abingdon, Oxon ; New York, NY : Routledge, 2019. | Includes bibliographical references and index.
Identifiers: LCCN 2018055565| ISBN 9780815362685 (hardback) | ISBN 9780815362692 (pbk.) | ISBN 9781351111591 (ebook)
Subjects: LCSH: Sports--Psychological aspects--Case studies. | Sports injuries--Psychological aspects--Case studies. | Sports injuries--Rehabilitation--Case studies. | Sports medicine--Case studies.
Classification: LCC GV706.4 .P7846 2019 | DDC 617.1/027--dc23
LC record available at https://lccn.loc.gov/2018055565

ISBN: 978-0-8153-6268-5 (hbk)
ISBN: 978-0-8153-6269-2 (pbk)
ISBN: 978-1-351-11159-1 (ebk)

Typeset in Bembo
by Taylor & Francis Books

Äidin ei niin pienelle enkelille, Amielle (to Mom's not so little angel, Amie) and all those healthcare professionals who just know when their patient needs some explicit 2Pac to get through the treatment. You rock.
Monna

Family is everything and without you all, I am nothing. This book is a testament and direct reflection of your unwavering support of me and my career goals.
Damien

CONTENTS

ILLUSTRATIONS

Figure

Tables

ABOUT THE CONTRIBUTORS

Monna Arvinen-Barrow (PhD, CPsychol, AFBPsS, UPV sert.) is Associate Professor in the Department of Kinesiology - Integrative Health Care & Performance Unit, at the University of Wisconsin-Milwaukee, USA and an online contributing faculty at the University of St Augustine for Health Sciences, USA. Monna is a chartered psychologist (CPsychol), an associate fellow (AFBPsS) of the British Psychological Society, a Finnish Psychological Association certified mental performance coach and exercise practitioner (UPV sert.), and an elected expert member of the Finnish Sport Psychology Association. She is a former professional figure- and synchronized-skating coach, and regularly consults with athletes from different sports and competitive levels. She is also an active member of the Association for Applied Sport Psychology (AASP), and received the 2016 Dorothy V. Harris award from AASP for her distinguished contributions in the field of sport and exercise psychology as a scholar/practitioner. Monna has a specialist interest and expertise in biopsychosocial aspects of sport and performance injury occurrence, rehabilitation, and return to participation process. Her research and practice is transdisciplinary, and in her work, she draws from her diverse professional and personal experiences. Monna has one daughter, Amie, and enjoys traveling, Orangetheory® Fitness workouts, and sewing.

Theresa Bianco (PhD) is Senior Lecturer in the Department of Psychology at Concordia University in Montreal, Canada, where she teaches sport psychology, health psychology, and research methodology. Her research interests center on recovery from sport injury, with a special focus the role of coach support in the recovery process. Theresa's work has been published in research articles and book chapters, and presented at international conferences. Theresa balances her teaching with sport psychology consulting, providing sport psychology services mainly to varsity and elite level athletes. She also serves on the Science and Innovation

Committee of the Institut National du Sport in Montreal. Theresa enjoys landscape photography and watercolor painting – and most of all, nature walks with Bella, her Bernese Mountain dog.

William Brown (PhD, RN, FNP-BC) is a Lieutenant Colonel in the U.S. Army Nurse Corps and Chief, Center for Nursing Science and Clinical Inquiry (CNSCI) at Womack Army Medical Center, Fort Bragg, NC. His primary research interests are motivation (Self Determination Theory) and exercise behavior. Other research interests include bone stress injuries, injury prevention and rehabilitation, blood flow restriction (BFR) training, and human performance optimization. He also sees patients on a limited basis in the Department of Family Medicine.

Damien Clement (PhD, ATC, NCC, CMPC) is Assistant Dean in the Honors College and Associate Professor at West Virginia University, USA. Damien is a certified athletic trainer (ATC) and a national certified counselor (NCC) as well as an Association for Applied Sport Psychology certified mental performance consultant (CMPC). He is an active member in the Association for Applied Sport Psychology (AASP), National Athletic Trainers' Association (NATA), and West Virginia Athletic Trainers' Association (WVATA). In 2014, Damien was the recipient of the Dorothy V. Harris award from the Association for Applied Sport Psychology for his distinguished contributions in the field of sport and exercise psychology as a scholar/practitioner. In 2015, Damien was one of the recipients of West Virginia University's Foundation Award for Outstanding Teaching. His research interests span both sport and exercise psychology and athletic training. Damien is married with two children and he enjoys hanging out with his family, gardening, running, and playing and watching soccer.

Ashley Coker-Cranney (PhD, CMPC) is Adjunct Instructor of Sport, Exercise, and Performance Psychology in the College of Physical Activity and Sport Sciences at West Virginia University, USA. She is also owner and sport performance consultant at MindRight Performance Consulting, LLC, USA. Ashley is a member of the Association for Applied Sport Psychology, North American Society for the Sociology of Sport, and American Psychological Association, Division 47 (Society for Sport, Exercise and Performance Psychology). She has research and practical interests and expertise in sport deviance, specifically with regards to overconformity to the sport ethic and related sub-clinical indicators. Ashley's professional goals include elucidating the intricacies of sport conformity and developing practical methods for addressing sport overconformity to maximize participant performance and satisfaction. Ashley is a mother of three small children and enjoys being outdoors with her husband and children as often as possible.

Jessica Ford (MS) is a PhD student in the Department of Kinesiology - Integrative Health Care & Performance Unit at the University of Wisconsin-Milwaukee, USA, studying sport and performance psychology with a cognate in community counseling. Jessica has taught psychological aspects of sport and exercise at the undergraduate level, and she is working toward her Certified Mental Performance Consultant (CMPC) certification from the Association for Applied Sport Psychology. Her research interests primarily concern novel applications of sport psychology to nontraditional populations, such as performing artists. In her free time, Jessica enjoys singing, playing guitar, and running marathons.

Päivi Frantsi (PhD) is a certified sport psychologist (Finland), work- and occupational health psychologist, and an Eye Movement Desensitization and Reprocessing (EMDR) trained therapist. She is the co-owner of her family company, Consultants Frantsi in Vierumäki, Finland. She has been working with athletes for almost three decades, and has consulted with shooters, rally drivers, figure skaters, and aesthetic group gymnasts. Her main interests include helping athletes reach their best and promoting their well- being. Päivi has wealth of experience as a coach educator/trainer and she offers professional guidance to sport coaches. Päivi has published several articles, books, and book chapters in mental training and sport psychology.

Leanne Griffiths (PhD) is Head of Department for Sport and Exercise Science at St Mary's University in Twickenham, London. She contributes to teaching on the BSc/MSc Sport Rehabilitation and MSc Physiotherapy programs, whilst also supporting students with post-graduate research projects. Leanne is a charted physiotherapist with the Health Care & Professions Council (HCPC) and is a member of the Chartered Society of Physiotherapy (CSP). She has a special interest in lower limb biomechanics, neuromuscular electrical stimulation (NMES) for rehabilitation, and recreational return to sport after injury. Leanne is a mother of two young boys, and uses running as a means of relaxation and brain space generation!

Jordan Hamson-Utley (PhD, ATC) is Program Director of the Master of Health Science and Associate Professor in the College of Health Sciences at the University of St. Augustine for Health Sciences (USAHS), USA. She designed the degree program to expand the role of the athletic trainer on the interprofessional healthcare team. Jordan was instrumental in starting the interprofessional education (IPE) effort at USAHS and aligns her research agenda with studying the effectiveness of IPE to create behavioral change in practicing athletic trainers. She has a special interest and expertise in biopsychosocial aspects of sport injury rehabilitation, recovery, and return to sport/school/life following concussion. Jordan is a certified athletic trainer (ATC) and a member of the National Athletic Trainers' Association (NATA). Jordan serves the NATA as a committee member of the Post Professional Education Committee (PPEC) and has previously served on the Professional Development Committee and various workgroups. Clinically, she has worked with athletes from all levels, including the United States soccer teams, Olympic athletes, and extreme sport athletes.

Allison Hetrick (MEd, ATC) is a certified athletic trainer (ATC) and strength and conditioning specialist. She is the program director for the Athletic Training program at West Virginia University after previously serving as the clinical coordinator. She worked in Division I athletics for 15 years with a variety of sports such as football, baseball, women's basketball, tennis, cheerleading, men's and women's soccer, and gymnastics. Her academic interests include rehabilitation of injury, injury prevention, and emergency medicine. Allison is an avid adventurer who is always planning the next excursion into the great outdoors.

Ken Ildefonso (MA, LAT) is a PhD student in the Department of Kinesiology – Integrative Health Care & Performance Unit at the University of Wisconsin-Milwaukee, USA, studying the psychological aspects of sports medicine. His primary research interests pertain to the psychological aspects of chronic athletic injury. Ken is a certified athletic trainer (ATC) and a member of the National Athletic Trainers' Association, and provides outreach athletic training coverage in the Milwaukee area. Ken is also a Wisconsin Area Health Education Centers alumni, an organization that aims to educate and facilitate community-based health care in Wisconsin's less fortunate communities. Ken spends his leisure time endurance training and is a three-time Ironman triathlete.

Russ Johnson (MFA) is Associate Professor and Director of Jazz Studies at the University of Wisconsin-Parkside, USA and Adjunct Instructor of Trumpet at Carthage College, WI, USA. In 2016, Russ was honored with the "Stella Gray Teaching Excellence Award" by University of Wisconsin-Parkside. As a jazz trumpeter and composer, Russ has produced eight recordings as a leader or co-leader, and has appeared on more than 100 recordings as a sideman. His recordings consistently receive critical acclaim from all major jazz publications, and he appeared in Down Beat magazine's critics' poll as a rising star in the trumpet category in 2018. Russ has performed in more than 40 countries across the globe.

Cindra Kamphoff (PhD, CMPC) is Professor in the Department of Human Performance at Minnesota State University, Mankato where she helps coordinate the graduate program in Sport and Exercise Psychology. Cindra is also the Director and Founder of the Center for Sport and Performance Psychology. She is a Certified Mental Performance Consultant (CMPC) with the Association for Applied Sport Psychology and operates her own private practice where she provides mental training with the Minnesota Vikings. Her first book, *Beyond grit: Ten powerful practices to gain the high-performance edge*, was an Amazon bestseller. Cindra lives in Minnesota with her husband and two boys and enjoys boating, marathoning and going to sporting events.

Satu Kaski (PhD) is a certified sport psychologist (Finland), and an Eye Movement Desensitization and Reprocessing (EMDR) trained therapist. Satu is the owner of Clear mind Oy, Helsinki, Finland. She has over 20 years of experience working as psychotherapist and sport psychologist. Satu has extensively studied therapeutic change of athletes dealing with competition anxiety, and her doctoral dissertation focused on coaches' well-being. She has also developed mental health survey and clinical interview protocols that are widely used in Finnish sport settings. She has published several articles, books, and book chapters in sport psychology and athletes' mental health.

Corey Oshikoya (MEd, ATC, CSCS, EMT-B) is Assistant Athletic Director for Sports Medicine/Head Athletic Trainer at Loyola University Chicago, USA. Oshikoya comes to Chicago after spending 16 seasons as an assistant athletic trainer with the Denver Broncos Football Club of the National Football League. Oshikoya has presented at many national, district and state sports medicine symposiums. He has been a committee member on the Ethnic Diversity Advisory Committee of the National Athletic Trainers' Association and committees for the Board of Certification. He has also been a board member for the Professional Football Athletic Trainers Society, Colorado Athletic Trainers' Association and Rocky Mountain Athletic Trainers' Association. He has also served on executive boards and in leadership positions for two faith-based congregations. He earned his Bachelor of Arts degree from West Virginia University and his Master of Education degree in Athletic Training/Sports Medicine from the University of Virginia. He is currently pursuing his doctorate in Education at the University of St. Augustine.

Melissa Paré is a masters student in the Department of Kinesiology and Physical Education at Wilfrid Laurier University, Waterloo, Ontario, Canada. Her career as a varsity athlete inspired her to pursue an education in sport psychology and human performance. Her current research is focused on athlete retirement transition, psychological responses to stress in sport, and coping styles and behaviors in the performance environment. Melissa has a passion for sport, coaching and wellness.

Leslie Podlog (PhD)'s research focuses on health psychology issues, primarily the psychological aspects of injury rehabilitation and athlete burnout. He has published over 85 peer reviewed journal articles and book chapters. His interests in the psychology of injury recovery stem from his personal injury experiences as a former amateur wrestler at Simon Fraser University in Burnaby, British Columbia, Canada. Following completion of his doctoral studies (2006) at the University of Western Australia, Les held faculty positions at Charles Sturt University (Bathurst, Australia), the German Sport University (Cologne, Germany), and Texas Tech University (Lubbock, Texas). He has been a faculty member at the University of Utah since 2011 where teaches classes in sport psychology and the psychology of sport injury. Outside of work, Les enjoys hiking, skiing, and spending time with his family.

Nettie Puglisi Freshour (RDN) is Teaching Associate Professor and Director of the Graduate Dietetic Internship in the Davis College at West Virginia University,

USA. She is a licensed and registered dietitian with the Academy of Nutrition and Dietetics as well as a certified specialist in Sports Dietetics. Nettie is also a member of the Nutrition Registry for the US Olympic Committee. Before moving to the Davis College, Nettie was the Director of Sports Nutrition at WVU in the Athletic Department for five years and served as their nutrition consultant for ten years prior. In her private practice, Nettie specializes in athletes and eating disorders. She lives in Morgantown with her husband and two children. Nettie enjoys her children's many activities, reading, exercise, good food, and family time.

Claudio Robazza (PhD) is Associate Professor in the Department of Medicine and Aging Sciences at the University of Chieti-Pescara, Italy. As a sport psychologist, he has been working with top level athletes of different sports, including golf, archery, modern pentathlon, rugby, track and field, and shooting. He has conducted field-based studies in physical education, motor learning, and sport performance domains, and his primary research interest is in the area of performance-related emotions, performance optimization, and motor learning. In the 2015, Claudio received the Ema Geron Award from the FEPSAC (European Federation of Sport Psychology) in recognition of his national contribution to the development of sport and exercise psychology. In the same year, he also received the Diploma of Honour – Bronze Medal from the ISSF (International Shooting Sport Federation) in appreciation of his service to the shooting sports. Claudio has two sons and enjoys challenging them, without much chance of success, in a number of sports, including running, biking, swimming, and rugby.

Arielle Rousseau (BMSc, BSc, CAT) is an athletic therapist in Montreal, Canada. She is a retired competitive gymnast and former gymnastics coach. Arielle has worked as a therapist with multiple teams at national and international sporting events, and served as head athletic therapist for the McGill University soccer team. Arielle recently joined a practice where she treats athletic and non-athletic populations, and also provides strength and conditioning coaching. She continues to serve as Head Athletic Therapist for a local swim club, providing therapy, leading injury prevention initiatives, and designing strength and conditioning programs for entry up to elite level athletes. Arielle keeps fit by cycling and hiking nature trails with her dog. She also enjoys playing music, especially in the company of friends.

Montse C. Ruiz (PhD, UPV sert.) is Senior Lecturer of sport and exercise psychology at the Faculty of Sport and Health Sciences of the University of Jyväskylä, Finland. Her research interests involve emotional regulation and the study of emotional and motivational components of performance-related experiences. She is a Finnish Psychological Association certified mental performance coach and exercise practitioner (UPV sert.), and has worked with athletes in different sports, levels, and countries. Montse is a board member of national and international Sport and Exercise Psychology associations.

Hayley Russell (PhD) is Assistant Professor in the Department of Health and Exercise Science at Gustavus Adolphus College in Saint Peter, MN. Her research interests are in psychosocial aspects of sport-related injury and lifelong health and physical activity behavior of athletes. Hayley enjoys running, reading, and traveling.

Jessica Tidswell (DPT) is Assistant Professor in the Department of Physical Therapy and Athletic Training at the University of Utah in Salt Lake City, USA where she is also the clinical education coordinator for the Athletic Training Program and a physical therapist and athletic trainer for Utah Athletics. She is a physical therapist, athletic trainer, board-certified clinical specialist in Sports Physical Therapy, corrective exercise specialist and certified strength and conditioning specialist. Jessica has been involved with Paralympic sports since 2002 and has been an international classifier since 2009. She currently serves on the Classification Advisory Panel for Para Alpine Skiing and Para Snowboard for the International Paralympic Committee. Jessica has been involved with Para Surfing with the International Surfing Association since 2016. She is an avid skier, photographer, outdoor enthusiast and animal lover.

Jill Tracey (PhD) is Associate Professor in the Department of Kinesiology and Physical Education at Wilfrid Laurier University, Waterloo, Ontario, Canada. She is an active member of the Association for Applied Sport Psychology (AASP). Her research program is focused on the psychosocial aspects of injury and rehabilitation, ranging from issues surrounding sustaining an injury, through rehabilitation, to return to sport. As well, she is interested in transition and retirement from sport and lifelong physical activity behaviors. Jill enjoys running, road cycling, mountain biking, spending as much time as possible in nature, and is a voracious reader.

Dana K. Voelker (PhD, CMPC) is Assistant Professor of Sport, Exercise, and Performance Psychology in the College of Physical Activity and Sport Sciences at West Virginia University, USA. As a researcher, Dana is committed to generating scientific knowledge to inform the psychosocial wellbeing and performance of children, adolescents, and young adults in sport, exercise, and physical activity contexts. She has been the recipient of over 25 academic honors and awards, including the West Virginia University Foundation Award for Outstanding Teaching and the 2018 Dorothy V. Harris Memorial Award from the Association for Applied Sport Psychology. She was a University Distinguished Fellow at Michigan State University. Dana enjoys the outdoors including hiking and biking, spends her spare time completing DIY projects, and is passionate about animal rescue.

Ross Wadey (PhD) is Reader in Sport Psychology at St Mary's University (London) and a chartered psychologist with the British Psychological Society. His research operates at the intersection of psychology and sociology, and at the forefront of advancing knowledge on three themes: well-being following amputation(s) and the role of physical activity; prevention of and rehabilitation from sporting injuries; and post-traumatic growth following adversity. He is Chair of the Injury and Rehabilitation Research Group (IRRG) at St Mary's University and is also a trustee to the charity LimbPower that aims to engage amputees and individuals with limb impairments in physical activity to improve quality of life and aid lifelong rehabilitation. Ross is married to Becky and has two children, Phoebe and George.

David Zilberman (MEd) is a physical education teacher at Vanier College in Montreal Canada. David is also an eight-time Canadian wrestling champion, and a 2008 Olympian. He is a level 3 NCCP (National Coaching Certification Program) certified coach and is the head wrestling coach (men) at Concordia University, and also an assistant coach (men and women) with the Montreal Wrestling Club. David has coached multiple national champions, national team athletes and world medalists. He is also a published photographer and accomplished musician, with a grade 10 classical piano certification from the McGill University Music Conservatory.

FOREWORD

Earlier in my life, I worked as a coach for a competitive male handball team in Sweden. One year, at the beginning of the pre-season, my team played several friendly games aimed to improve the team's level of fitness for the forthcoming competitive season. In one of these games, two of my players unfortunately sustained similar severe injuries, that is, a torn anterior cruciate ligament (ACL) injury and a torn ACL and meniscus injury. Since both players were physically strong and skilled individuals, this was a major drawback for the team, but above all, this was a stressful situation for the injured players. Even though they experienced similar injuries, during the same game, had similar levels of fitness, their speed of recovery was very different. In fact, the player who suffered the torn ACL and meniscus injury rehabilitated faster than expected and came back to play at the end of the season without complications. The player with the ACL injury never managed to get back to play. A key question to ask at this point of the story is: "How is this possible given the above background?" An important piece of the answer relates to the psychological profiles of the players, their surrounding support network, and the quality of support given during the demanding rehabilitation period.

The Psychology of Sport and Performance Injury: An Interprofessional Case-Based Approach presents several important answers to the above-stated question. It is grounded on, and centered around, the importance and organization of a well-composed and communicative support team for injured performers. The book postulates that any and all individuals involved in the process of helping injured athletes and performers undergoing a demanding rehabilitation period should work together. The underpinning theme of the book is that the process of working together is a team-based approach, aimed at identifying key factors of concern, as well as to design and deliver multidimensional treatment plans and interventions. In the nine "real-life inspired" fictional cases presented, the book creatively provides central and systematic answers to the above-stated question.

The Psychology of Sport and Performance Injury: An Interprofessional Case-Based Approach highlights the importance of working together in an interprofessional manner during sport and performance injury rehabilitation. The book also captures the synergies of this process, by creating and sharing each other's expertise fields for the patient's best. The dictum "the whole is greater than the sum of its parts," formulated by the German-American psychologist Kurt Lewin in the 1940s, certainly applies to the logic of this book. The holistic perspective of the injury, consisting of biopsychosocial ingredients, also adds an expectation that different fields of expertise should work together during the rehabilitation, which is clearly outlined in the book.

For each of the nine cases presented, there is a repeated and appealing structure of sub-headings that helps the reader to follow and compare the development of an appropriate psychological intervention to address the identified key factors. Within applied sport psychology practice, one issue of concern is addressing clinical psychological issues when such arise in the consultancy process, and how these are professionally handled. In this book, each chapter author carefully discusses the issues of ethical considerations and need(s) for referral in relation to the case presented, adding credibility to the narrative of the stories and the process of referral.

Two special matters caught my attention whilst reading the manuscript. The first matter relates to the importance to scientifically position each case in a theoretical model to facilitate applied work. As such, the integrated model of psychological responses to the sport injury and rehabilitation process (Wiese-Bjornstal, Smith, Shaffer, & Morrey, 1998) appears to be a suitable framework advocated by many of the authors. Another example of a suitable theoretical model used is the multilevel model of sport injury (Wadey, Day, Cavallerio, & Martinelli, 2018). Using appropriate theoretical models can help explain injured performers' responses to their situation, and assist the reader in understanding the development of the interprofessional plan of care. It is my conviction that combining *science* (e.g., theoretical model and empirical evidence) and *art* (e.g., ability to listen and to communicate credibly) in a balanced way creates good conditions for constructive team-based work and can facilitate beneficial rehabilitation outcomes. An interesting note in this context is that recent research found the incidence of severe injuries for players in European elite football clubs was significantly higher for teams with a low quality of communication between the head coach/manager and the medical team than teams with moderate or high-quality communication scores (Ekstrand, Lundqvist, Davison, D'Hooghe, & Pensgaard, 2018).

The second matter that caught my attention relates to the possible outcomes of the "real-life inspired" fictional sport and performance injury cases, the plans of care, and the case updates. My own applied experience of helping long-term injured athletes indicates that, in most cases, the rehabilitation results in beneficial biopsychosocial outcomes such as increased quality of life and a safe return to sport. However, in some cases, physical and psychosocial complications arise that challenge and prolong the rehabilitation process. For some, the injury can ultimately lead to an end of a career, a case that is suitably described in Chapter 10. This is a great addition to the book, as it is important for the reader to understand how to assist injured athletes and performers in such vulnerable situations (prolonged rehabilitation and/or career ending injury) in an interprofessional manner.

Circling back to the story told at the beginning of the foreword, it is tempting to conclude that the player who did not succeed in his rehabilitation might have had a different outcome had his rehabilitation been an interprofessional, and case-based in nature. After reading *The Psychology of Sport and Performance Injury: An Interprofessional Case-Based Approach,* I am convinced that the player in question could have returned back to competitive handball had his rehabilitation plan been designed in close collaboration with experts from sports medicine, sport psychology, and other relevant and related disciplines. It is my humble opinion that this type of cooperation is the future of sport and performance injury, and the big winner in the process is the injured individual.

Urban Johnson
Professor of Psychology and Sport
Halmstad University, Sweden

References

Ekstrand, J., Lundqvist, D., Davison, M., D'Hooghe, M., & Pensgaard, A. M. (2018). Communication quality between the medical team and the head coach/manager is associated with injury burden and player availability in elite football clubs. *British Journal of Sports Medicine*, 1–6. doi:10.1136/bjsports-2018-099411.

Wadey, R., Day, M., Cavallerio, F., & Martinelli, L. (2018). The multi-level model of sport injury: Can coaches impact and be impacted by injury? In R. Thelwell & M. Dicks (Eds.), *Professional advances in sports coaching: Research and practice.* Abingdon: Routledge.

Wiese-Bjornstal, D. M., Smith, A. M., Shaffer, S. M., & Morrey, M. A. (1998). An integrated model of response to sport injury: Psychological and sociological dynamics. *Journal of Applied Sport Psychology, 10*(1), 46–69. doi:10.1080/10413209808406377.

PREFACE

Monna Arvinen-Barrow and Damien Clement

Even in our individually oriented culture, teams are now ubiquitous in most areas of science, work, and art—teams predominate in aviation, the military, business, space exploration, academia, and health care. (McDaniel & Salas, 2018, p. 305)

Harm to the human body sustained while participating in sport and performance-related activities is a commonly known health concern worldwide for participants of all ages (Conn, Annest, & Gilchrist, 2003; Konttinen et al., 2011; Maffulli, Giuseppe Longo, Gougoulias, Caine, & Denaro, 2010; Uitenbroek, 1996). Specifically within the context of sport and performance, injuries are generally defined as "trauma to the body or its parts that result in at least temporary, but sometimes permanent physical disability and inhibition of motor function" (Berger, Pargman, & Weinberg, 2007, p. 186). Sport and performance related injuries are typically associated with a range of biopsychosocial antecedents and post-injury responses. Some of the more prominent injury antecedents include, but are not limited to, poor training methods, musculoskeletal deficiencies, unsafe exercising environments, and a wide range of biopsychosocial factors (Prentice, 2017). Post-injury responses, on the other hand, include a range of cognitive appraisals of self, the injury, rehabilitation, and return to sport process, emotional responses such as anger, denial, and frustration, as well as behavioral responses such as restricted mobility, adherence compliance problems, and affected interpersonal relationships (Johnston & Carroll, 1998; Ruddock-Hudson, O'Halloran, & Murphy, 2012; Tracey, 2003).

Building on existing psychology of injury literature (for more details on the theoretical foundations, empirical evidence, and applied applications to date, please see Arvinen-Barrow & Walker, 2013; Brewer & Redmond, 2017; Granquist, Hamson-Utley, Kenow, & Stiller-Ostrowski, 2014; Heil, 1993; Kolt & Andersen,

2004; Pargman, 2007; Ray & Wiese-Bjornstal, 1999; Taylor, Stone, Mullin, Ellenbecker, & Walgenbach, 2003; Taylor & Taylor, 1997), this book is founded on the premise that sport and performance injury prevention, rehabilitation, and return to participation should be interprofessional, person-centered, and a case-based process. The book postulates that by adopting such an approach, any and all individuals involved in the process should work together in a team-based manner to identify key factors of concern, as well as design and deliver multidimensional treatment plans and interventions.

While most areas of science, work, and art, including healthcare in general, have moved towards more holistic and interprofessional approaches (McDaniel & Salas, 2018), the corresponding shift in sport and performance injury rehabilitation has occurred primarily at elite levels of competition (Ray & Wiese-Bjornstal, 1999; Taylor et al., 2003). According to Hess, Gnacinski, and Meyer (forthcoming), most of the sport and performance injury rehabilitation research has been focused on either theoretical conceptualizations (i.e., high level of abstraction; Aoyagi & Poczwardowski, 2013) or specific techniques and interventions (i.e., low level of abstraction; Aoyagi & Poczwardowski, 2013), and has failed to investigate professional practice frameworks (medium level of abstraction; Aoyagi & Poczwardowski, 2013) in detail.

The above is somewhat problematic. Conceptualizing injury rehabilitation experience through the biopsychosocial paradigm, by default, calls for a team-approach to care and the implementation of holistic, multidimensional interventions informed by different disciplines (Hess et al., forthcoming). However, this rarely happens in practice, as many practitioners still work in isolation using unidimensional techniques or interventions (Hess et al., forthcoming), or in some cases, dabble in using strategies they are not adequately trained to use with the aim to address the biopsychosocial aspects of the rehabilitation (e.g., Arvinen-Barrow, Penny, Hemmings, & Corr, 2010; Heaney, 2006; Zakrajsek, Fisher, & Martin, 2016).

It is the aim of this book to address this gap in the literature. First, Chapter 1 aims to make a case for interprofessional care by providing the reader with an introduction to the core conceptualizations that underpin the subsequent injury case chapters. The chapter will highlight the importance of adopting an interprofessional, person-centered, case-based approach to sport and performance injury prevention, rehabilitation, and return to participation process.

Chapters 2–10 will present nine "real-life inspired" fictional sport and performance injury cases. Loosely adopting a structure of a "pedagogical case" (Armour, 2014), each chapter will provide a case narrative of an injured performer, focused on a particular phase of the injury rehabilitation process (Kamphoff, Thomae, & Hamson-Utley, 2013). It is within this narrative that the wider context of the individual will be explained, along with information related to key factors affecting the individual's cognitive-affective-behavioral reactions to their particular situation.

Within each case chapter, the reader will find a brief section outlining the broad details of the injury. Given the psychological focus of this book, the injury details provided are general in nature, aimed to provide the reader some contextual clarity of what is going on with the athlete physically. Depending on the case in question, these details include injury characteristics, typical symptoms of the injury, common physical limitations associated with the injury, and a general description of the treatment (i.e., type, amount, and duration of care). The injury section is followed by the presentation of three interdependent factors considered pertinent to the success of the case. First, the factor is defined, followed by an evidence-based description of how the factor relates to the case. For each factor, the authors also provide evidence-based suggestions on how practitioners could assess/evaluate the factor at baseline and/or during the different phases of rehabilitation.

Somewhat consistent with the structure for a "pedagogical case" (Armour, 2014) and the three levels of abstraction (Aoyagi & Poczwardowski, 2013), each case is also evaluated from a theoretical (high level) and an interprofessional (medium level) perspective to generate an appropriate plan of care for the injured performer. This is then followed by three different perspectives on how the relevant psychosocial factors were addressed and what psychosocial interventions were used (low level; Aoyagi & Poczwardowski, 2013). It is the goal of these perspectives to demonstrate how a variety of professionals and significant others can work alongside and with each other to provide holistic psychological care for the injured performer within their own (professional) competencies. To find out more on the different psychological interventions used, the reader is directed to other core readings such as Arvinen-Barrow and Walker (2013) and Brewer and Redmond (2017). At the end of each chapter, key ethical issues and potential need(s) for referral are presented, and an update and overall conclusion of the injury case is provided. The chapters also include critical thinking and research questions, aimed to challenge the readers' knowledge on the topics discussed. Lastly, Chapters 2–10 will also contain two key publications relevant to the case to further readers' knowledge in the area. The book concludes with Chapter 11, which aims to synthesize the key points raised in the earlier chapters and to provide researchers and applied practitioners alike with some tangible suggestions for both academic and clinical settings.

Consistent with existing definitions (e.g., Merriam-Webster, 2018), throughout the text, performance is defined as an *act of doing something*, and *any activity or gathering of reactions that leads to an outcome or has an impact on the surroundings*. In the context of this book, this can mean the actual performance where the injury occurred, as well as performance related to rehabilitation and return to participation activities. The book also adopts a philosophy that injury and performance (be it circus, military, music, sport, or other) should be viewed on a continuum (Arvinen-Barrow, 2018; Dijkstra, Pollock, Chakraverty, & Alonso, 2014), where injury and high performance stand at opposite ends. At any given time, a performer is able to operate at a level somewhere along the continuum, with the goal of moving toward the high-performance end. By viewing injury and performance in this way, researchers and applied practitioners are able to meet the performers where they are at, and to account for natural fluctuations in their performance as they are working their way back to full participation in their respective domain.

Given the continued confusion over terminology used within the interprofessional field (*Journal of Interprofessional Care*, 2018), and consistent with existing interprofessional terminologies (Barr, Koppel, Reeves, Hammick, & Freeth, 2005; Melvin, 1980; Reeves, Lewin, Espin, & Zwarenstein, 2010), this book has adopted the following definitions: *Interprofessional* refers to the collaborative efforts undertaken by individuals from different disciplines such as kinesiology, medicine, psychology, theology, or other. At times, these collaborations are *transdisciplinary* (i.e., the team members share the responsibility of addressing the issue of concern), *interdisciplinary* (i.e., members work together interdependently and collaboratively toward a common goal for the single injured performer), or *multidisciplinary* (i.e., members work independently toward their own discipline specific goals for the single injured performer). It is the aim of the book to demonstrate how these *interprofessional* teams can work in an *interdisciplinary*, or, in some cases, *transdisciplinary* or *multidisciplinary* manner to use appropriate *psychological interventions* to address the identified *key factors* within their own professional competencies to achieve mutually agreed goals for each injured performer.

When referring to *psychological interventions*, we use this to collectively describe psychological techniques such as goal setting, imagery, range of physical and mental relaxation strategies, patient education, and social support (Arvinen-Barrow & Walker, 2013; Ayers & de Visser, 2018). The term *key factors* is used to describe a range of personal, social, and contextual factors affecting the injured performer. These can include personality traits and states, cognitive appraisals, emotional and/or behavioral responses, injury-related factors, and a plethora of environmental and/or organizational factors.

Since the book presents injury cases from different cultural contexts (Canada, Finland, United Kingdom, United States), we have purposefully used different occupational titles to describe the professionals working together in an interprofessional manner. To ensure effective biopsychosocial care, we would encourage all of our readers to do their research and find out (a) who is qualified to provide the services required, and (b) what is the appropriate occupational title to use for each professional group in different cultural/country contexts. Not only do such actions demonstrate unity and communication across the different professionals but they also highlight the value and respect toward teamwork, collaboration, and all those involved in the process.

References

Aoyagi, M. W., & Poczwardowski, A. (2013). Models of sport psychology practice and delivery. In S. D. Mellalieu & S. Hanton (Eds.), *Professional practice issues in sport psychology: Critical reviews* (pp. 5–30). New York, NY: Routledge.

Armour, K. (2014). Pedagocial cases explained. In K. Armour (Ed.), *Pedagogical cases in physical education and youth sport* (pp. 6–21). Abingdon: Routledge.

Arvinen-Barrow, M. (2018). Injury prevention in sport and performance psychology. In O. Braddick (Ed.), *Oxford research encyclopedia of psychology*. Oxford: Oxford University Press.

Retrieved from http://psychology.oxfordre.com/view/10.1093/acrefore/9780190236557. 001.0001/acrefore-9780190236557-e-171. doi:10.1093/acrefore/9780190236557.013.171.

Arvinen-Barrow, M., Penny, G., Hemmings, B., & Corr, S. (2010). UK chartered physiotherapists' personal experiences in using psychological interventions with injured athletes: An interpretative phenomenological analysis. *Psychology of Sport & Exercise*, 11(1), 58–66. doi:10.1016/j.psychsport.2009.05.004.

Arvinen-Barrow, M., & Walker, N. (Eds.). (2013). *Psychology of sport injury and rehabilitation.* Abingdon: Routledge.

Ayers, S., & de Visser, R. (2018). *Psychology for medicine and healthcare* (2nd ed.). Thousand Oaks, CA: Sage Publications.

Barr, H., Koppel, I., Reeves, S., Hammick, M., & Freeth, D. (2005). *Effective interprofessional education: Argument, assumption and evidence.* Oxford: Blackwell.

Berger, B. G., Pargman, D., & Weinberg, R. S. (2007). *Foundations of exercise psychology* (2nd ed.). Morgantown, WV: Fitness Information Technology.

Brewer, B. W., & Redmond, C. J. (2017). *Psychology of sport injury.* Champaign, IL: Human Kinetics.

Conn, J. M., Annest, J. L., & Gilchrist, J. (2003). Sports and recreation related injury episodes in the US population, 1997–1999. *Injury Prevention*, 9(2), 117–123. doi:10.1016/j.jsams.2006.03.004.

Dijkstra, P. H., Pollock, N., Chakraverty, R., & Alonso, J. M. (2014). Managing the health of the elite athlete: A new integrated performance health management and coaching model. *British Journal of Sports Medicine*, 48(7), 523–531. doi:10.1136/bjsports-2013-093222.

Granquist, M. D., Hamson-Utley, J. J., Kenow, L. J., & Stiller-Ostrowski, J. L. (2014). *Psychosocial strategies for athletic training.* Philadelphia, PA: FA Davis.

Heaney, C. (2006). Physiotherapists' perceptions of sport psychology intervention in professional soccer. *International Journal of Sport and Exercise Psychology*, 4, 67–80. doi:10.1080/1612197x.2006.9671785.

Heil, J. (1993). *Psychology of sport injury.* Champaign, IL: Human Kinetics.

Hess, C. W., Gnacinski, S. L., & Meyer, B. B. (forthcoming). A review of the sport injury and rehabilitation literature: From abstraction to application. *Journal of Applied Sport Psychology*.

Johnston, L. H., & Carroll, D. (1998). The context of emotional responses to athletic injury: A qualitative analysis. *Journal of Sport Rehabilitation*, 7(3), 206–220. doi:10.1123/jsr.7.3.206.

Journal of Interprofessional Care. (2018). Instructions for authors: Terminology. Retrieved September 26, 2018, from https://www.tandfonline.com/action/authorSubmission?journalCode=ijic20&page=instructions.

Kamphoff, C., Thomae, J., & Hamson-Utley, J. J. (2013). Integrating the psychological and physiological aspects of sport injury rehabilitation: Rehabilitation profiling and phases of rehabilitation. In M. Arvinen-Barrow & N. Walker (Eds.), *Psychology of sport injury and rehabilitation* (pp. 134–155). Abingdon: Routledge.

Kolt, G. S., & Andersen, M. B. (Eds.). (2004). *Psychology in the physical and manual therapies.* Philadelphia: Churchill Livingstone Inc.

Konttinen, N., Mononen, K., Pihlaja, T., Sipari, T., Arvinen-Barrow, M., & Selanne, H. (2011). Urheiluvammojen esiintyminen ja niiden hoito nuorisourheilussa - Kohderyhmänä 1995 syntyneet urheilijat [Sport injury occurrence and treatment in youth sports - athletes born in 1995 as a target population]. *KIHUn julkaisusarjanro25(PDF-julkaisu)*, 1–16. http://www.kihu.jyu.fi/tuotokset/haku/index.php?hae=Tee+haku#TOC2011.

McDaniel, S. H., & Salas, E. (2018). The science of teamwork: Introduction to the special issue. *American Psychologist*, 73(4), 305–307. doi:10.1037/amp0000337.

Maffulli, N., Giuseppe Longo, U., Gougoulias, N., Caine, D., & Denaro, V. (2010). Sport injuries: A review of outcomes. *British Medical Bulletin*, 97, 47–80.

Melvin, J. L. (1980). Interdisciplinary and multidisciplinary activities and the ACRM. *Archives of Physical Medicine and Rehabilitation*, 61, 379–380.

Merriam-Webster (Ed.). (2018) *Merriam-Webster Dictionary*. Merriam-Webster Inc.

Pargman, D. (Ed.). (2007). *Psychological bases of sport injuries* (3rd ed.). Morgantown, WV: Fitness Information Technology.

Prentice, W. E. (2017). *Principles of athletic training: A guide to evidence-based clinical practice* (16th ed.). New York, NY: McGraw-Hill Education.

Ray, R., & Wiese-Bjornstal, D. M. (Eds.). (1999). *Counseling in sports medicine*. Champaign, IL: Human Kinetics.

Reeves, S., Lewin, S., Espin, S., & Zwarenstein, M. (2010). *Interprofessional teamwork for health and social care*. London: Blackwell-Wiley.

Ruddock-Hudson, M., O'Halloran, P., & Murphy, G. (2012). Exploring psychological reactions to injury in the Australian Football League (AFL). *Journal of Applied Sport Psychology*, 24(4), 375–390. doi:10.1080/10413200.2011.654172.

Taylor, J., Stone, K. R., Mullin, M. J., Ellenbecker, T., & Walgenbach, A. (2003). *Comprehensive sports injury management: From examination of injury to return to sport* (2nd ed.). Austin, TX: Pro-Ed.

Taylor, J., & Taylor, S. (1997). *Psychological approaches to sports injury rehabilitation*. Gaithersburg, MD: Aspen.

Tracey, J. (2003). The emotional response to the injury and rehabilitation process. *Journal of Applied Sport Psychology*, 15(4), 279–293. doi:10.1080/714044197.

Uitenbroek, D. G. (1996). Sports, exercise, and other causes of injuries: Results of a population survey. *Research Quarterly for Exercise and Sport*, 67, 380–385. doi:10.1080/02701367.1996.10607969.

Zakrajsek, R. A., Fisher, L. A., & Martin, S. B. (2016). Certified athletic trainers' understanding and use of sport psychology in their practice. *Journal of Applied Sport Psychology*. doi:10.1080/10413200.2016.1231722.

ACKNOWLEDGEMENTS

To the amazing group of interprofessional healthcare professionals who authored the case chapters this book. Your collective efforts are an excellent proof of teamwork in action. We express our gratitude for your time, effort, expertise, and attention to detail.

To the true pioneers of psychology of sport and performance injury. Mark Andersen, Britton Brewer, Lynne Evans, Frances Flint, Sandy Gordon, Charles Hardy, John Heil, Urban Johnson, Gregory Kolt, David Lavallee, David Pargman, Aynsley Smith, Ron Smith, Frank Smoll, Jim Taylor, Judy Van Raalte, Maureen Weiss, Diane Wiese-Bjornstal, and Jean Williams. Your outstanding efforts have been pivotal in developing a solid theoretical and empirical foundation for interprofessional, biopsychosocial sport injury research and applied work. Thank you for all that you have done and continue to do for our field. Your work has taught us, challenged us, and inspired us.

To our mentors. Edward F. Etzel, Brian Hemmings, Barbara B. Meyer, Andrew C. Ostrow, Jack C. Watson II, and Sam Zizzi. Collectively, you have been instrumental in shaping our academic careers. We are grateful for all your encouragement, guidance, and support.

To Routledge and our publishing team. Thank you for making our vision a reality by commissioning this book and for helping us every step of the way.

To our families. You know who you are and we appreciate you. Thank you for your continued, unconditional support throughout the process of getting this book to print. It is you who make us work hard toward our goals.

Kiitos Amie for brightening my day with your smile. Just keep swimming; just keep swimming (Dory, 2003) through life to find your happy place (Monna). Many thanks and sincere appreciation to my wife Mariah, who took care of our kids, Isla and Asa, while I was at the office working on this project. Without your constant support, this dream would not have become a reality (Damien).

Monna and Damien

1

A CASE FOR INTERPROFESSIONAL CARE

Monna Arvinen-Barrow and Damien Clement

Interest in understanding psychological aspects of sport and performance injuries – a sub-discipline within sport psychology – dates back to the late 1960s when applied sport psychology practitioners documented first accounts of *Problem athletes and how to handle them* (Ogilvie, 1966), followed by research aiming to understand the relationship between personality and injury (e.g., Jackson et al., 1978; Valiant, 1981). These efforts were soon enriched with a plethora of research investigating the role of stress in injury, culminating in a seminal paper proposing the first theoretical model depicting the relationship between stress and athletic injury occurrence (Andersen & Williams, 1988). Other pivotal moments in the development of the field include the publication of the first textbook on psychology of sport injury (Heil, 1993), the emergence of grief response and cognitive appraisal-based models aimed to explain psychological responses to injury (e.g., Brewer, 1994; Evans & Hardy, 1995), and the development of the integrated model of psychological response to sport injury and rehabilitation process (Wiese-Bjornstal, Smith, Shaffer, & Morrey, 1998).

Following a similar trajectory during the 1960s, sports medicine also emerged as a specialized area of study (Heil, 1993). Like general medicine, sports medicine has been predominantly underpinned by the biomedical model, where injury (and illness) are defined as biological defects (Engel, 1977). Thus, much of sports medicine, i.e., the diagnosis, treatment, prevention, and performance related efforts (Heil, 1993), have been focused on eliminating these biological defects, and not considering the individual's psychological, social, or contextual factors that may influence the injury occurrence, rehabilitation, and recovery process (Engel, 1977).

The disparate growth of the two fields is not surprising, as ambiguity still exists in how sport and performance injuries are defined and reported (Timpka et al., 2014). Verhagen and van Mechelen (2010) have argued that sport and performance injury definitions can be discussed both theoretically and operationally. In theoretical definitions, the focus is on the abstract conceptualization of *what is* sport and performance injury. Even though it has been long established that sport and performance injuries have psychological antecedents and consequences (for more details, see Arvinen-Barrow & Walker, 2013; Brewer & Redmond, 2017; Ivarsson et al., 2017; Wiese-Bjornstal, 2014), theoretical definitions still fail to account for those factors (Arvinen-Barrow & Walker, 2013). The International Olympic Committee manual of sport injuries, for example, defines sport injuries as a "damage to the tissues of the body that occurs as a result of sport or exercise" (Bahr, Engebretsen, Laprade, McCrory, & Meeuwisse, 2012, p. 1). Operational definitions, on the other hand, are focused on the *properties of injury*, such as the injury location, mechanics of onset, time taken for tissue to become injured, tissue type affected, and injury severity (Granquist, Hamson-Utley, Kenow, & Stiller-Ostrowski, 2014). Like the theoretical definitions, the operational definitions also do not account for any psychological onset factors such as stress, attentional focus shifts, or somatic state anxiety, to name a few.

Nevertheless, and in the absence of unified and all-encompassing sport and performance injury definition, the two fields have grown closer toward a more holistic, biopsychosocial approach (Kolt & Andersen, 2004; Taylor, Stone, Mullin, Ellenbecker, & Walgenbach, 2003). The first model aimed to bridge the gap between the medical and psychological approaches to sport injury rehabilitation was proposed by Brewer, Andersen, and Van Raalte (2002). Drawing from other existing health outcome models (Cohen & Rodriguez, 1995; Matthews et al., 1997), the biopsychosocial model of sport injury rehabilitation aims to "broaden the scope of sport injury rehabilitation research, augmenting, rather than replacing current models of relevance to sport injury rehabilitation" (Brewer et al., 2002, p. 47). Since the publication of the biopsychosocial model, ample evidence exists in support of the different components of the theoretical biopsychosocial conceptualizations (Brewer & Redmond, 2017; Hess, Gnacinski, & Meyer, forthcoming), and as a consequence, the importance of treating a person and not just the injury (or illness) is now globally recognized as the best approach to patient care (Ayers & de Visser, 2018). However, very little is known about how a biopsychosocial approach, when delivered by an interprofessional team of healthcare professionals, works in practice when rehabilitating sport and performance injuries (Arvinen-Barrow & Clement, 2015, 2017; Clement & Arvinen-Barrow, 2013; Hess, 2015; Ogilvie & Tutko, 1966).

Integrating physical with the psychological: Three phases of rehabilitation

Traditionally, sport injury rehabilitation is viewed as consisting of a series of physiological phases (acute, repair, and remodeling) closely aligned to the healing process (Prentice & Arnheim, 2014). Flint (1998) was one of the first sports medicine researcher-practitioners to propose an integrated approach to rehabilitation. The integrated rehabilitation model (Flint, 1998, 2007) aimed to match the above-mentioned physical healing stages with psychosocial strategies to match, but failed to discuss how psychological responses are linked with patients' physical healing process and the transition from one phase to another. To address the above gap, Kamphoff, Thomae, and Hamson-Utley (2013) proposed a conceptual framework to better understand the relationship between physical and psychosocial responses to injuries. Once injured, an individual will go through three interconnected phases, namely reactions to injury, reactions to rehabilitation, and reactions to return to participation (Kamphoff et al., 2013).

The *reaction to injury* phase is said to represent the injured performer's initial psychosocial responses to their injury (Hamson-Utley, 2010). These responses are typically influenced by the physical characteristics of the injury, such as type, location, history, severity and the associated physiological consequences (Kamphoff et al., 2013). These include, but are not limited to, swelling, discoloration, muscle spasm, pain, and lack of mobility. The *reaction to rehabilitation* phase is said to start when the injured performer has dealt with the initial impact of the injury and they transition into the rehabilitation phase of the process. This typically means a decrease in physical injury complications, and the performer begins to engage in activities aimed to increase strength, balance, and mobility (Kamphoff et al., 2013). The engagement in new behaviors will typically elicit a number of new cognitive appraisals, emotional, and behavioral responses, often triggered by specific rehabilitation activities and associated physiological responses (Clement & Arvinen-Barrow, in press-b). The final phase, the *reaction to return to participation*, incorporates the reactions the injured performers are experiencing in relation to their physical and psychosocial readiness to return to participation (Hamson-Utley, 2010). Individuals in this phase react to challenges associated with setbacks in the healing process, and the process of returning back to performance (Kamphoff et al., 2013).

Thus far, limited research has explicitly investigated the different phases of rehabilitation (Clement, Arvinen-Barrow, & Fetty, 2015; Ruddock-Hudson, O'Halloran, & Murphy, 2014); however, what does exist supports the theoretical conceptualizations put forth by Kamphoff et al. (2013). In general, it appears that when the performers are expected to engage in new behaviors during their injury rehabilitation and return to participation process, they will make new cognitive appraisals of the situation, its demands, consequences, and available resources. These appraisals will then influence any subsequent emotional and behavioral responses, and ultimately, both the psychosocial and physical outcomes (Verhagen & van Mechelen, 2010). These appraisals, as previous theoretical conceptualizations indicate (Brewer, 1994; Brewer et al., 2002; Wiese-Bjornstal et al., 1998), are also influenced by a number of personal and situational factors which in turn will also influence the individual's subsequent emotional and behavioral responses. Depending on the outcome of this bidirectional interaction between thoughts, emotions, and behaviors, this process can be either recovery-facilitating or recovery-debilitating (Verhagen & van Mechelen, 2010).

Psychology in sport and performance injury rehabilitation: A case for interprofessional care

Although a strong case for addressing both physical and psychological aspects of sport and performance injuries has been made in the literature (for a thorough review of evidence to date, see Brewer & Redmond, 2017), ambiguity still exists with regards to which professionals are best qualified to diagnose and treat a range of psychological concerns during the sport and performance injury rehabilitation process. For example, the National Collegiate Athletics Association states:

> All collegiate athletics programs should have both an athletic trainer and designated team physician who will serve as core members of the mental health team. These individuals may not be mental health experts, but they can serve as a "point person" for referring student-athletes to the appropriate professional for evaluation and treatment. (Klenck, 2014, p. 101)

Support for the above has been found in the literature. Athletes, athletic trainers, and sport psychology professionals all perceive athletic trainers as being best suited to act as the point person during injury rehabilitation (Arvinen-Barrow & Clement, 2015, 2017b, 2017a). However, athletic trainers in the United States (Clement & Arvinen-Barrow, in press-a; Clement, Granquist, & Arvinen-Barrow, 2013; Cormier & Zizzi, 2015; Estepp, 2013; Zakrajsek, Fisher, & Martin, 2016; Zakrajsek, Martin, & Wrisberg, 2016), physiotherapists in the United Kingdom (Arvinen-Barrow, Hemmings, Weigand, Becker, & Booth, 2007; Arvinen-Barrow, Penny, Hemmings, & Corr, 2010; Heaney, 2006; Jevon & Johnston, 2003) and Australia (Francis, Andersen, & Maley, 2000; Gordon, Milios, & Grove, 1991), and physicians in the United States (Mann, Grana, Indelicato, O'Neill, & George, 2007) all have reported feeling underprepared in addressing psychological concerns during injury rehabilitation, while also perceiving it as important element of successful rehabilitation. As such, inclusion of a qualified mental health professional as part of the interprofessional health care team is critically important to ensure competent, ethical, and holistic care to injured performers.

In an ideal world, each injury rehabilitation setting would have access to a plethora of healthcare professionals representing a range of professions. However, this rarely happens outside of elite sports (Clement & Arvinen-Barrow, 2013; Ray & Wiese-Bjornstal, 1999), and as a result, many healthcare settings are left to be creative in how they ensure their patients' biopsychosocial care needs are best met. Bahr et al. (2012) suggested that in collegiate athletic settings, in the United States, core members to include in an interprofessional care team to diagnose and treat psychological concerns should include a psychiatrist, a clinical psychologist, or a licensed clinical social worker with experience in mental health counseling. However, depending on a country's context, who should be involved can differ, as scope of practice for different professionals is dependent on educational and core competency requirements. It is therefore imperative to know what (a) qualifications are required to treat a range of psychological concerns, and (b) occupations are associated with these qualifications.

Interprofessional approach to care

For comprehensive sport and performance injury management, different professional approaches have been proposed in the literature. Within sports medicine, Prentice (1991) was one of the first to propose a "group approach" to care where individuals representing different professions would work together for the benefit of the injured performer. Since then, few interprofessional practice models have been proposed in the sport psychology literature (Hess et al., forthcoming), namely the multidisciplinary approach to sport injury rehabilitation (Clement & Arvinen-Barrow, 2013), the integrated performance health management and coaching model (Dijkstra, Pollock, Chakraverty, & Alonso, 2014), and the Meyer athlete performance management model (Meyer, Merkur, Ebersole, & Massey, 2014).

The multidisciplinary approach to sport injury rehabilitation (Clement & Arvinen-Barrow, 2013) is based on the premise that during injury rehabilitation, the injured performer is typically surrounded by a range of professionals and significant others, forming a "dual-layered" approach to care. The primary team typically consist of all those professionals who interact with the injured performer directly in rehabilitation related activities on a day-to-day basis. The secondary team consist of professionals, and significant others, who have an integral role in the injured performer's rehabilitation, but may or may not be involved in the day-to-day processes of rehabilitation. Depending on the injured performer's needs, the secondary team members will interact with them directly or indirectly. The multidisciplinary approach to sport injury (Clement & Arvinen-Barrow, 2013) also presumes that the individuals involved in the rehabilitation process should be "working closely together for the benefit of the athletes" (p. 150).

The integrated performance health management and coaching model (Dijkstra et al., 2014) considers sport injury and athletic performance on a continuum and emphasizes the need to incorporate the performer as part of the interprofessional team. The model also calls for the collaboration between its two core domains (i.e., performance enhancement and injury/health management) and those involved in these domains. The model proposes an overlap between performance coaching and performance health management, as well as the two sub-disciplines of performance health management: medicine and therapy, and associated sciences of nutrition, physiology, psychology, biomechanics, podiatry (Dijkstra et al., 2014). The Meyer athlete performance management model (Meyer et al., 2014) proposes that for optimal elite sport performance outcomes, all members of the team representing different aspects of the performance (i.e., mental, physical, technical, and senior management operations) should work together in an performer-centered, interdependent, and collaborative manner (Meyer et al., 2014).

While all of the above models have their own intricacies, they are all underpinned by the same core philosophy: each case should be evaluated, diagnosed, and treated in a holistic, patient-centered manner. Thus far, evidence in support of the models is limited. Existing research has confirmed the dual-layered structure of the multidisciplinary approach to sport injury rehabilitation; however, discrepancies in which professionals should be part of the primary team have also been noted (Arvinen-Barrow & Clement, 2015, 2017b, 2017a). The integrated performance health management and coaching model has only been tested by UK Athletics in preparation for the 2012 London Olympic and Paralympic Games (Dijkstra et al., 2014). Although the Meyer athlete performance management model is founded on decades of professional practice evidence in diverse domains, its applicability to injury rehabilitation has only been explored in elite, Olympic-level sport (Hess, 2015). Nevertheless, each of the models outlined above has potential to serve as a useful framework for interprofessional sport and performance injury rehabilitation.

Conclusion

Recognizing the inherent relationship between psychology of injury and sports medicine, the authors adopt the above philosophy and aim to make a case for a team-based, interprofessional approach to sport and performance injury rehabilitation as the best practice model. Depending on the organizational structures of the healthcare setting, this approach can be multi-, inter-, or transdisciplinary in nature. More specifically, this book aims to demonstrate how *interprofessional* teams can work in an *interdisciplinary*, or, in some cases, *transdisciplinary* or *multidisciplinary* manner to use appropriate *psychological interventions* to address the identified *key factors* within their own professional competencies to achieve mutually agreed goals for each injured performer. Anchored in the three phases of rehabilitation (Kamphoff et al., 2013), the book provides the reader with nine, "real-life inspired" fictional sport and performance injury cases. Each case analysis is theory driven, and provides an evidence-based example of how different interprofessional practitioners can work together in "the real world" in an integrated fashion. It is the hope of the editors that this book provides its readers additional insight and practical nuances on how psychological aspects of sport and performance injury rehabilitation can be best addressed in an interprofessional, person-centered manner.

References

Andersen, M. B., & Williams, J. M. (1988). A model of stress and athletic injury: Prediction and prevention. *Journal of Sport & Exercise Psychology*, 10(3), 294–306. doi:10.1123/jsep.10.3.294.

Arvinen-Barrow, M., & Clement, D. (2015). A preliminary investigation into athletic trainers' views and experiences of a multidisciplinary team approach to sports injury rehabilitation. *Athletic Training and Sports Health Care*, 7(3), 97–107. doi:10.3928/19425864-20150422-05.

Arvinen-Barrow. M., & Clement, D. (2017a). A preliminary investigation into previously injured athletes' views and experiences of a rehabilitation team approach to sport injury rehabilitation. Unpublished manuscript.

Arvinen-Barrow, M., & Clement, D. (2017b). A preliminary investigation into sport and exercise psychology consultants' views and experiences of an interprofessional care team approach to sport injury rehabilitation. *Journal of Interprofessional Care, 31*(1), 66–74. doi:10.1080/13561820.2016.1235019.

Arvinen-Barrow, M., Hemmings, B., Weigand, D. A., Becker, C. A., & Booth, L. (2007). Views of chartered physiotherapists on the psychological content of their practice: A national follow-up survey in the United Kingdom. *Journal of Sport Rehabilitation*, 16(2), 111–121. doi:10.1123/jsr.16.2.111.

Arvinen-Barrow, M., Penny, G., Hemmings, B., & Corr, S. (2010). UK chartered physiotherapists' personal experiences in using psychological interventions with injured athletes: An interpretative phenomenological analysis. *Psychology of Sport & Exercise*, 11(1), 58–66. doi:10.1016/j.psychsport.2009.05.004.

Arvinen-Barrow, M., & Walker, N. (Eds.). (2013). *Psychology of sport injury and rehabilitation*. Abingdon: Routledge.

Ayers, S., & de Visser, R. (2018). *Psychology for medicine and healthcare* (2nd ed.). Thousand Oaks, CA: Sage Publications.

Bahr, R., Engebretsen, L., Laprade, R., McCrory, P., & Meeuwisse, W. H. (Eds.). (2012). *The IOC manual of sports injuries: An illustrated guide to the management of injuries in physical activity*. New York, NY: John Wiley & Sons.

Brewer, B. W. (1994). Review and critique of models of psychological adjustment to athletic injury. *Journal of Applied Sport Psychology, 6*, 87–100. doi:10.1080/10413209408406467.

Brewer, B. W., Andersen, M. B., & Van Raalte, J. L. (2002). Psychological aspects of sport injury rehabilitation: Toward a biopsychological approach. In D. L. Mostofsky & L. D. Zaichkowsky (Eds.), *Medical aspects of sport and exercise* (pp. 41–54). Morgantown, WV: Fitness Information Technology.

Brewer, B. W., & Redmond, C. J. (2017). *Psychology of sport Injury*. Champaign, IL: Human Kinetics.

Clement, D., & Arvinen-Barrow, M. (2013). Sport medicine team influences in psychological rehabilitation: A multidisciplinary approach. In M. Arvinen-Barrow & N. Walker (Eds.), *The psychology of sport injury and rehabilitation* (pp. 156–170). Abingdon: Routledge.

Clement, D., & Arvinen-Barrow, M. (in press-a). Athletic trainers' views and experiences of discussing psychosocial and mental health issues with athletes: An exploratory study. *Athletic Training and Sports Health Care*.

Clement, D., & Arvinen-Barrow, M. (in press-b). Psychosocial strategies for the different phases of sport injury rehabilitation. In A. Ivarsson & U. Johnson (Eds.), *Psychological bases of sport injuries* (4th ed.). Morgantown, WV: Fitness Information Technology.

Clement, D., Arvinen-Barrow, M., & Fetty, T. (2015). Psychosocial responses during different phases of sport-injury rehabilitation: A qualitative study. *Journal of Athletic Training*, 50(1), 95–104. doi:10.4085/1062-6050-49.3.52.

Clement, D., Granquist, M. D., & Arvinen-Barrow, M. (2013). Psychosocial aspects of athletic injuries as perceived by athletic trainers. *Journal of Athletic Training*, 48(4), 512–521. doi:10.4085/1062-6050-49.3.52.

Cohen, S., & Rodriguez, M. S. (1995). Pathways linking affective disturbance and physical disorders. *Health Psychology*, 14(5), 374–380. doi:10.1037//0278-026133.14.5.374.

Cormier, M. L., & Zizzi, S. J. (2015). Athletic trainers' skills in identifying and managing athletes experiencing psychological distress. *Journal of Athletic Training*, 50(12), 1267–1276.

Dijkstra, P. H., Pollock, N., Chakraverty, R., & Alonso, J. M. (2014). Managing the health of the elite athlete: A new integrated performance health management and coaching model. *British Journal of Sports Medicine*, 48(7), 523–531. doi:10.1136/bjsports-2013-093222.

Engel, G. L. (1977). The need for a new medical model: A challenge for biomedicine. *Science*, 196(4286), 129–136.

Estepp, M. K. (2013). NCAA division I athletic trainers' perceptions and use of psychological skills during injury rehabilitation. (Master's degree). University of Tennessee, Knoxville.

Evans, L., & Hardy, L. (1995). Sport injury and grief response: A review. *Journal of Sport & Exercise Psychology*, 17, 227–245.

Flint, F. A. (1998). Integrating sport psychology and sports medicine in research: The dilemmas. *Journal of Applied Sport Psychology*, 10(1), 83–102. doi:10.1080/10413209808406379.

Flint, F. A. (2007). Matching psychological strategies with physical rehabilitation: Integrated rehabilitation. In D. Pargman (Ed.), *Psychological bases of sport injuries* (3rd. ed., pp. 319–334). Morgantown, WV: Fitness Information Technology.

Francis, S. R., Andersen, M. B., & Maley, P. (2000). Physiotherapists' and male professional athletes' views on psychological skills for rehabilitation. *Journal of Science & Medicine in Sport*, 3(1), 17–29. doi:10.1016/S1440-2440(00)80044-80044.

Gordon, S., Milios, D., & Grove, J. R. (1991). Psychological aspects of the recovery process from sport injury: The perspective of sport physiotherapists. *Australian Journal of Science & Medicine in Sport*, 23, 53–60.

Granquist, M. D., Hamson-Utley, J. J., Kenow, L. J., & Stiller-Ostrowski, J. L. (2014). *Psychosocial strategies for athletic training*. Philadephia, PA: FA Davis.

Hamson-Utley, J. J. (2010). Psychology of sport injury: A holistic approach to rehabilitating the injured athlete. *Chinese Journal of Sports Medicine*, 29(3), 343–347.

Heaney, C. (2006). Physiotherapists' perceptions of sport psychology intervention in professional soccer. *International Journal of Sport and Exercise Psychology*, 4, 67–80. doi:10.1080/1612197x.2006.9671785.

Heil, J. (1993). *Psychology of sport injury*. Champaign, IL: Human Kinetics.

Hess, C. W. (2015). The lived experiences of an injured athlete and members of a performance management team during injury rehabilitation: An interpretative phenomenological analysis. (Master's thesis) *Department of Kinesiology - Integrated Health Care and Performance Unit, University of Wisconsin–Milwaukee*, 170. http://dc.uwm.edu/cgi/viewcontent.cgi?article=2038&context=etd.

Hess, C. W., Gnacinski, S. L., & Meyer, B. B. (forthcoming). A review of the sport injury and rehabilitation literature: From abstraction to application. *The Sport Psychologist*.

Ivarsson, A., Johnson, U., Andersen, M. B., Tranaeus, U., Stenling, A., & Lindwall, M. (2017). Psychosocial factors and sport injuries: Meta-analyses for prediction and prevention. *Sports Medicine, Training and Rehabilitation*, 47(2), 353–365. doi:10.1007/s40279-40016-0578-x.

Jackson, D. W., Jarrett, H., Barley, D., Kausch, J., Swanson, J. J., & Powell, J. W. (1978). Injury prediction in the young athlete. *American Journal of Sports Medicine*, 6, 6–14. doi:10.1177/036354657800600103.

Jevon, S. M., & Johnston, L. H. (2003). The perceived knowledge and attitudes of governing body chartered physiotherapists towards the psychological aspects of rehabilitation. *Physical Therapy in Sport*, 4(2), 74–81.

Kamphoff, C., Thomae, J., & Hamson-Utley, J. J. (2013). Integrating the psychological and physiological aspects of sport injury rehabilitation: Rehabilitation profiling and phases of rehabilitation. In M. Arvinen-Barrow & N. Walker (Eds.), *Psychology of sport injury and rehabilitation* (pp. 134–155). Abingdon: Routledge.

Klenck, C. (2014). Best practices for athletics departments. In G. T. Brown (Ed.), *Mind, body and sport: Understanding and supporting student-athlete mental wellness*. National Collegiate

Athletics Association. Retrieved from www.ncaapublications.com/productdownloads/MindBodySport.pdf.

Kolt, G. S., & Andersen, M. B. (Eds.). (2004). *Psychology in the physical and manual therapies.* Philadelphia: Churchill Livingstone Inc.

Mann, B. J., Grana, W. A., Indelicato, P. A., O'Neill, D. F., & George, S. Z. (2007). A survey of sports medicine physicians regarding psychological issues in patient-athletes. *American Journal of Sports Medicine, 35,* 2140–2147.

Matthews, K. A., Shumaker, S. A., Bowen, D. J., Langer, R. D., Hunt, J. R., Kaplan, R. M., & Ritenburg, C. (1997). Women's health initiative: Why now? What is it? What's new? *American Psychologist, 52*(2), 101–116. doi:10.1037//0003-0066X.52.2.101.

Meyer, B. B., Merkur, A., Ebersole, K. T., & Massey, W. V. (2014). The realities of working in elite sport. What they didn't teach you in graduate school. In A. M. Lane, R. J. Godfrey, M. Loosemore & G. P. Whyte (Eds.), *Applied sport science and medicine: Case studies from practice* (pp. 137–142): CreateSpace: Self-published.

Ogilvie, B. C. (1966). *Problem athletes and how to handle them.* London: Pelham.

Ogilvie, B. C., & Tutko, T. A. (1966). *Problem athletes and how to handle them.* London: Pelham.

Prentice, W. E. (1991). The athletic trainer. In F. Mueller & A. Ryan (Eds.), *Prevention of athletic injuries: The role of the sports medicine team.* Philadelphia, PA: F A Davis.

Prentice, W. E., & Arnheim, D. D. (2014). *Principles of athletic training: A competency-based approach* (15th ed.). New York, NY: McGraw-Hill.

Ray, R., & Wiese-Bjornstal, D. M. (Eds.). (1999). *Counseling in sports medicine.* Champaign, IL: Human Kinetics.

Ruddock-Hudson, M., O'Halloran, P., & Murphy, G. (2014). The psychological impact of long-term injury on Australian football league players. *Journal of Applied Sport Psychology, 26*(4), 377–394. doi:10.1080/10413200.2014.897269.

Taylor, J., Stone, K. R., Mullin, M. J., Ellenbecker, T., & Walgenbach, A. (2003). *Comprehensive sports injury management: From examination of injury to return to sport* (2nd ed.). Austin, TX: Pro-Ed.

Timpka, T., Jacobsson, J., Bickenbach, J., Finch, C. F., Ekberg, J., & Nordenfelt, L. (2014). What is a sports injury? *Sports Medicine, 44*(4), 423–428. doi:10.1007/s40279-40014-0143-0144.

Valiant, P. M. (1981). Personality and injury in competitive runners. *Perceptual and Motor Skills, 53*(1), 251–253. doi:10.2466/pms.1981.53.1.251.

Verhagen, E., & van Mechelen, W. (2010). *Sports injury research.* Oxford: Oxford University Press.

Wiese-Bjornstal, D. M. (2014). Reflections on a quarter-century of research in sports medicine psychology. *Revista de Psicología del Deporte, 23*(2), 411–421.

Wiese-Bjornstal, D. M., Smith, A. M., Shaffer, S. M., & Morrey, M. A. (1998). An integrated model of response to sport injury: Psychological and sociological dynamics. *Journal of Applied Sport Psychology, 10*(1), 46–69. doi:10.1080/10413209808406377.

Zakrajsek, R. A., Fisher, L. A., & Martin, S. B. (2016). Certified athletic trainers' understanding and use of sport psychology in their practice. *Journal of Applied Sport Psychology.* doi:10.1080/10413200.2016.1231722.

Zakrajsek, R. A., Martin, S. B., & Wrisberg, C. A. (2016). National collegiate athletic association division I certified athletic trainers' perceptions of the benefits of sport psychology services. *Journal of Athletic Training, 51*(5), 398–405. doi:10.4085/1062-6050-51.5.13.

2

REACTIONS TO A FOOTBALL INJURY

Adrian Jones, a freshman collegiate football player

Ken Ildefonso, Monna Arvinen-Barrow, and Damien Clement

Key Words: 19-year-old male, out-of-state freshman, personality, history of stressors, coping skills, grade II lateral ankle sprain

Case description

Adrian Jones (this name is a pseudonym and used for descriptive purposes only), a 19-year-old football player has recently relocated to Tucson, Arizona from Chicago, Illinois to attend division I university on a football scholarship. He was born and raised in the Midwest; the first five years of his life, he lived in Madison, Wisconsin before relocating to suburban Chicago. His parents are Larry (45) and April (43) and he has three older siblings: Daniel (27), Christina (25) and Benjamin (24). Adrian's siblings have already moved away from home a few years earlier. Adrian comes from a family with a long history of collegiate and professional sports. His grandfather played professional football for the Green Bay Packers, and his father used to be a goaltender for the Minnesota Wild ice hockey team. Both of his brothers have followed their father's footsteps playing professional hockey, Daniel is currently playing for the Chicago Blackhawks, and Benjamin for the Winnipeg Jets. Adrian's mother used to be a collegiate and national level track runner, and his sister Christina was an Olympic level basketball player until her retirement two years ago.

Adrian got involved in football at a young age. At first, he dabbled in it with his friends, while also playing baseball. As a high school freshman, Adrian also played basketball during the baseball off-season. During his sophomore year, the coaches felt that his talents would be best utilized in football as a linebacker. After much deliberation, Adrian made a tough decision to focus on one sport in the hopes of increasing his chances of getting a college scholarship. "Choosing football wasn't about me loving the sport the most, it was more about odds. I know I am an excellent player and I know I can contribute to the team. I am fast, strong, and more skilled than most, and I know I should easily become one of the key players on the team. I know I can excel, I know I can do very well."

When Adrian moved to Tucson in late May, he felt overwhelmed. The weather was very different from back home in Chicago, and even the food was different. "There is way more rice based food than back home and it is spicier." Adrian found it hard to adjust to sharing a room with a teammate, who had a habit of leaving clothes on the floor, half-eaten food on the table, and not making his bed. Adrian found it to be very unsettling, and distracting. The team as a whole and the coaches seemed nice. Adrian did feel the pressure to perform, as he soon realized that many athletes on the team were much faster, stronger, and skilled than he was.

Two weeks after Adrian arrived in Tucson, he developed a rash on his torso. It was painful, but doctors could not find a real cause for it. They suspected that it was a result of the drastic change in climate, and that Adrian's body was simply trying to adjust to the heat. When it did not subside, his athletic trainer suggested that it could be "stress related." Soon after, Adrian also got sick with a cold, which wiped him out for three weeks. "Who gets sick in June? In this heat?" On his return to practice, he also noticed that he was really far behind the other players in the team physically, which made him very tense and nervous. "How am I going to catch up with them? At this rate, I am never going to make the starting lineup."

In July, during a regular practice session, a few weeks before the season opener, Adrian tripped and twisted his ankle. The injury was diagnosed as a grade II lateral ankle sprain, and the team doctor estimated that it would take Adrian six or so weeks to fully recover. This meant he would miss at least four games at the start of the season. Adrian called home, and his father was obviously worried about his chances of playing this season and suggested he should redshirt this year. At that point, having never experienced a sport injury before, Adrian, with some encouragement from an assistant coach, decided to seek assistance from the team's certified mental performance consultant for two reasons: (a) to help him make a decision about redshirting this season; and (b) to help him get his confidence as a player back.

The injury

The lateral ankle sprain (LAS) is the most common ankle injury amongst athletes. It occurs when the foot rolls inwards, stretching or tearing one or more of the lateral ankle ligaments: anterior talofibular ligament (ATF), calcaneofibular ligament (CF), and posterior talofibular ligament (PTF) (van den Bekerom, Kerkhoffs, McCollum, Calder, & Niek van Dijk, 2013). A grade II lateral ankle sprain indicates that the disruption sustained to the ligaments on the outer portion of the joint is severe enough to significantly decrease the stability of an athlete's lower leg, and is characterized by immediate swelling, persistent pain, and difficulty walking (van den Bekerom et al., 2013). Early treatment (approximately four to five days) will consist of rest, ice, compression, elevation of the foot, and utilizing crutches to walk. Upon decreases in swelling and pain, rehabilitation will consist of exercises aimed to increase range of motion, strength, and stability, with the aim to return to sport in four to six weeks (van den Bekerom et al., 2013). It is known, however, that the ligament itself may not start to heal for up to three months after the injury, and that it can take over a year to completely heal, thus the risk of re-injury is high (van den Bekerom et al., 2013).

Key factor 1: Personality

One of the key factors to consider in Adrian's case is his personality. Defined as "the psychological qualities that contribute to an individual's enduring and distinctive patterns of feeling, thinking and behaving" (Cervone & Pervin, 2010, p. 8). A range of personality factors have been found to significantly increase an individual's suscept-ibility to injury. For example, anxiety as a personality trait can elicit both cognitive (e.g., worry, apprehension) and somatic symptoms (e.g., perspiration, increased heart-rate) without a situationally specific onset (Smith & Smoll, 1990). These symptoms, if not controlled appropriately by the individual in question, can amplify one's stress response to a stressful situation thus increasing their risk of encountering an injury (Ivarsson et al., 2017). Previous research also suggests that personality traits such as hardiness (Wadey, Evans, Hanton, & Neil, 2012) and mental toughness (Petrie, Deiters, & Harmison, 2014) help combat feelings of dispiritedness and thus, posi-tively influence athletes' perceptions of stress pertaining to athletic injury.

To better understand Adrian's anxious personality and how it may have con-tributed to his injury occurrence as well as, reactions to the injury, we recom-mend utilizing the trait subscale of the State-Trait Anxiety Inventory (STAI; Spielberger, Gorsuch, & Lushener, 1970). The trait subscale consists of 20 items rated on a 4-point Likert scale (1 = not at all; 4 = very much so). Respondents identify how they would typically feel (e.g., tense, nervous, worried) in hypo-thetical situations (Martin, Craib, & Mitchell, 1995).

Key factor 2: History of stressors

Adrian's case also reveals that in the months leading up to his injury, he experi-enced a range of significant life events (i.e., moving away from home, new food, new school, new teammates, new climate, and new daily routine). All of the above are considered either major life events or daily hassles, both have been found to negatively influence one's stress response, and in turn, increase the likelihood of injury occurrence (Ivarsson et al., 2017; Ivarsson, Johnson, Lindwall, Gustafsson, & Altemyr, 2014). A recent meta-analysis found negative life event stress to be the strongest predictor of athletic injury (Ivarsson et al., 2017), as it can impede an athlete's ability to focus on the task at hand and thus, increase their likelihood of sustaining an injury (Johnson & Ivarsson, 2011). It is also possible that recurrent daily hassles can cause athletes to develop anxious thoughts, that can hinder an athlete's ability to focus on the task at hand and in turn, increase the risk of injury (Ivarsson, Johnson, & Podlog, 2013).

To gain insight into Adrian's major life events, using the Life Events Survey for Collegiate Athletes (LESCA; Petrie, 1992) is recommended. It is a 69-item measure, aimed to capture: (a) the number of major life events that have occurred in the past 12 months, and (b) the perceived impact of said event's occurrence. The impact responses are rated on an 8-point Likert scale ranging from −4 (extremely negative) to +4 (extremely positive).

Key factor 3: Coping skills

Another important factor to consider in Adrian's case is his coping skills. In general, coping refers to the cognitive and behavioral efforts of managing internal and external demands with consideration to one's resources (Madrigal & Gill, 2014). Coping is a dynamic process that often incorporates multiple strategies to address a single stressor (Madrigal & Gill, 2014), and is typically classified into three main types: problem-focused coping (i.e., direct addressment), emotion-focused coping (i.e., emotional regulation), and avoidant coping (Kowalski & Crocker, 2001). It is clear that Adrian has not coped well with his transition to college. This is an important factor to consider because now Adrian's injury itself will only add to his existing stressors. Without adequate coping skills, Adrian's injury rehabilitation and return to sport process could be affected. Previous research has shown weak psychological coping skills such as denial and wishful thinking (i.e., hoping an injury will improve on its own) to mediate the intensity and frequency of athletes' anxiety, as well as negative psychological outcomes such as worry or return to sport concerns (Wadey et al., 2014).

To formally assess Adrian's coping skills, using the Athletic Coping Skill Inventory-28 (ACSI-28; Smith, Schutz, Smoll, & Ptacek, 1995) is recommended. The ACSI-28 is a valid and reliable 28-item measure consisting of seven subscales measured on a 4-point Likert scale (1 = almost never; 4 = almost always).

Theoretical considerations

As evidenced in the case, Adrian's initial responses to injury are rooted in his pre-injury experiences. How these experiences interact can be explained through the integrated model of psychological response to sport injury and rehabilitation (from now on, referred to as the integrated model; Wiese-Bjornstal, Smith, Shaffer, & Morrey, 1998), with a particular focus on the role of pre-injury factors in post-injury psychological responses. Adapted from the model of stress and athletic injury (Andersen & Williams, 1988), the integrated model posits that a range of personality characteristics, history of stressors, coping strategies, and use of cognitive-behavioral interventions contribute to sport injury occurrence, and continue to influence athletes' post-injury cognitive appraisals. These cognitive appraisals are also influenced by a range of personal and situational factors and have a bidirectional relationship with emotional and behavioral responses, ultimately affecting overall physical and psychosocial recovery outcomes.

In Adrian's case, he sustained an ankle sprain as a result of a tripping mechanism from not meeting the situational demands required to maintain his balance. It is likely that the injury incident was influenced by potential impairments in his attentional focus and inappropriate assessment of the kinesthetic demands required to keep his footing (an example of a cognitive-physiological stress response), resulting in his inability to maintain an upright position. The case also highlights that at the time of the injury, he was anxious about competing against his team-mates for a playing position and self-confidence was lower than when first arriving to Tucson (i.e., personality factor). Adrian was also struggling to cope with his move from Chicago to Tucson, and with no previous history of injuries he was unsure what to do (i.e., stress history). Although Adrian appeared to have the full support of his assistant coach and his father (i.e., coping resource), the case does not provide any evidence of additional cognitive-behavioral strategies Adrian is using to cope with his anxiety and/or life stressors. Equally, given his history of physical (e.g., rash, catching a cold in June) and psychological (e.g., feeling pressures to perform, worries about "falling behind" his teammates) stress symptoms, it is likely that pre-injury stress influenced Adrian's injury-incidence, and if not addressed, will impede his post-injury reactions as well.

Support for the above can be found in previous literature. A recent meta-analysis (Ivarsson et al., 2017) provided support for the role of stress in injury occurrence. In particular, the findings from a path-analysis found all three injury antecedents (personality, stress history, and coping resources) to indirectly influence injury occurrence through the stress response (Ivarsson et al., 2017). The results also revealed that the stress response and history of stressors have the strongest associations with injury incidences (Ivarsson et al., 2017). Furthermore, utilizing behavioral interventions to help alleviate the stress response does decrease injury occurrences (Ivarsson et al., 2017).

Interprofessional plan of care

Following his conversation with the assistant coach, Adrian approached the team's certified mental performance consultant (CMPC) with the goal of (a) making a decision about redshirting, and (b) getting his playing confidence back before returning to the field after his injury rehabilitation. During their first meeting, it was decided that in order to meet Adrian's goals, the CMPC would need to collaborate with his primary treatment provider (athletic trainer, AT), and his strength and conditioning coach (CSCS), both of whom would be instrumental in ensuring Adrian's physical and psychosocial readiness to return to the football field.

Once the care team was established, with Adrian's permission, the professionals from the team met to discuss his case and agree on the plan of action. The meeting was successful in that it helped the professionals to clarify their roles and responsibilities, get an understanding of Adrian's rehabilitation, and overall recovery needs. It was agreed that one of the key issues to address was Adrian's awareness of how stress can influence injury occurrence, what factors in his case appear to exacerbate his stress response, and teach Adrian strategies to better cope with stressors. Based on the meeting, it was also decided that the CMPC would be best suited to pro-vide psychoeducation, facilitate Adrian's self-awareness and self-regulatory skills, as well as, teach him cognitive-behavioral stress management strategies. The AT would focus on Adrian's physical rehabilitation goals, while reinforcing the cogni-tive-behavioral stress management skills during rehabilitation. The CSCS would focus on improving Adrian's overall strength and conditioning beyond the injury to ensure Adrian's confidence in his overall physical capabilities remained the same, if not increased, during the rehabilitation process. Like the AT, the CSCS would also focus on educating Adrian about his progress and reinforce the cognitive-behavioral stress management skills during conditioning workouts. The team also agreed that before implementation of the plan, Adrian would be consulted to ensure he was comfortable with the approach.

Perspective 1:
The certified mental performance consultant's perspective

The CMPC's main goal was to assist Adrian in developing skills to manage physical and psychological stress. To achieve this goal, Adrian needed to learn how a range of psychological and physical factors interact to create an individual's response to stressful situations. He also needed to understand how he as a person could learn to self-regulate his thoughts, emotions, and behaviors to reduce the stress response. To achieve these aims, the CMPC developed a client-specific program for Adrian consisting of four components: (a) psychoeducation pertaining to Adrian's health and mood states; (b) identification and increasing Adrian's awareness of his mala-daptive thoughts and mood states; (c) teaching Adrian self-regulatory skills to control his physical and mental states; and (d) re-configuration of Adrian's cogni-tive-affective-behavioral responses to stressful situations.

When the CMPC met with Adrian for the first time, it was apparent that he was highly stressed. Based on Adrian's account, it became apparent that the most influential factor of his stress response was his personality, and more specifically, his somewhat unidimensional identity. Adrian also lacked previous injury experiences, thus increas-ing his stress. It was also apparent that Adrian felt that his family expected him to perform well, he overtly worried about not making the team's starting line-up, and that he had not adapted well to his collegiate life. It also became apparent that Adrian was unaware that there is a link between the above factors and injury occurrence, and that these factors can influence injury rehabilitation, recovery, and return to sport success. As a consequence, over the next few weeks, the CMPC met with Adrian regularly to implement psychoeducation (Hamson-Utley, Arvinen-Barrow, & Granquist, 2014; Hoffman & Hanrahan, 2012).

During these early meetings, the CMPC explained how the existing research has demonstrated a bidirectional dynamic relationship among an individual's thoughts, feelings, and behaviors. The CMPC also explained how a range of factors, like those identified above, could influence this interaction, and if left unmanaged, lead to an injury or an illness (Andersen & Williams, 1988; Ivarsson et al., 2017; Williams &

Andersen, 1998). After the CMPC had provided Adrian with this information, he said: "I had no idea that all of these things can be so connected. Kind of scary, but also cool." The CMPC then asked Adrian to complete a journaling exercise where he was asked a series of questions related to his best and worst athletic performances, his thoughts and feelings related to his move to Tucson, and identify any possible pertinent thoughts that were currently occupying his mind. Upon completing this exercise, the CMPC and Adrian broke down his answers, and discussed how these factors could be classified, for example as a thought, emotion, or a behavior, or other (personal or a situational factor). They then discussed how these may relate and how these factors may (or may not) have influenced his injury experience. Once the injury-relevant factors were identified, the CMPC and Adrian worked to identify which of the factors were helping him and which were hindering his rehabilitation progress and well-being. It was through these discussions that it became apparent that Adrian's unidirectional identity was also feeding his anxiety (a personality factor), which, together with his stress history (a situational factor) were facilitating the development of a range of negative thought patterns. These thoughts also influenced the creation of unrealistic expectations (i.e., the need to be best on the team) and emphasized things beyond his control (i.e., the weather, athleticism of his team-mates). To help Adrian control his newly identified maladaptive thought patterns, the CMPC taught Adrian two cognitive-behavioral stress management strategies: positive self-talk, and relaxation strategies.

Typically defined as "what athletes say to themselves either out loud or as a small voice inside their head" (Theodorakis, Weinberg, Natsis, Douma, & Kazakas, 2000, p. 254), self-talk has been found beneficial during sport injury rehabilitation for athletes to heal faster, remain positive (Ievleva & Orlick, 1991), and help with coping (Gould, Eklund, & Jackson, 1993; Gould, Finch, & Jackson, 1993). Use of self-talk has also been found to have a positive effect on cognitive anxiety (Tod, Hardy, & Oliver, 2011). To help Adrian change his maladaptive thoughts into positive ones, the CMPC first reviewed his journal responses identified as negative, cognitive constructs. Then, the CMPC and Adrian came up with a thought-stopping strategy that Adrian could use when he finds himself thinking these negative constructs. Adrian chose to use an imaginary alarm buzzer, which would go off at the recognition of a maladaptive thought. Lastly, the CMPC and Adrian developed a series of positive self-talk sentences to counteract his maladaptive thoughts identified earlier. These included but were not limited to: (a) changing *I can't* to *I will* (i.e., reframing; Podlog, Heil, & Schulte, 2014); and (b) establishing a *go to phrase* for when he feels anxious: *Improve today for a better tomorrow* (i.e., a mantra; McCormick, Meijen, & Marcora, 2018). It appeared that these self-talk strategies had somewhat positive effect on Adrian, as during one of the sessions he explained: "I feel they are helping me. But at times, when I am just overly tense, I mean, when I can feel the muscle tension in my shoulders and arms and legs and everywhere, these thoughts just are not helping. And when you have the racing heart on top of it all … forget any talking as my mind and body are not listening. I just need to calm myself down physically."

Prompted by the above conversation, the CMPC discussed relaxation techniques with Adrian. Defined as a "temporary deliberate withdrawal from everyday activity that aims to moderate the functions of the sympathetic nervous system, which is usually activated during stress" (Hill, 2001; cited in Walker & Heaney, 2013, p. 87), a range of relaxation strategies can be beneficial in helping Adrian to manage his physical symptoms of stress (e.g., chest tightness, shortness of breath). Adrian was keen to try simple breathing strategies, so the CMPC worked with him to identify his physical symptoms in times of stress. The CMPC taught Adrian how to use *ratio breathing* to help alleviate chest tightness, and *centering breaths* to help him remain grounded and balanced when feeling flustered or overwhelmed (Walker & Heaney, 2013). Adrian was quick to learn the techniques, and soon after he was very comfortable in pairing the two breathing strategies together. For example, when Adrian found out he would not be able to return to sport as quickly as he anticipated, thus forcing him to redshirt his freshman season, he became light-headed and short of breath. He responded by taking a centering breath, followed by ratio breathing. "Within minutes," Adrian explained during his next session, "I felt like a different person. I was noticeably calmer and felt in control."

The CMPC then encouraged Adrian to combine the skills learned. The CMPC explained how centering and ratio breathing during times of stress would influence his physical stress symptoms, and how using thought-stopping, reframing, and mantras would influence his cognitive symptoms of stress. The CMPC emphasizes the importance of alleviating the psychophysiological stress response, both in sport and in life. Learning these skills demonstrated to Adrian that he was capable of controlling his stress responses, both cognitively and physically. During the next session Adrian explained: "yesterday, I attended practice. It was so hard to watch my teammates play when I cannot. It was overwhelming, and I could feel my heart racing. So, I just closed my eyes. I took a centering breath, then a couple of ratio breaths, and while doing so, I said to myself: *improve today, for a better tomorrow.* And then I kept on breathing. It felt great."

Perspective 2:
The athletic trainer's perspective

As the football team's onsite sports medicine professional, the athletic trainer (AT) has the most contact time with Adrian. The AT's main goal is to assist Adrian back to his pre-injury health or better. Considering the duration required to treat a lateral ankle sprain injury, the AT is in an ideal position to assist in: (a) educating Adrian about his injury; (b) working with Adrian to establish appropriate physical reha-bilitation goals; (c) monitoring overall rehabilitation progress, and (d) reinforcing the cognitive-behavioral stress management skills Adrian had learned from the CMPC during rehabilitation.

Because Adrian had no previous injury experiences, the AT felt it was important to ensure he understood his injury and rehabilitation well. According to MacClean (2010), patient education is one of the key factors healthcare professionals can use to "achieve shared decision making, improve understanding and adherence, motivate, and encourage self-management" (p. 721). First, the AT educated Adrian about the injury and its mechanics (e.g., anatomy of the ankle and the injury characteristics). Then, the AT educated Adrian about the importance of adherence when it came to using crutches to minimize setbacks and prevent further injury. Lastly, the AT and Adrian spent time reviewing specific expectations pertaining to rehabilitation duration (i.e., at least four weeks), the possibility of setbacks, and the potential of re-injury. When asked if he had any questions, Adrian responded no, but seemed agitated and nervous. Drawing from the initial interprofessional team meetings, the AT encouraged Adrian to take his time to collect his thoughts. The AT stated: "We are in this together; I will help you step by step. Now, focus on your breathing and finding your balance. Just like the CMPC said."

To help Adrian better cope with his injury, the AT also spent considerable time working with Adrian to set appropriate rehabilitation goals. The goal-setting program aimed to provide Adrian direction and purpose, as well as help alleviate his stress response to his injury and rehabilitation situation (Arvinen-Barrow & Hemmings, 2013). The AT and Adrian worked together to set goals that would systematically focus Adrian's attention toward personally controllable pre-set physical performance (e.g., balancing on injured foot without pain for 5, 10, 15, and later 20 seconds) throughout the duration of treatment (Arvinen-Barrow & Hemmings, 2013). The overall rehabilitation goal was a successful return to play (Arvinen-Barrow & Hemmings, 2013).

Adrian was quick to note that returning to play would take a lot of work; however, the thought of "short-term goals" confused him. "I want to be out there [on the field] as soon as possible," he said. The AT responded by saying, "That would be great, but there are several things we need to have you accomplish before you get to that point. You need to take things step-by-step, and ensure you follow a plan. A physical goals map will identify distinct indicators needed to get you one step closer to the field each day." Adrian paused for a moment then responded abruptly, "So, it's like a check list! Let's do it!" Together, the AT and Adrian worked to set Adrian short-, medium-, and long-term goals. The AT asked Adrian "What do you need to be physically capable of in order to return to play?" This launched a discussion pertaining to the physical challenges Adrian would endure to progress in his recovery, which were then organized in a manner that provided Adrian a sense of direction, as well as an indication of an approximate timeline for recovery. These goals were then frequently monitored and evaluated, to ensure they were matching Adrian's progress and possible setbacks (Flint, 1998; Heil, 1993). Adrian seemed to really embrace this systematic, detailed and visual approach to his rehabilitation. During one of his sessions he stated: "I really like to see what is coming next. I mean … I know I can be a little pedantic, and not knowing makes me anxious. This, just by writing things down in a visual way helps me cope with the injury, this rehabilitation, and everything really."

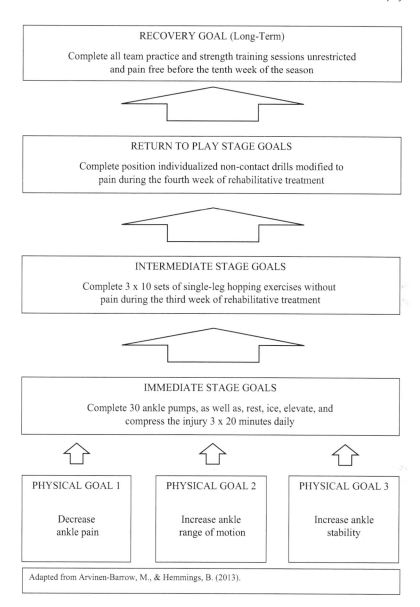

RECOVERY GOAL (Long-Term)

Complete all team practice and strength training sessions unrestricted
and pain free before the tenth week of the season

RETURN TO PLAY STAGE GOALS

Complete position individualized non-contact drills modified to
pain during the fourth week of rehabilitative treatment

INTERMEDIATE STAGE GOALS

Complete 3 x 10 sets of single-leg hopping exercises without
pain during the third week of rehabilitative treatment

IMMEDIATE STAGE GOALS

Complete 30 ankle pumps, as well as, rest, ice, elevate, and
compress the injury 3 x 20 minutes daily

PHYSICAL GOAL 1	PHYSICAL GOAL 2	PHYSICAL GOAL 3
Decrease ankle pain	Increase ankle range of motion	Increase ankle stability

Adapted from Arvinen-Barrow, M., & Hemmings, B. (2013).

FIGURE 2.1 Sample physical goals map
Adapted from Arvinen-Barrow, M., & Hemmings, B. (2013).

Reinforcing the cognitive-behavioral stress management skills Adrian had learned from the CMPC was also one of the key strategies the AT used with Adrian. Knowing Adrian's personality, his tendencies of not coping well with stress, and the need to know what is coming next, the CMPC and the AT established a few ground rules. First, the AT would communicate with Adrian in a manner that would focus on rehabilitation exercises at the present moment (i.e., not talk about events too much in the future), while also giving him a "heads up" at the end of each session about what was on the agenda for the next session. Second, the AT would reinforce self-talk strategies developed with the CMPC during rehabilitation sessions. Third, the AT would build in time for Adrian to use his centering breaths and ratio breathing before, during, and in-between his rehabilitation exercises. For example, Adrian and the AT developed a pre-exercise routine for use prior to completing challenging, painful, and/or stress inducing exercises, such as the 20-second single-leg balance exercise. To start, Adrian would first gaze at the clock on the wall. Then, he would inhale for five seconds, hold for one, exhale over a seven count. Once ready, Adrian would balance on his injured foot, keeping the same breathing rhythm. Once mastered, Adrian also incorporated his self-talk mantras to the activity — after each attempt, Adrian would say to himself "Got it!"; a phrase Adrian chose to represent the fact that "I control my balance."

Perspective 3:
The strength and conditioning coach's perspective

At Adrian's university, the strength and conditioning coach (CSCS) holds a prominent role as a full-time member of the football team. As such, the CSCS, who typically has extensive training in the physiological aspects of sport performance, will be an integral part of Adrian's rehabilitation (National Strength and Conditioning Association, 2009). While injured, the AT and CSCS agreed that Adrian would be able to participate in the team strength and conditioning sessions, provided he would not participate in lower extremity exercises. Instead, the CSCS and Adrian would focus on core and upper extremity exercises, with the goal of making Adrian stronger upon return than he was prior to the injury. This goal was aimed at complementing the work conducted by the CMPC and the AT. If Adrian increases his strength, it could help eliminate some of his stressors, thus helping him cope better with the rehabilitation and the return to sport process. To achieve this goal, it was imperative to ensure the CSCS and the AT continued to work closely in designing Adrian's strength, conditioning, and rehabilitation exercises. The CSCS and the AT met on a regular basis to discuss Adrian's progression through the physiological phases of rehabilitation (i.e., immediate, intermediate, advanced, return to function; Reiman & Lorenz, 2011). This allowed for better communication and collaboration between Adrian's treatment and training programs.

To help Adrian cope with his injury, the CSCS worked with Adrian to develop a goal-setting program to increase his core and upper extremity strength. Consistent with the goal-setting theory (Locke & Latham, 1985; Locke, Shaw, Saari, & Latham, 1981), the CSCS set SMARTER goals with Adrian (for more details on SMARTER goals, please see Locke et al., 1981), aimed to reinforce his existing strengths and building on to them. Given Adrian's personality and tendency to worry, it was important that the CSCS monitored and evaluated the set goals with Adrian and the AT regularly. Integrating sport-related performance goals to Adrian's rehabilitation could be of benefit in number of ways. First, they could help Adrian identify potential areas of improvement and focus on them while undergoing rehabilitation (Taylor & Taylor, 1997). Setting strength-related goals could also provide Adrian new incentives during rehabilitation, thus helping him remain motivated during rehabilitation. Equally, directing Adrian's attention towards his strengths instead of only his injury could promote self-belief (Ludlam, Bawden, Butt, Lindsay, & Maynard, 2017).

Having Adrian be part of the strength and conditioning workouts proved effective. For example, when Adrian seemed discouraged after completing a set of exercises, the CSCS noticed his frustration, and deflated body posture. The CSCS casually reminded Adrian: "You know, usually, when I see you here, you have always found a way to get things done, no matter what. That's a great strength of yours! Now, let's find a way to get this set done!" The CSCS also brought in much needed humor to Adrian's life. By playing different songs in the background during workouts, and making the sessions fun, Adrian found a way to get his mind off the injury. One day he explained to the CMPC: "The CSCS is great. Just yesterday, we joked around about our favorite pro teams. I cannot remember last time I had that much fun bantering. It was almost like … the injury did not exist."

Lastly, much like the AT, the CSCS also reinforced the cognitive-behavioral stress management skills Adrian had learned from the CMPC. Like with the AT, the CMPC and the CSCS established few ground rules. First, the CSCS would communicate with Adrian in a manner that would focus on the strength exercises at the present moment (i.e., not talk about activities too much in the future), while also giving him a "heads up" at the end of each session about what was on the agenda for the next session. Second, the CSCS would reinforce self-talk strategies developed with the CMPC during strength and conditioning workouts. Third, the CSCS would allocate time for Adrian to use his centering breaths and ratio breathing before, during, and in-between his strength exercises. Lastly, the CSCS would ensure their sessions were challenging but fun, and focused on sport performance and not Adrian's injury. For example, the CSCS would encourage Adrian to control his inhalations and exhalations to breathe through the sticking point of every exercise (e.g., bench-press), while mentally saying "get it!" as he exhaled.

Ethical considerations and need(s) for referral

This case study asserts that all members of the interprofessional care team collaborate in a manner that best exemplifies their individual competencies, while recognizing the overlapping areas. Each professional is responsible for conducting himself or herself legally and ethically in accordance to the statutes set forth by their respective governing bodies.

For example, ATs have expertise and competences in clinical examination, diagnosis and use of range of therapeutic interventions (National Athletic Trainers' Association, 2011). A CSCS is expected to be proficient in the coaching of strength and conditioning design and exercise technique (National Strength and Conditioning Association, 2009). Because of the obvious overlap in these proficiencies, it is imperative to ensure the AT and CSCS communicate effectively and regularly to ensure competent and optimal patient care.

The CMPC's competencies include teaching and application of mental and/or self-regulatory skills to optimize sport performance and personal development (Association for Applied Sport Psychology, 2017). Since key factors affecting Adrian's reactions to injury (and possibly his injury occurrence), included personality factors (e.g., unidimensional identity and anxiety), major life stressors, and apparent lack of appropriate coping skills, all three members of the team need to be mindful of the possible need for extended mental health support for Adrian. In such case, it would be the CMPC's responsibility to assess whether the mental health concerns extend beyond their own competencies, followed by facilitating a mental health referral to a clinically trained professional (e.g., licensed clinical psychologist, psychiatrist, licensed mental health counselor).

Case update

As noted above, Adrian redshirted his first year. After the initial shock, Adrian took it really well, and worked diligently with his interprofessional care team throughout the rehabilitation. Five months on, Adrian continues to use self-talk and relaxation techniques daily, and has independently started to use them outside of sport as well. He also meets with the CMPC regularly and continues to strive toward his goal of receiving and maintaining a starting position on the team.

Conclusion

Adrian Jones is a 19-year-old university football player who sustained a grade II lateral ankle sprain during his freshman collegiate season. Adrian recently moved to Arizona from the Midwest on a football scholarship, and was faced with a range of stressors he had not anticipated. Inevitably, these stressors disrupted his focus during practice and possibly contributed to the occurrence of his injury. Grounded in the integrated model (Wiese-Bjornstal et al., 1998), an interprofessional care approach was utilized to ensure Adrian's successful return to sport. Despite redshirting his freshman year, Adrian feels confident in his ability to earn a starting position for next season. He also proclaims that much of this confidence is due to the collaborative efforts of the interprofessional team, particularly as they relate to stress management, and his ability to stay present in the moment working towards one goal at the time.

KEY POINTS

- Adrian Jones, a college freshman football player sustained a grade II lateral ankle sprain injury.
- The physiological mechanism of Adrian's injury was an unbalanced "rolling of the ankle."
- Adrian's stress experiences suggest psychological concerns related to his personality life stress, and coping skills negatively influenced his overall biopsychosocial health, and possibly influenced his injury occurrence.
- An interprofessional care team assisted Adrian in raising his awareness of how stress can influence injury occurrence, what factors in his case appeared to exacerbate stress his response, and taught him strategies to better cope with stressors.
- Most notably, Adrian stated, "The work I have done with the interprofessional care team has made me comfortable in my own skin."

CRITICAL THINKING QUESTIONS

1. In what ways might Adrian transfer the psychological skills he learned during his rehabilitation experience to stressful life situations, such as completing school, and/or starting a career outside of sports?
2. What environmental factors influenced Adrian's injury and rehabilitation experiences and how?
3. Adrian's interprofessional care team comprised of a CMPC, AT, CSCS. If the university did not have access to a CMPC, which other professionals could have been included in Adrian's care team to ensure similar outcomes could be reached? Justify your answer.

RESEARCH QUESTIONS

1. What are antecedents to athletic injury and how do they influence injury occurrence?
2. What is cognitive-behavioral therapy and why is it beneficial for athletes during athletic injury rehabilitation?
3. Describe the pros and cons of integrated methods of patient centered care, such as interprofessional sports medicine teams.

KEY PUBLICATIONS

1. Andersen, M. B. & Williams, J. M. (1988). A model of stress and athletic injury: Prediction and prevention. *Journal of Applied Sport Psychology, 10,* 294–306. doi: 10.1123/jsep.10.3.294.

This paper is one of the seminal papers in psychological aspects of sport injury. Drawing from the stress and illness literature, the paper proposes a theoretical model in which sport injury is seen as a potential consequence of a stress response to a stressful situation.

2. Ekstrand, J., Lundqvist, D., Davison, M., D'Hooghe, M., & Pensgaard, A. M. (2018). Communication quality between the medical team and the head coach/manager is associated with injury burden and player availability in elite football clubs. *British Journal of Sports Medicine*, 1–6. doi:10.1136/bjsports-2018-0994.

This paper investigates the relationship between elite soccer team medical staff member's perceptions of the internal communication quality and athletes' injury-incidence and/or time lost due to injury occurrence. Thirty-six elite football clubs among 17 European countries produced 77 reports. Incidents of severe injuries were significantly higher in teams with low quality of communication between the head coach and the medical team. Teams with low communication scores had 4%–5% lower training attendance compared to teams with moderate or high communication quality scores. Results suggest that the quality of internal communication among a team and its medical staff is related to the team's injury rates, training attendance and match availability.

References

Andersen, M. B., & Williams, J. M. (1988). A model of stress and athletic injury: Prediction and prevention. *Journal of Sport & Exercise Psychology*, 10(3), 294–306. doi:10.1123/jsep.10.3.294.

Arvinen-Barrow, M., & Hemmings, B. (2013). Goal setting in sport injury rehabilitation. In M. Arvinen-Barrow & N. Walker (Eds.), *Psychology of sport injury and rehabilitation* (pp. 56–70). Abingdon: Routledge.

Association for Applied Sport Psychology (2017). Certification. Retrieved September 16, 2018, from https://appliedsportpsych.org/certification/.

Cervone, D., & Pervin, L. (2010). *Personality: Theory and research* (11th ed.). New York, NY: Wiley.

Flint, F. A. (1998). Specialized psychological interventions. In F. A. Flint (Ed.), *Psychology of sport injury* (pp. 29–50). Leeds: Human Kinetics.

Gould, D., Eklund, R. C., & Jackson, S. A. (1993). Coping strategies used by US Olympic wrestlers. *Research Quarterly for Exercise and Sport*, 64, 83–93.

Gould, D., Finch, L. M., & Jackson, S. A. (1993). Coping strategies used by national champion figure skaters. *Research Quarterly for Exercise and Sport*, 64(4), 453–468.

Hamson-Utley, J. J., Arvinen-Barrow, M., & Granquist, M. D. (2014). Psychosocial strategies: Effectiveness and application. In M. Granquist, J. J. Hamson-Utley, L. J. Kenow & J. Stiller-Ostrowski (Eds.), *Psychosocial strategies for athletic training* (pp. 231–263). Philadelphia, PA: F A Davis.

Heil, J. (1993). *Psychology of sport injury*. Champaign, IL: Human Kinetics.

Hoffman, S. L., & Hanrahan, S. J. (2012). Mental skills for musicians: Managing music performance anxiety and enhancing performance. *Sport, Exercise, and Performance Psychology*, 1(1), 17–28. doi:10.1037/a0025409.

Ievleva, L., & Orlick, T. (1991). Mental links to enhance healing: An exploratory study. *The Sport Psychologist*, 5(1), 25–40. doi:10.1123/tsp.5.1.25.

Ivarsson, A., Johnson, U., Andersen, M. B., Tranaeus, U., Stenling, A., & Lindwall, M. (2017). Psychosocial factors and sport injuries: Meta-analyses for prediction and prevention. *Sports Medicine, Training and Rehabilitation*, 47(2), 353–365. doi:10.1007/s40279-40016-0578-x.

Ivarsson, A., Johnson, U., Lindwall, M., Gustafsson, H., & Altemyr, M. (2014). Psychosocial stress as a predictor of injury in elite junior soccer: A latent growth curve analysis. *Journal of Science and Medicine in Sport*, 17(4), 366–370. doi:10.1016/j.jsams.2013.10.242.

Ivarsson, A., Johnson, U., & Podlog, L. (2013). Psychological predictors of injury occurrence: A prospective investigation of professional Swedish soccer players. *Journal of Sport Rehabilitation*, 22(1), 19–26. doi:10.1123/jsr.22.1.19.

Johnson, U., & Ivarsson, A. (2011). Psychological predictors of sport injuries among junior soccer players. *Scandanavian Journal of Medicine and Science in Sports*, 21(1), 129–136. doi:10.1111/j.1600-0838.2009.01057.x.

Kowalski, K., & Crocker, P. (2001). Development and validation of the coping function questionnaire for adolescents in sport. *Journal of Sport & Exercise Psychology*, 23(2), 136–155. doi:10.1123/jsep.23.2.136.

Locke, E. A., & Latham, G. P. (1985). The application of goal setting to sports. *Journal of Sport Psychology*, 7, 205–222.

Locke, E. A., Shaw, K. N., Saari, L. M., & Latham, G. P. (1981). Goal setting and task performance: 1969–1980. *Psychological Bulletin*, 90(1), 125–152. doi:10.1037//0033-002909.90.1.125.

Ludlam, K., Bawden, M., Butt, J., Lindsay, P., & Maynard, I. M. (2017). Perceptions of engaging with a super-strengths approach in elite sport. *Journal of Applied Sport Psychology*, 29(3), 251–269. doi:10.1080/10413200.2016.1255278.

MacClean, K. (2010). Patient education: sharing a passion, sharing resources. *Canadian Family Physician ● Le Médecin de famille canadien*, 56, 721.

McCormick, A., Meijen, C., & Marcora, S. (2018). Effects of a motivational self-talk intervention for endurance athletes completing an ultramarathon. *The Sport Psychologist*, 32(1), 42–50. doi:10.1123/tsp.2017-0018.

Madrigal, L., & Gill, D. L. (2014). Psychological responses of division I female athletes through injury recovery: A case study approach. *Journal of Clinical Sport Psychology*, 8(3), 276–298. doi:10.1123/jcsp.2014-0034.

Martin, J. J., Craib, M., & Mitchell, V. (1995). The relationships of anxiety and self-attention to running economy in competitive male distance runners. *Journal of Sports Sciences*, 13(5), 371–376.

National Athletic Trainers' Association. (2011). *Athletic training educational competencies* (5th ed.). Dallas, TX: National Athletic Trainers' Association.

National Strength and Conditioning Association. (2009). Areas of proficiency covered by the CSCS. Retrieved September 15, 2018, from https://www.nsca.com/education/high-school-athletic-directors-resources/what-are-the-competencies-of-a-qualified-strength-and-conditioning-professional/.

Petrie, T. A. (1992). Psychosocial antecedents of athletic injury: The effects of life stress and social support on female collegiate gymnasts. *Behavioral Medicine*, 18(3), 127–138. doi:10.1080/08964289.1992.9936963.

Petrie, T. A., Deiters, J., & Harmison, R. (2014). Mental toughness, social support, and athletic identity: Moderators of the life stress-injury relationship in collegiate football players. *Sport, Exercise, and Performance Psychology*, 3(1), 13–27. doi:10.1037/a0032698.

Podlog, L., Heil, J., & Schulte, S. (2014). Psychosocial factors in sports injury rehabilitation and return to play. *Physical Medicine and Rehabilitation Clinics*, 25(4), 915–930. doi:10.1016/j.pmr.2014.06.011.

Reiman, M. P., & Lorenz, D. S. (2011). Integration of strength and conditioning principles into a rehabilitation program. *The International Journal of Sports Physical Therapy*, 6(3), 241–253.

Smith, R. E., Schutz, R. W., Smoll, F. L., & Ptacek, J. T. (1995). Sport psychology development and validation of a multidimensional measure of sport-specific psychological skills: The athletic coping skills inventory-28. *Journal of Sport & Exercise Psychology*, 17(4), 379–398.

Smith, R. E., & Smoll, F. L. (1990). Sport performance anxiety. In H. Leitenberg (Ed.), *Handbook of social and evaluation anxiety* (pp. 417–454). Boston, MA: Springer.

Spielberger, C. R., Gorsuch, R. L., & Lushener, E. (1970). *The state-trait anxiety inventory (test manual)*. Palo Alto, CA: Consulting Psychologists Press.

Taylor, J., & Taylor, S. (1997). *Psychological approaches to sports injury rehabilitation*. Gaithersburg, MD: Aspen.

Theodorakis, Y., Weinberg, R., Natsis, P., Douma, I., & Kazakas, P. (2000). The effects of motivational versus instructional self-talk on improving motor performance. *The Sport Psychologist*, 14(3), 253–271. doi:10.1123/tsp.14.3.253.

Tod, D., Hardy, J., & Oliver, E. (2011). Effects of self-talk: A systematic literature review. *Journal of Sport and Exercise Psychology*, 33, 666–687.

van den Bekerom, M. P. J., Kerkhoffs, G. M. M. J., McCollum, G. A., Calder, J. D. F., & Niek van Dijk, C. (2013). Management of acute lateral ankle ligament injury in the athlete. *Knee Surgery, Sports Traumatology, Arthroscopy*, 21(6), 1390–1395. doi:10.1007/s00167-00012-2252-2257.

Wadey, R., Evans, L., Hanton, S., & Neil, R. (2012). An examination of hardiness throughout the sport injury process. *British Journal of Health Psychology*, 17(1), 103–128. doi:10.1111/j.2044-8287.2011.02025.x.

Wadey, R., Podlog, L., Hall, M., Hamson-Utley, J. J., Hicks-Little, C., & Hammer, C. (2014). Reinjury anxiety, coping, and return-to-sport outcomes: A multiple mediation analysis. *Rehabilitation Psychology*, 59(3), 256–266. doi:10.1037/a0037032.

Walker, N., & Heaney, C. (2013). Relaxation techniques in sport injury rehabilitation. In M. Arvinen-Barrow & N. Walker (Eds.), *Psychology of sport injury and rehabilitation* (pp. 86–102). Abingdon: Routledge.

Wiese-Bjornstal, D. M., Smith, A. M., Shaffer, S. M., & Morrey, M. A. (1998). An integrated model of response to sport injury: Psychological and sociological dynamics. *Journal of Applied Sport Psychology*, 10(1), 46–69. doi:10.1080/10413209808406377.

Williams, J. M., & Andersen, M. B. (1998). Psychosocial antecedents of sport injury: Review and critique of the stress and injury model. *Journal of Applied Sport Psychology*, 10(1), 5–25. doi:10.1080/10413209808406375.

3

REACTIONS TO A CIRCUS INJURY

Jan Smith, an aerial performer, Cirque du Soleil

Jordan Hamson-Utley, Cindra Kamphoff, and Corey Oshikoya

Key Words: 24-year-old female, circus aerialist, concussion history, denial, spirituality, sport-related concussion, post-concussion syndrome

Case description

Jan Smith, (this name is a pseudonym and used for descriptive purposes only), a 24-year-old former gymnast, had always dreamed of being part of Cirque du Soleil since first seeing them perform 15 years earlier. Ever since she was little, she had been drawn to extreme sports and liked the thrill of danger. Five years ago, her dream became a reality when she was hired by Cirque du Soleil as an aerialist. "I love my job. It is my dream come true in so many ways!" Being part of an aerial stunt team was not without risk. Over the past five years, Jan has experienced multiple concussions, and following each incident she has noticed subtle changes in herself. Over time, she has become somewhat detached from her boyfriend of six years, who is not part of the troupe, and she feels that a long-distance relationship is no longer worth it. Jan has noticed that she prefers to be alone, cries a lot, and for the first time, feels she has difficulty in keeping up with her life. She is also experiencing lingering headaches, increased general fatigue, problems managing sleep, and overall, just feeling different.

Jan has downplayed her symptoms and not shared them with anyone, not even the troupe's athletic trainer. Instead, she has continued to tour the world with Cirque du Soleil, typically performing in two to five shows a week depending on location. She has bonded well with her house troupe and production staff, but often chooses to stay in her hotel room after each show when others go out to dinner. "I just don't have the energy to go out in a big crowd. It makes me feel uneasy." Within the troupe, Jan has found one member in particular, the troupe manager Rob (who is also an ordained minister), to be her confidant. Jan does not consider herself religious, or spiritual for that matter, but has recently started asking

Rob questions related to faith, and how it could help her cope with the increasing changes she has been experiencing over past years. Jan has always looked to solve every problem or obstacle placed in front of her, without anyone's assistance. However, with increased social isolation, sadness, and worsening physical symptoms, Jan realized that she needed help. With long travel hours on tour, she began to open up to Rob, stating to him: "I fight daily with fatigue and headaches, and sometimes I lose my concentration during a show. Why is this happening to me? I feel like I'm drowning and there's no one on shore." Jan also told Rob that on few occasions, she had been blacking out on high tosses and when she has taken an inverted pose on top of the formation. Then it happened. Jan fell during an act in Las Vegas one month later, and hit her head again.

Following a visit to the troupe's physician, Jan was diagnosed with a sport-related concussion (SRC). Jan was devastated, knowing her own history of head injuries and increased symptoms over the previous years. She struggled with the thought of being injured and missing show performances. Talking with the troupe's athletic trainer (AT) she stated:

> I feel out of control. For the first time in my life, I feel like I'm not able to get back on my own. I have to perform. I need to perform. This is my life. The headaches and sleeping issues I can work through. But what if my blackouts get worse and never go away? They are affecting my ability to perform. I get dizzy when I stand up. I need help. I need to get back to what I know, to who I am.

Everything seemed overwhelming to Jan, and she was easily irritated and seemed emotionally unsteady. She began to avoid social interactions with her troupe, even Rob. It was clear that she struggled with having an invisible injury, stating to the AT:

> I wish I just had an arm in a cast or something, so it was visible to everyone. Feeling foggy and dizzy isn't an injury. This is not a big deal. I can cope with it fine and still perform. I mean … why is this happening to me? Give me a real injury. Why doesn't God answer (my) prayers?

It became clear to the healthcare team that Jan was experiencing post-concussion syndrome (PCS) and she was diagnosed this way by the troupe physician. Concerned about Jan, the AT suggested she meet with a clinically trained licensed psychologist who is also a certified mental performance consultant (CMPC) they had on staff at the Cirque du Soleil. Jan had previously attended several of the consultant's mental training workshops and liked them, so she agreed.

The injury

A sport-related concussion (SRC) occurs when a force impacts the head or moves through the body (via impact with a hard surface), jostling the brain against the bony cavity of the skull causing a bruise-like injury (McCrory et al., 2017).

Symptoms typically include headache, fogginess, irritability, as well as abnormalities in balance and gait, memory and reaction time; the injury can also present with loss of consciousness or blacking out. Symptoms can persist beyond a normal recovery timeframe; however, they usually resolve in seven to ten days (McCrory et al., 2017). In Jan's case, her symptoms from her previous concussions have persisted, and instead of returning to baseline, have worsened. Following her recent concussion, and taking into account her history of concussion, it is plausible for her medical team to diagnose Jan with a post-concussion syndrome (PCS). Post-concussion syndrome is characterized by symptoms that persist beyond the normal recovery timeframe, sometimes for months to years, and are commonly paralleled with depressed mood or depression (Kontos, Covassin, Elbin, & Parker, 2012). Pre-disposing risk factors for developing PCS include having a history of concussion, increasing age, life stress, anxiety, trauma, and pain (Hanna-Pladdy, Berry, Bennett, Phillips, & Gouvier, 2001). Additionally, returning to participation prior to symptoms resolving can be fatal (McCrory et al., 2017).

Key factor 1: Concussion history

When considering treatment for Jan, one of the important factors to consider is her concussion history. Having a history of SRCs poses increased risk for repeated injury, and with repeated SRCs, patients tend to experience heightened cognitive, emotional, and physical symptoms (McCrory et al., 2017). In Jan's case, her symptoms have progressively worsened with each SRC. At first, she experienced sleep issues and headaches, which were manageable; however, more recently her symptoms have progressed to increased isolation and sadness, and dizziness and blacking out when upside down. This is a typical symptom progression pattern of patients suffering from multiple SRCs (Ponsford et al., 2002). As patients' number of SRC injuries increases, so does the recovery time to clinical normal (McCrory et al., 2017).

To gain a full picture of Jan's history of SRC injuries, the medical professionals working with her would need to gather information to this effect from her, and possibly from the medical professionals who worked with her during the prior injuries. The troupe physician would be able to request/order documents related to Jan's care and attempt to place each of the puzzle pieces into a picture of Jan's current health. In Jan's case, patient notes (SOAP notes) related to her care at prior facilities might provide insight into her response to prior concussion injuries. In particular, the following documents could be beneficial: (a) any documentation/ medical records from high school and college gymnastics; (b) any previous results of diagnostic testing performed post-concussion injury; and (c) any details and outcomes of prior post-concussion rehabilitation programs.

Key factor 2: Denial

Although it appears that Jan recognizes the significance of her current concussion, a factor that will significantly influence her recovery is her history of denial. Over the years, Jan has downplayed and denied her increasing concussion symptoms, even though they can be fatal; she has experienced blacking out on high tosses and in poses on the top of the formation. Denying injury occurrence, or severity is not unusual; as when injured, many athletes report denial as a typical response post-injury occurrence (Tracey, 2003). Addressing Jan's internal cognitions about her injury and its possible consequences are important as in many cases, such as Jan's, continuing in their sport too soon post SRC can be fatal. Thus, helping athletes like Jan accept their injury is essential to their life, overall health, and their ability to continue in the sport long-term.

One way to evaluate the extent of Jan's appraisals of denial is to use motivational interviewing (MI; Rollnick & Miller, 1995). According to Rollnick and Miller, MI is a "directive, client-centered counseling style for eliciting behavior change by helping clients to explore and resolve ambivalence." (p. 325). It has been suggested that when used appropriately, MI can be an effective tool for sport psychology consultants, as it can help the client find internal motivation they need to change even if they start off as unmotivated or unprepared to change (Mack, Breckon, Butt, & Maynard, 2017). Using MI has also been reported as an effective way for consultants to demonstrate empathy, reflective listening, and to take a nonprescriptive, guiding role in helping the athlete change (Hardcastle & Hagger, 2011).

Key factor 3: Spirituality

Given Rob's role as Jan's confidant while on tour and Jan's reliance on prayer to help her cope with her symptoms, one factor to consider is the role of spirituality and prayer in her life. For some athletes, spirituality and prayer can be an important way to cope with their injuries (Czech, Wrisberg, Fisher, Thompson, & Hayes, 2004; Koenig, 2012; Mittenberg, Tremont, Zielinski, Fichera, & Rayls, 1996; Watson & Czech, 2005). While not always contained in a structured religious framework, having faith and spirituality are also often associated with a higher power or life purpose (Bergamo & White, 2016). Research also suggests that individuals who practice religion and/or identify with being spiritual are mentally and physically healthier than their non-spiritual or non-religious counterparts (Barton & Miller, 2015).

To understand how Jan wishes to integrate spiritualty and prayer into her rehabilitation, it would be imperative to discuss the role of spirituality and prayer in her care early on in the rehabilitation process. This should be followed by careful consideration of possible ethical issues pertinent to Jan and the professionals working with her. In addition, practitioners working with Jan should also consider self-assessing their own religious/spiritual stance, the nature of the professional relationship, timing of the integration, assessment of Jan's spiritual needs, practicalities of implementation, and potential cultural considerations (for more details, see Clement, Arvinen-Barrow, & LaGuerre, 2019).

Theoretical considerations

Jan's responses to her concussion injury can be explained through the integrated model of psychological response to sport-related concussion injury and rehabilitation (Wiese-Bjornstal, White, Russell, & Smith, 2015). The model is an adapted version of the integrated model of psychological response to sport injury and rehabilitation process (Wiese-Bjornstal, Smith, Shaffer, & Morrey, 1998), and aims to provide a conceptual framework for understanding the role of psychosocial factors in concussion injury. In Jan's case, her history of concussion likely influenced her most recent concussion injury. Equally, it is likely that her concussion history also influenced the severity of her most recent injury and any subsequent neurobiological, psychogenic, and pathophysiological causes, which, together with range of personal and situational factors affected her cognitive symptoms and appraisals of her injury. Although Jan cannot deny her dizziness and blacking out, she has appeared to appraise these as something she can "perform through," suggesting that she is in denial about her injury and its severity. Such appraisals could be influenced by the culture surrounding aerial performers, where she is expected to approach all challenges with the mindset that there is no roadblock that she cannot overcome. Equally, it is likely that Jan's unidimensional identity as a circus performer is also influencing her desires to continue to "perform through" and downplaying her injury severity.

The model also emphasizes that Jan's affective and behavioral responses influence each other, the persistence of symptoms, and subsequent injury appraisals. As you can see, this becomes a downward spiral for Jan, with negative appraisals feeding negative outcomes. One way to halt the negative spiral is intervention from an interprofessional care team. The model depicts post-injury psychological care strategies that aim to influence the re-appraisal cycle, including affective and behavioral symptoms and responses, ultimately affecting Jan's satisfaction with life, return to sport and performance quality, and PCS. In Jan's case, the interprofessional care team includes an athletic trainer (AT), a certified mental performance consultant (CMPC), and an ordained minister.

Interprofessional plan of care

Given that Jan had a history of previous concussions, and to ensure she would be closely monitored during her rehabilitation, it was decided that her AT would be best positioned to serve as her case coordinator. The AT, who travels with the troupe, would also be Jan's primary treatment provider, responsible for her daily care. Since Jan's AT was also trained in vestibular therapy, they would be able to take charge of this aspect of recovery. Additionally, the AT would collaborate closely with the troupe's physician throughout Jan's rehabilitation to ensure appropriate care, and eventually successful return to the circus act.

Upon their initial conversation with Jan, the AT had observed clear behavioral and cognitive signs of denial and distress, and consequently felt that the inclusion of a clinically trained licensed psychologist who is also a Certified Mental Performance Consultant (CMPC) would be imperative for Jan's care and recovery. It was also evident that Jan had developed a close relationship with the troupe's manager, Rob. Rob's background as an ordained minister brings a unique skill set to Jan's care team. As a troupe manager, ordained minister, and Jan's closest confidant, Rob can ease any pressures to return to the circus act too soon, facilitate potential spiritual needs Jan might have, and provide her different types of social support during her rehabilitation and recovery.

To start Jan's care plan, with Jan's permission, the AT called a meeting with the team's CMPC and Rob, the troupe manager. The three had not previously collaborated on patient care, and given Rob's divided role in Jan's care, the team established roles, responsibilities, and boundaries prior to discussing Jan's case. Once established, they shared pertinent information about Jan's case: the AT highlighted the need for Jan to be educated on concussion injury, post-concussion syndrome, and potential consequences of continuing to perform through symptoms. The CMPC emphasized that such education needed to take into consideration Jan's denial of the injury, as if not addressed, it would continue to undermine any educational attempts the AT would implement. As the CMPC was also trained on post-concussion syndrome, it was agreed that patient education would be part of both the AT's and the CMPC's role. Addressing Jan's denial about the severity of her symptoms would be something the CMPC would work with Jan during their one-on-one sessions.

During the care team discussions on Jan's case, Rob mentioned that Jan had been growing closer to God over the previous months, explaining how she had repeatedly requested to pray with Rob prior to her performances. The AT chimed in, outlining Jan's initial reactions to her injury including a spiritual component and direct reference to God. It was decided that Rob's role as a spiritual support would be imperative for Jan's care, particularly as the troupe was on the road again and Jan's access to her family was limited, and her relationship with her long-term boyfriend offered unstable social support. As a final step, the team invited Jan to discuss the proposed care plan, to which Jan agreed: 'Thank you so much for all you do. I know I did not want any help, as I should be able to get through this on my own. But I realize that it is OK to ask for help. God willing, I will heal and can continue my path as normal soon."

Perspective 1:
The athletic trainer's perspective

After the first few meetings with Jan, the AT had gained a sense of Jan's approach to her injuries. Jan is a performer who rarely seeks assistance prior to training, or after a performance. She leads on that she is in full control of her body and her performance. At the elite level, this is a mindset that exists and controls the behavior of many athletes; they have gotten to this level *this way* (Burke, Fralick, Nejatbakhsh,

Tartaglia, & Tator, 2015). When Jan fell during an act, this prompted her first *real* encounter with the AT since she joined the troupe.

To ensure their work with Jan was off to a great start, the AT wanted to gain a better understanding of Jan's expectations of the AT and the rehabilitation they would provide. It is known that patient expectations can affect recovery outcomes (Silverberg et al., 2013), and that such expectations can vary depending on gender, type of sport, previous experiences with the said professional, and nationality (Arvinen-Barrow et al., 2016; Silverberg et al., 2013). Existing research has highlighted that injured female athletes expect their ATs to provide them knowledge of the injury (Silverberg et al., 2013), which, in Jan's case might not be the case, given her history of denial about her injury and its severity.

Upon establishing Jan's expectations of rehabilitation, the AT, together with the SPC, designed an interactive patient education protocol for her. A well-designed and well-delivered patient education protocol has the potential to shift Jan's cognitive appraisal of the injury, resulting in more adherent behaviors and a better recovery (Wiese-Bjornstal et al., 2015). In Jan's case, the patient education included the use of traditional paper methods as well as some effective online apps and websites. One of the main goals of this early patient education was to help Jan gain a sense of control over her injury situation. As such, the content of the patient education at this early stage of injury was focused on (a) increasing awareness on range of signs and symptoms of SRC and PCS, (b) highlighting the importance of rehabilitation adherence, (c) understanding the consequences of returning to circus act too early, and (d) recognizing the importance of setting small yet attainable goals throughout the rehabilitation.

Along with patient education, to help Jan gain control of her situation, the AT also wanted Jan to monitor her SRC symptoms since they had worsened following her latest concussion. The symptoms had caused Jan to get out of rhythm with her sleep pattern and daily life. This is not surprising, as approximately 20% of patients diagnosed with concussion will develop chronic pain and/or sleep problems (Silverberg et al., 2013). To address the above, the AT wanted Jan to monitor her headaches, fatigue levels, and sleep patterns, as utilizing a sleep diary has been found to be an effective way to monitor sleep patterns and sleep efficiency (Mittenberg et al., 1996). To address fatigue and monitor sleep, the AT requested Jan keep a sleep journal via smartphone app. The app allowed Jan to track her sleep duration, quality, and any possible sleep disturbances during the night. The AT also encouraged Jan to use an app-based, pre-sleep, deep-breathing strategy to help her sleep easier. Jan seemed to like these approaches as they involved the use of her phone: "I really like these apps. I know I use my phone too much, but at least now I am using it for a purpose."

It must be noted that sleep management in post-concussion care is not yet evidence-based (Silverberg et al., 2013). However, it is known that poor sleep quality is associated with increased stress and mood disturbances and that good quality sleep can help alleviate stress (Ellis & Dryden, 1987). Using deep breathing presleep has also been linked with reduction in physiological symptoms that increase with stress (Hanna-Pladdy et al., 2001). In addition, patient education protocol combined with reassurance about prognosis can lower anxiety, reduce distress, and improve sleep (Ponsford et al., 2002). Taking the above into account, by addressing Jan's issues with sleep the AT can assist Jan very effectively during rehabilitation, and ensure she is able to minimize any stressors associated with the injury, rehabilitation, and ultimate return back to the act.

Perspective 2:
The clinical licensed psychologist/certified mental performance consultant's perspective

When the AT approached Jan about the possibility of working with a consultant trained in sport psychology, Jan was eager. She had previously attended several of the mental training workshops offered at the Cirque du Soleil, and found them beneficial. When working with Jan, the CMPC used motivational interviewing (MI; Mack et al., 2017) to guide her work as Jan shared her sport and injury history. During this session, Jan detailed her three concussions and the fall in Las Vegas. She shared that she missed performing with her "family" in Cirque and described how she felt "lonely" and "not herself." As she described her concussions, one by one, Jan came to recognize the severity of her situation, had many "ah-ha moments" with the CMPC and slowly over time began to accept her injury.

To better understand the root cause for Jan's denial, the CMPC continued the session by asking Jan how the news of having a SRC was affecting her. Jan told the CMPC that after the fall in Las Vegas, she was devastated. She said she was easily irritated, and anxious about losing her role and her "dream job." Jan stated: "The thought of not performing makes me physically sick. It is such a double edged sword … I mean I am afraid of falling again, and I do feel overwhelmed and more tired than normal. So it is easier to pretend I am fine than to think about the alternative." As Jan talked, the CMPC used the MI principles of showing empathy, developing discrepancy, dealing with resistance, supporting self-efficacy, and developing autonomy (Mack et al., 2017). As the CMPC listened and probed, Jan started to see the impact that denying her injury had had on her health. She verbalized her commitment to working through the recovery process with the CMPC. During the first meeting, Jan and the CMPC decided to meet weekly.

Given the CMPC's experience in clinical psychology and knowledge of the empirical evidence on use of psychological interventions with concussed patients, the CMPC implemented an evidence-based approach (Azulay, Smart, Mott, & Cicerone, 2013; Hamson-Utley, Arvinen-Barrow, & Clement, 2017) throughout her work with Jan. More specifically, the approach included cognitive behavioral therapy (CBT; Hsiao-Yean, Wen-Cheng, Yung-Hsiao, & Pei-Shan, 2014) and Mindfulness-Based Stress Reduction (MBSR; Tummers, 2013). Cognitive behavioral therapy is the most used and studied intervention within the evidence-based treatment of concussions (Burke et al., 2015), and it has been found to reduce the frequency, intensity and duration of post-concussion symptoms (Mittenberg et al.,

1996), decrease anxiety and depressive symptoms (Burke et al., 2015; Silverberg et al., 2013), and improve psychosocial functioning with concussed patients (Hanna-Pladdy et al., 2001).

The CMPC and Jan worked together by focusing on the relationship between Jan's thoughts, feelings, and behaviors. They explored how her maladaptive thinking patterns had contributed to her cognitive appraisals of her concussions (i.e., denial of severity and downplaying symptoms), and how these thoughts were connected to her behavioral (i.e., continued participation despite symptoms) and affective responses. During her sessions with the CMPC, Jan learned to challenge her thinking with more rational and realistic explanations, and reported being more self-aware of her thoughts and feelings. To achieve this goal, the CMPC used Albert Ellis's ABC cognitive restructuring (Ellis & Dryden, 1987) regularly with Jan. First, Jan would identify the (A) activating event, then describe the (B) beliefs or interpretations of the event, then identify the (C) consequences, feelings, behaviors and her bodily reactions to the event, and then (D) dispute her automatic thoughts by describing a rational response. Jan found cognitive restructuring helpful and reported that she had started using cognitive restructuring in other areas of her life.

Trained in Mindfulness-based stress reduction (MBSR), the CMPC also taught Jan MBSR techniques to reduce her stress, worry, and anxiety. Thus far, preliminary support for the use of MBSR in the recovery from concussion suggests the use of MBSR can improve concussed patients self-efficacy and quality of life post-intervention (Azulay et al., 2013). The exercises the CMPC did with Jan included the body scan, mindful eating, walking meditation, and progressive muscle relaxation. Jan committed to engaging in MBSR at least ten minutes each day and as her rehabilitation progressed, she reported less anxiety and worry.

Perspective 3:
Ordained minister's perspective

One of the most impactful factors helping performers to cope with their injuries and rehabilitation is social support (Arvinen-Barrow & Pack, 2013). Social support has been shown to mediate the stress-health relationship (Sarason, Sarason, & Gurung, 1997), and to facilitate successful recovery. The following should be considered when implementing social support: (a) social support is best provided by a network; (b) these networks should be developed and tested; and (c) the utilization of such networks should be constant (Richman, Hardy, Rosenfeld, & Callanan, 1989). In Jan's case, it is important to acknowledge that her social support network is limited. She has family (at a distance), her relationship with her boyfriend is failing, and her friends are members of her troupe (including Rob), some of whom are competing for the same positions on acts. As a result, Rob's role as Jan's main source of support becomes paramount, particularly as a source of spiritual guidance and support.

To help Jan better cope with the injury, Rob worked with Jan one-on-one to help her find a deeper connection with her own values and beliefs. Rob started this conversation with a few simple questions: "What is important to you?" "In what ways do you think your spirituality can help you to cope with your injury?," and "what can I do to support your coping with your injury spiritually?" (see Matthews, 1998). Together, they identified three main ways to incorporate spirituality into Jan's rehabilitation: (a) attending the troupe spiritual gatherings; (b) reading Bible passages that would provide Jan a sense of calm and hope during times of struggle; and (c) use of prayer to seek guidance, patience, and strength from God during Jan's journey toward full health.

Since Rob held spiritual gatherings for troupe members few days a week depending on their performance schedules, he invited Jan to join them. First, Jan was hesitant, but agreed to come. First, she mainly observed, but later she started feeling more comfortable sharing her thoughts. Over time Jan became more and more comfortable in the group, and it was clear that she found the spirituality gatherings beneficial. One day, during her one-on-one session with Rob, she stated: "it feels good not to just think about performing. I feel like the spiritual gatherings, I can just be Jan. Not Jan the aerialist, but just Jan … and I have met so many nice people that before, were just faces in the line-up. Who would have known that a clown has so much in common with me, an aerialist?"

Rob was pleased to see Jan becoming more comfortable in her own skin, and that she found the group as a source of support. To explore Jan's newfound identity simply as Jan and not Jan the aerialist, Rob also worked with Jan to identify appropriate Bible passages to help her explore this further. One in particular stood out for Jan: "Or do you not know that your body is a temple of the Holy Spirit within you, whom you have from God? You are not your own, for you were bought with a price. So glorify God in your body" (1 Corinthians 6:19–20). When Rob and Jan discussed the meaning of the passage, Jan started crying. Amidst her tears, she stated; "I never realized how harsh I have been on myself, and my body. By denying that my body hurts, I have just been hurting myself."

Lastly, Rob helped Jan to develop a prayer that Jan could use during times of stress. Jan wanted the prayer to focus on her desires to go back too early, and doing too much during rehabilitation. The result, in Jan's opinion was just right for her:

> Thank you, Lord, for hearing this prayer and helping me as I face this injury. I trust in you and submit to your will, and I know that you will never forsake me. Please give me the strength and discipline to persevere through my treatment and recovery, and the wisdom to participate constructively in my own treatment. Please guide the doctors in their care for me, and please bless my friends and family as they support me through this challenge. (Burke et al., 2015)

The spiritual work with Rob appeared to be helpful for Jan. In particular, including spiritual aspects to Jan's rehabilitation reinforced her existing beliefs, helped her accept her injury, gave her hope, alleviated stress and worry, expanded her social networks, and reinforced her adherence to her rehabilitation, all of which has proposed as having an association with spirituality (George, Ellison, & Larson, 2002; Mittenberg et al., 1996; Najah, Farooq, & Rejeb, 2017).

Ethical considerations and need(s) for referral

When working as part of an interprofessional care team, it is imperative to act within one's own scope of practice. It is also important to recognize that roles may overlap, and that can cause confusion, concerns, or other issues related to the patient care. When two practitioners possess same competencies and skills, the role of each must be decided prior to progressing with care, and any potential conflicts of interest must be identified and addressed. Additionally, when an individual has more than one role in the patients' life/care, any possible ethical or moral conflicts should be considered and addressed. It is also essential to evaluate any potential concerns over existing personal relationships between the patient and a member of the care team, and to ensure such members will be removed from the team if deemed necessary. Finally, if a team member begins to experience personal gains as a result of the therapeutic relationship, this should also be addressed and this team member be replaced. For additional ethical guidelines, the readers are encouraged to review the code of ethics relevant to the profession in question.

In Jan's case, two key ethical concerns are worthy of mention. First, Rob holds multiple roles; he is Jan's troupe manager, her spiritual leader, and her main confidant. Due to staffing constraints within the Cirque troupe, it is not possible to remove Rob from Jan's team, therefore establishing boundaries and role clarity is vitally important. Second, since Jan has a long history of concussions, her neurological, physical, and psychological symptoms may progressively worsen over time. Should that happen, those on the care team must be competent in making a referral to relevant healthcare professionals. For example, if Jan starts showing signs of maladaptive coping behaviors (e.g., restricting calorie intake, skipping meals) the AT and/or the CMPC must refer Jan to a professional who specializes in eating disorders.

Case update

Three months later, Jan was cleared to return to her troupe. By adhering to her rehabilitation plan, using psychological interventions, and trusting God, her PCS symptoms have diminished. Despite successfully returning back to her act, Jan decided to continue her consultations with the CMPC biweekly. Through these sessions, Jan has developed an understanding of the importance of listening to her body, training her brain alongside her body, and feeling like herself again. Jan feels one with her mind and body, more so than ever before. She continues to attend the spiritual gatherings, meets occasionally with Rob, and has found new friends from the troupe to hang with when not performing.

Conclusion

Jan, an aerial performer described in this case study, suffered a concussion during a circus act, while also experiencing symptoms suggestive of post-concussion syn-drome. She was unable to continue performing in her act, and struggled with understanding the severity of her injury. It became clear that for a long time she had been in denial about her concussion injury history and severity, and had limited support system due to being on the road consistently for performances. Jan's care team, consisting of the AT, the CMPC, and an ordained minister, worked with her to address key factors affecting her reactions to her concussion injury. The AT, provided Jan appropriate patient education and helped her to monitor her sleep. The SPC worked with Jan to address her denial, and used CBT and MBSR to teach her how to manage her thoughts, emotions, and behaviors. Finally, Rob, the ordained minister served as Jan's social support and spiritual guide, helping her to cope with her injury. It was through coordinated care efforts from her care team, Jan was able to successfully change her injury appraisals, adhere to her rehabilitation, and ultimately, successfully return to her act.

KEY POINTS

- Patient education during the reaction to injury phase is instrumental in ensuring the patient understands their injury, its severity, and potential outcomes of maladaptive behavioral responses to injury recovery.
- Elite performers such as professional circus aerialists may experience heightened levels of denial, stress, and anxiety associated with the injury.
- For performers who find comfort and hope from religion, spirituality, and prayer, incorporating these aspects to injury rehabilitation can be beneficial.
- As a clinician, be prepared to form and work as part of an interprofessional care team. Knowing your healthcare peers and through effective communication, adopting a team approach typically results in the most comprehensive patient care (Institute of Medicine).

CRITICAL THINKING QUESTIONS

1. What biopsychosocial factors can you identify that were not addressed in Jan's case?
2. How does competition/performance at the elite level influence the experience of denial as a reaction to injury?
3. In coordinating Jan's interprofessional team care, what do you perceive as the biggest challenge for the athletic trainer?

RESEARCH QUESTIONS

1. Does sleep deficiency prolong symptom resolution in PCS?
2. In what way does spirituality affect patient reactions to concussion injury, their expression of symptoms, and the rehabilitation process?

3.   Does social support (time spent with a CMPC, AT, minister) influence symptom reporting (lessen the magnitude or occurrence of reported symptoms) and how does it relate to recovery?

KEY PUBLICATIONS

1.   Clement, D., LaGuerre, D., & Arvinen-Barrow, M. (2019). Role of religion and spirituality in sport injury rehabilitation. In B. Hemmings, N. J. Watson & A. Parker (Eds.), *Sport, psychology and Christianity: Welfare, performance and consultancy*. Abingdon: Routledge.

To provide the best, most comprehensive patient care, practitioners need to diversify their approaches to meeting care goals. This chapter discusses how spirituality can be integrated into injury rehabilitation. The chapter also provides practical guidelines on how to implement religion and spirituality into rehabilitation. With strong focus on theory, empirical evidence, and practical application, this chapter is useful for all professionals working with injured patients to better understand the role of faith in their patient's rehabilitation.

2.   Hamson-Utley, J. J., Arvinen-Barrow, M., & Clement, D. (2017). Managing mental health aspects of post-concussion syndrome in the college athlete: Applying theory to practice. *Athletic Training and Sports Health Care, 9*(6), 263–270. doi: 10.3928/19425864-20171010-05.

This article takes an evidence-based approach to evaluation of a patient's case in relation to the Conceptual Model of Psychological Response to Sport Concussion (Wiese-Bjornstal et al., 2015) and resulting patient care. The article discusses factors that influence diagnosis and care, presents evidence-based psychosocial intervention for the patient, discusses the patient's needs for mental health referral, and highlights the interprofessional care approach by examining the roles of various professionals involved in a safe return back to sport.

References

Arvinen-Barrow, M., Clement, D., Hamson-Utley, J. J., Zakrajsek, R., Kamphoff, C., Lee, S. M., … Martin, S. B. (2016). Athletes' expectations about sport injury rehabilitation: A cross-cultural study. *Journal of Sport Rehabilitation*, 25(4), 338–347. doi:10.1123/jsr.2015-0018.
Arvinen-Barrow, M., & Pack, S. M. (2013). Social support in sport injury rehabilitation. In M. Arvinen-Barrow & N. Walker (Eds.), *Psychology of sport injury and rehabilitation* (pp. 117–131). Abingdon, UK: Routledge.
Azulay, J., Smart, C. M., Mott, T., & Cicerone, K. D. (2013). A pilot study examining the effect of mindfulness-based stress reduction on symptoms of chronic mild traumatic brain injury/postconcussive syndrome. *Journal of Head Trauma Rehabilitation*, 28(4), 323–331. doi:10.1097/HTR.0b013e318250ebda.

Barton, Y., & Miller, A. (2015). Spirituality and positive psychology go hand in hand: An investigation of multiple empirically derived profiles and related protective benefits. *Journal of Religion and Health*, 54(3), 829–843. doi:10.1007/s10943-10015-0045-0042.

Bergamo, D., & White, D. (2016). Frequency of faith and spirituality discussion in health care. *Journal of Religion and Health*, 55(2), 618–630. doi:10.1007/s10943-10015-0065-y.

Burke, M. J., Fralick, M., Nejatbakhsh, N., Tartaglia, M. C., & Tator, C. H. (2015). In search of evidence-based treatment for concussion: Characteristics of current clinical trials. *Brain Injury*, 29(3), 300–305.

Clement, D., Arvinen-Barrow, M., & LaGuerre, D. (2019). Role of religion and spirituality in sport injury rehabilitation. In B. Hemmings, N. J. Watson & A. Parker (Eds.), *Sport, psychology and Christianity: Welfare, performance and consultancy*. Abingdon: Routledge.

Czech, D. R., Wrisberg, C., Fisher, L., Thompson, C., & Hayes, G. (2004). The experience of Christian prayer in sport - An existential phenomenological investigation. *Journal of Psychology and Christianity*, 2, 1–19.

Ellis, A., & Dryden, W. (1987). *The practice of rational emotive behavior therapy*. New York, NY: Springer Publishing Company.

George, L. K., Ellison, C. G., & Larson, D. B. (2002). Explaining the relationships between religious involvement and health. *Psychological Inquiry*, 13(3), 190–200.

Hamson-Utley, J. J., Arvinen-Barrow, M., & Clement, D. (2017). Managing mental health aspects of post-concussion syndrome in the college athlete: Applying theory to practice. *Athletic Training and Sports Health Care*, 9(6), 263–270. doi:10.3928/19425864-20171010-05.

Hanna-Pladdy, B., Berry, Z. M., Bennett, T., Phillips, H. L., & Gouvier, W. D. (2001). Stress as a diagnostic challenge for postconcussive symptoms: Sequelae of mild traumatic brain injury or physiological stress response. *The Clinical Neuropsychologist*, 15(3), 289–304.

Hardcastle, S., & Hagger, M. S. (2011). "You Can't Do It on Your Own": Experiences of a motivational interviewing intervention on physical activity and dietary behaviour. *Psychology of Sport and Exercise*, 12(3), 314–323. doi:10.1016/j.psychsport.2011.01.001.

Hsiao-Yean, C., Wen-Cheng, L., Yung-Hsiao, C., & Pei-Shan, T. (2014). The effects of sleep on the relationship between brain injury severity and recovery of cognitive function: A prospective study. *International Journal of Nursing Studies*, 51(6), 892–899. doi:10.1016/j. ijnurstu.2013.10.020.

Koenig, H. G. (2012). Religion, spirituality, and health: The research and clinical implications. *International Scholarly Research Network, ISRN Psychiatry*, 1–33. doi:10.5402/2012/278730.

Kontos, A. P., Covassin, T., Elbin, R. J., & Parker, T. (2012). Depression and neurocognitive performance after concussion among male and female high school and college athletes. *Archives of Physical Medicine and Rehabilitation*, 93, 1751–1756.

Mack, R., Breckon, J. D., Butt, J., & Maynard, I. (2017). Exploring the understanding and application of motivational interviewing in applied sport psychology. *The Sport Psychologist*, 31(4), 1–36. doi:10.1123/tsp.2016-0125.

McCrory, P., Meeuwisse, W., Dvorak, J., Aubry, M., Bailes, J., Broglio, S ...Vos, P. E. (2017). Consensus statement on concussion in sport—the 5th international conference on concussion in sport held in Berlin, October 2016. *British Journal of Sports Medicine*, 51(11), 838–847. doi:10.1136/bjsports-2017-097699.

Matthews, D. A. (1998). Religious commitment and health status: A review of the research and implications for family medicine. *Archives of Family Medicine*, 7(2), 118–124.

Mittenberg, W., Tremont, G., Zielinski, R. E., Fichera, S., & Rayls, K. R. (1996). Cognitive-behavioral prevention of postconcussion syndrome. *Archives of Clinical Neuropsychology*, 11(2), 139–145.

Najah, A., Farooq, A., & Rejeb, R. B. (2017). Role of religious beliefs and practices on the mental health of athletes with anterior cruciate ligament injury. *Advances in Physical Education*, 7(2), 181–190.

Ponsford, J., Willmott, C., Rothwell, A., Cameron, P. A., Kelly, A. M., Nelms, R., & Curran, C. (2002). Impact of early intervention on outcome following mild head injury in adults. *Journal of Neurology, Neurosurgery and Psychiatry*, 73(3), 330–332. doi:10.1136/jnnp.73.3.330.

Richman, J. M., Hardy, C. J., Rosenfeld, L. B., & Callanan, R. A. E. (1989). Strategies for enhancing social support networks in sport: A brainstorming experience. *Journal of Applied Sport Psychology*, 1, 150–159.

Rollnick, S., & Miller, W. R. (1995). "What is Motivational Interviewing?". *Behavioural and Cognitive Psychotherapy*, 23(4), 325–334. doi:10.1017/S135246580001643X.

Sarason, B. R., Sarason, I. G., & Gurung, R. A. R. (1997). Close personal relationships and health outcomes: A key to the role of social support. In S. Duck (Ed.), *Handbook of personal relationships* (pp. 547–573). New York, NY: Wiley.

Silverberg, N. D., Hallam, B. J., Rose, A., Underwood, H., Whitfield, K., Thornton, A. E., & Whittal, M. L. (2013). Cognitive-behavioral prevention of post-concussion syndrome in at-risk patients: A pilot randomized controlled trial. *Journal of Head Trauma Rehabilitation*, 28(4), 313–322.

Tracey, J. (2003). The emotional response to the injury and rehabilitation process. *Journal of Applied Sport Psychology*, 15(4), 279–293. doi:10.1080/714044197.

Tummers, N. E. (2013). *Stress management: A wellness approach*. Champaign, IL: Human Kinetics.

Watson, N., & Czech, D. R. (2005). The use of prayer in sport: Implications for sport psychology consulting. *Athletic Insight: The Online Journal of Sport Psychology*. Retrieved from www.athleticinsight.com/Vol7Iss4/PrayerinSports.htm.

Wiese-Bjornstal, D. M., Smith, A. M., Shaffer, S. M., & Morrey, M. A. (1998). An integrated model of response to sport injury: Psychological and sociological dynamics. *Journal of Applied Sport Psychology*, 10(1), 46–69. doi:10.1080/10413209808406377.

Wiese-Bjornstal, D. M., White, A. C., Russell, H. C., & Smith, A. M. (2015). Psychology of sport concussions. *Kinesiology Review*, 5, 169–189. doi:10.1123/kr.2015-0012.

4

REACTIONS TO A WRESTLING INJURY

Jenna Cousteau, a senior high school wrestler

Theresa Bianco, Arielle Rousseau, and David Zilberman

Key Words: 16-year-old female, high school student, return-to-sport (RTS) concerns, life stress, limited social support, season-ending ulnar collateral ligament tear

Case description

Jenna Cousteau (this name is a pseudonym and used for descriptive purposes only), is a 16-year-old high school student in Montreal, Canada, considered to be a rising star in the sport of wrestling until her injury occurred. Introduced to the sport by her father, a former elite wrestler, she started wrestling competitively at the age of 10. In her first competition, as a cadet wrestler, she placed second, and continued to place in the top three throughout her elementary and high school competitions. By age 16, her success on the mat had earned her the title of athlete of the year and Jenna's coach believed she had Olympic potential. Jenna was looking forward to turning 17, when she could try for Olympic qualification.

Jenna's father has been very involved in her wrestling career from the start, but even more so after recently losing his wife, Jenna's mother, to cancer. He attends most practices, and never misses a tournament. Being an only child, Jenna is very close to her dad. She appreciates his support but finds it sometimes overbearing. He has told her multiple times about how his own wrestling career was cut short due to injury, and how he is counting on her to "bring home the Olympic medal that slipped through his fingers." Jenna promised her father she would do her best to make that happen.

The injury occurred at a tournament in which Jenna tried a new move her coach insisted she do. Unfortunately, her opponent got the upper hand and threw Jenna in such a manner that she landed on her outstretched arm. Instantly, she heard a pop and felt a sharp pain run up her arm. She tried to continue wrestling; she prides herself on being tough, but the referee ended the match.

The athletic therapist (AT) on site assessed Jenna and determined that she had most likely torn her ulnar collateral ligament (UCL). She recommended Jenna not wrestle until she was able to consult with an orthopedic surgeon. Jenna was devastated by the news. She did not want to miss out on upcoming Olympics qualifications. So she told her coach that the AT had recommended she ice her elbow, skip a few practices, and would then be good to go. That strategy did not go well for Jenna; the instant she tried to wrestle a sharp pain would run up her arm. She finally decided to consult a surgeon and a magnetic resonance imaging (MRI) confirmed that she did indeed have a UCL tear and surgery was recommended.

Surgery meant the end of the competitive season for Jenna and she worried about the impact of the surgery on her wrestling career. An honor roll student, Jenna was also worried about her grades slipping were she to take time off school for surgery and rehabilitation. She discussed these concerns at length with her surgeon, her coach, and her father. The surgeon informed Jenna of possible complications and explained that the full extent of recovery could only be determined post-operatively. Everyone agreed that because of Jenna's young age, it was best to try to reconstruct the elbow rather than risk further irreparable damage.

The surgery went well, with no obvious complications and Jenna began her recommended rehabilitation program as prescribed by her surgeon. Jenna worked hard with her AT to ensure a quick return to wrestling but something was not quite right. Two months post-surgery, Jenna was still having difficulty weight-bearing on her newly reconstructed arm. A second MRI revealed the reconstruction had not healed properly. Going in for a second surgery was not an option. Instead, Jenna's surgeon recommended she just take the necessary time to let her reconstructed elbow heal on its own. Jenna received this news on the anniversary of her mother's death. She was devastated – and also overwhelmed by the weight of having let her father down.

To complicate matters, Jenna's father was furious and lashed out at everyone. He felt the surgeon botched the surgery and he blamed the coach for putting Jenna in a precarious situation. Jenna could not reason with her father, and she felt very alone. She had no siblings and all her friends were on the wrestling team. She really needed someone to talk to but she didn't want to burden her teammates with her problems. Jenna confided in her coach that she was afraid of never being able to wrestle again and that was making her panic.

The injury

The ulnar collateral ligament (UCL) of the elbow is a broad ligament located on the medial side of the elbow (Morrey, Llusá-Pérez, & Ballesteros-Betancourt, 2017). A traumatic tear of the UCL occurs with an abrupt valgus force to the elbow, common in contact sports, resulting in an acute rupture of the ligament (Hodgins, Ahmad, & Conway, 2017). Signs and symptoms of a UCL tear include hearing a snap, crack, or pop when injury occurs, pain and swelling on medial side of elbow, bruising and instability (Dines, Camp, & Elattrache, 2017). When a full rupture occurs, the UCL often does not heal on its own and surgical reconstruction is required. In order to return to full contact, an athlete must typically engage in 8–12 months of rehabilitation and reconditioning post-surgery (Ellenbecker, Wilk, Altchek, & Andrews, 2009). In Jenna's case, recovery time will likely be extended an additional three to six months due to complications experienced post-surgery.

Key factor 1: Return-to-sport concerns

With no prior injuries, Jenna was unable to imagine how it would be possible to continue wrestling, let alone be an Olympic contender with a "defective" elbow. "What's the point of continuing in my sport if I can't make it to the top and bring the medal home for my dad? I would just be letting everybody down." This type of questioning and distorted thinking is commonplace among injured athletes. They are often overwhelmed by concerns about being able to continue in their sport, and more importantly whether they will recover fully such that they can perform at and eventually surpass pre-injury levels (Evans, Wadey, Hanton, & Mitchell, 2012; Tracey, 2003). Such apprehensions are further exacerbated when the course of injury recovery does not go as planned, as was the case with Jenna. Setbacks can give rise to a number of cognitive errors (e.g., distortions, catastrophizing, all-or-none thinking, and focusing on the negative), which consequently can hamper the rehabilitation process and further delay full recovery (Brewer, 2010).

Two instruments that can be particularly useful in assessing the psychological impact of Jenna's injury are the Psychological Response to Injury Inventory (PRII; Evans, Hardy, Mitchell, & Rees, 2008) and the Cognitive Distortions Questionnaire (CD-QUEST; de Oliveira, 2015). The PRII comprises 19-items representing six psychological response subscales: devastation, dispirited, reorganization, feeling cheated, restlessness, and isolation. Items are scored on a 5-point Likert scale (1 = strongly disagree, 5 = strongly agree), with higher scores indicating greater psychological distress. With the 15-item CD-Quest, one can gain valuable insight into the frequency and intensity of specific cognitive distortions. Each item is scored from zero to five, with five representing greater intensity and frequency of the cognitive error in question. Both the PRII and the CD-Quest are simple and easy to administer, and although the CD-Quest was developed for general populations, the items are easily modified to suit the sport injury context.

Key factor 2: Life stress

The stress Jenna was experiencing with her recovery was further compounded by challenges she faced in other significant life domains. Being an honor roll student, Jenna felt the pressure of having to maintain academic excellence. "There's just so much you need to worry about; being excellent in sport, being excellent in class. It can be really overwhelming at times." Researchers have observed that compared to their non-athlete counterparts, student-athletes face the unique stressors of having to balance heavy academic demands with the rigors of training and competition (e.g., Etzel, 2009; Jolly, 2008). They also must contend with the interpersonal challenges associated with navigating coach–athlete relationships and intergroup dynamics.

A significant source of stress for Jenna was her father's over-involvement in her sport, and his expectations that she fulfill his own sport aspirations. This coupled with his apparent fury towards her coach and surgeon made it very difficult for Jenna to effectively communicate her needs to her father, thus putting a strain on their otherwise good relationship. "I love my dad, but he is always there. At training, at my doctor's appointments, just yelling at people. It's really not helping." Parental involvement is common in youth sport, but as Kanters, Bocarro, and Casper (2008) pointed out, parents and children often disagree as to whether parental behaviors translate into support or pressure. Jenna's father, although well-meaning, was unintentionally causing her additional stress rather than alleviating it. Jenna's father's behavior only compounded the grief Jenna was experiencing over the recent loss of her mother, leaving her in a vulnerable state. Stress and bereavement have been shown to compromise neuroendocrine functions associated with immunocompetency (Calabrese, Kling, & Gold, 1987) and given the key role these processes play in tissue healing (Kelc, Naranda, Kuhta, & Vogrin, 2013), Jenna's recovery could be adversely affected if these issues are left unaddressed.

The 24-item College Student-Athletes' Life Stress Scale (Lu, Hsu, Chan, Cheen, & Kao, 2012) can be used to assess the extent of stress Jenna is experiencing in her sport and non-sport life domains. Respondents rate the daily frequency with which they encounter various stressors on a 6-point Likert scale (1 = never, 6 = always). Scores are generated for both general and sport life stress, with higher scores reflecting greater degrees of stress. Regarding Jenna's grief experience, the Reactions to Loss Scale (Cooley, Toray, & Roscoe, 2010) can also prove quite informative. Albeit lengthy with 65 items, the scale intended for youth specifically offers insight into both grief intensity and coping strategies. The items representing three response subscales (loss of control, positive reappraisal, and avoidance) are scored on the 6-point Likert scale. Alternatively, the 13-item "present" scale of the widely used Texas Revised Inventory of Grief (Faschingbauer, 1981) can be used to assess Jenna's current pattern of grieving and determine whether it falls into the realm of normal grieving or requires further clinical intervention. Respondents indicate their level of agreement (on a 5-point Likert scale (1 = completely false, 5 = completely true) with statements describing difficulties with accepting loss. Higher scores reflect a more intense grief experience that ought to be addressed. Although intended for use with college age students, both these scales can be readily adapted for use with an adolescent population.

Key factor 3: Limited social support

Another major factor impacting Jenna's adjustment to her injury was her limited support network. Being an only child with a deceased mother and an over-involved father who was more of a burden than a source of support, Jenna was lacking in the support one normally receives from close ties, such as parents or siblings (Bianco, 2001). Further, as typically happens with athletes (Miller & Kerr, 2002), Jenna's social network was composed principally of her fellow wrestlers. Paradoxically, when the support of teammates is needed most, as in the case of injury, athletes tend to isolate themselves for fear of being a burden to their compatriots (Bianco, 2001). "I can't talk to my dad because he is so angry all the time and I don't want to be a downer around my teammates. So, it's really hard because I really would love to have someone to talk to—I just feel so all alone." This is all rather unfortunate because there is strong research evidence indicating that social support plays a key role in adjustment to injury, beliefs about and motivation for rehabilitation, and overall well-being (Bianco, 2001; Lu & Hsu, 2013). By buffering the impact of the stressors associated with injury, social support allows athletes to direct their energies toward engaging with their rehabilitation in a more positive and focused manner (Bianco, 2001; Mitchell, 2011).

The Social Support Survey (SSS; Richman, Rosenfeld, & Hardy, 1993) is an instrument that could be very useful in examining various aspects of Jenna's perceptions of social support. The SSS assesses eight dimensions of support, including listening support, task appreciation, task challenge, emotional support, emotional challenge, reality confirmation, tangible assistance, and personal assistance. For each of these eight categories, participants first indicate who provides them with that support type, and then, on a 5-point Likert scale (1 = not at all, 5 = very), rate their (a) satisfaction with that support type, (b) the ease of obtaining more of that support type, and (c) the impact of that support type on their overall well-being. Investigations of the utility of the SSS in sport settings (e.g., Rees, Hardy, & Evans, 2007) have suggested that perhaps only some and not all of the support types assessed by the instrument are relevant to athletes. Nonetheless, the SSS remains a valid and reliable tool to use in the sport injury context.

Theoretical considerations

Jenna's case nicely illustrates the principles of cognitive appraisal theory (Lazarus & Folkman, 1984; Lazarus, 2000). The theory posits that individuals will experience distress when they perceive that (a) an event (e.g., injury) poses an actual (e.g., thwarting of goals) or perceived threat (e.g., loss of sport career), and (b) that the coping demands of the situation (e.g., presence of multiple stressors) outweigh available resources (e.g., social support). The role that cognitive appraisal plays in the sport injury setting is well captured in the Biopsychosocial Model of Sport Injury Rehabilitation (from now on referred to as the biopsychosocial model; Brewer, Andersen, & Van Raalte, 2002), which serves to further explain Jenna's psychosocial reactions to her injury and recovery setbacks.

The biopsychosocial model ascribes a central role to cognitive appraisals, recognizing that they are influenced by a host of personal (e.g., age, injury history) and situational determinants (e.g., timing and severity of the injury, life stress, support network). The cognitive appraisals, in turn, influence emotional responses (e.g., fear and panic) and behavioral responses during rehabilitation (e.g., adherence). Further, the model recognizes that the process is dynamic in that psychological factors affect and are affected by intermediate (e.g., pain, endurance, rate of recovery) and final rehabilitation outcomes (e.g., functional performance and readiness to return to sport). For instance, while an athlete may initially have doubts about recovery, progress in rehabilitation can allay these concerns and lead to a further commitment to rehabilitation, which in turn can lead to a timely and successful recovery. On the other hand, setbacks in rehabilitation can further exacerbate the initial concerns, causing the athlete to lose faith in the rehabilitation process, and perhaps show adherence deficits. Treatment non-adherence, in turn, will further delay recovery and thus cause greater emotional distress.

Applying the biopsychosocial model to Jenna's case, one can see how a serious first-time injury (personal factor) combined with stresses in multiple domains and limited social support (pre-injury, social factor) put Jenna in a precarious situation at the onset of her injury. This resulted in Jenna feeling overwhelmed by her injury, which then translated into poor injury management at the start of the injury (i.e., not listening to her AT's advice). Even when Jenna did adhere to her treatment program post-surgically, there were complications, causing her to panic and question her recovery prognosis. "I don't understand! I'm doing everything I'm being asked to do. Why isn't it getting better? Is it ever going to get better?" To help Jenna from this point forward, adopting a biopsychosocial approach to rehabilitation as advocated by Brewer (2010) and suggested by the model would be essential. Such a stance recognizes that injury recovery is affected by a constellation of factors related to the biological aspects of the injury itself, the psychological responses to injury and rehabilitation, and the social factors that can either facilitate or hamper coping and recovery.

Interprofessional plan of care

Implementing a plan of care anchored in a biopsychosocial approach typically requires a multifaceted approach in which professionals and other individuals work together to address client issues (Clement & Arvinen-Barrow, 2013). In Jenna's case, the interprofessional care team included her coach, the school athletic therapist (AT), and the team sport psychology consultant (SPC). Research shows that support from these three types of professionals is important to athlete recovery (Bianco, 2001; Bricker Bone & Fry, 2006; Clement & Shannon, 2011).

The care team's tasks were to (1) determine intervention needs and objectives, (2) assign specific roles to team members, (3) establish an intervention timeline, (4) schedule follow-up meetings to monitor Jenna's progress, (5) share key information, and (6) adjust the intervention plan as needed. With the biopsychosocial model (Brewer et al., 2002) as a guiding framework and taking into account the three key factors hampering Jenna's progress, the team agreed that any intervention implemented would need to allay Jenna's concerns about the future, help her manage the stressors in her life, and mobilize social support. It was reasoned that doing so would result in more balanced cognitive appraisals, decreased emotional intensity, favorable rehabilitation behaviors, and better overall recovery outcomes.

Based on relative competencies, it was decided that the AT and coach were both well-placed to address Jenna's concerns about her future; the AT through education about injury and recovery, and the coach through education about various trajectories in wrestling. Further, the two could work together to develop an adapted training plan to maximize Jenna's future performance capabilities. The SPC would focus mainly on addressing Jenna's psychological distress and implementing stress management strategies, while also reinforcing the messages conveyed by the AT and coach. In fact, this was the approach all three professionals agreed to use when working one on one with Jenna; that is, they would capitalize on opportunities to support one another's efforts. Doing so would communicate to Jenna that she was benefiting from a targeted and coordinated treatment plan. The team felt that this knowledge would further allay Jenna's concerns about recovery, and generate confidence in the overall plan of care.

The care team recognized that although they, and the coach in particular, would become important sources of informational and emotional support for Jenna throughout the intervention, it was important to ensure Jenna cultivate a wider support network. It was also agreed that it would be necessary to get Jenna's father on board with the proposed intervention program, not only because Jenna was a minor (Sori & Hecker, 2015), but because of the negative impact he was having on her recovery. Jenna's father's difficulty accepting her injury was counterproductive and he likely needed help coming to terms with own his own grief and unresolved issues surrounding the termination of his athletic career as well as the death of his wife and becoming a single parent. It was decided that it would be best to take an educational approach (led by the AT) with Jenna's father to tackle the issues concerning his daughter's injury, and to refer him out to counseling (by the SPC) for assistance with his other issues.

Perspective 1:
Sport psychology consultant's perspective

Trust and rapport are the cornerstones of an effective intervention (Leach, 2005). The SPC used a client-centered approach to communicate empathy and acceptance, and thus create a safe environment for genuine exploration and expression. In their initial session, Jenna expressed relief at "finally" being able to speak openly about her injury. Jenna let it all out:

> I'm freaking out! I'm so scared I won't be able to wrestle again. I mean, how can I? Look at this arm, it's useless! I'll never be able to go to the Olympics. My poor dad, he wanted it so bad. I've totally let him down. And now, my grades are slipping. I'm going to be a failure at school as well. I don't know what to do! And I can't tell my dad any of this, he just flies off the handle every time.

The SPC recognized that at the root of such appraisals was Jenna's desire to aim for perfection in all aspects of her life (perfect wrestler, perfect student, and a perfect daughter). This aspect of her self-identity had now been challenged, and it was her inability to meet these self-imposed standards that resulted in a great degree of self-criticism and discontent, and a distorted pattern of thinking. Striving for perfection in sport is common but if left unchecked can become maladaptive and lead to depression (Gustafsson & Lundqvist, 2016). The SPC introduced Jenna to the concept of practicing self-compassion as an antidote to her perfectionist leanings. Self-compassion involves being caring and understanding with oneself rather than harshly critical, recognizing imperfection as part of the human condition and not unique to you, and confronting your failures with acceptance and forgiveness (Baltzell, 2016). The practice has been applied successfully in a variety of sport settings, including sport injury (Huysmans & Clement, 2017), and has also been linked to better coping with life stressors such as academic failure (Neff, Hsieh, & Dejitterat, 2005).

For Jenna to become comfortable with the practice, she was asked to complete a worksheet (as shown below) by reflecting on the situations causing her distress, her interpretation of them, and how she would comfort a friend confiding the same in her. Researchers have found that people have a tendency to be kinder and more forgiving towards others than themselves (Neff, 2011). Doing this type of "what I would say to a friend" exercise helps elicit people's compassionate tendencies and encourages them to turn their kindness onto themselves.

Doing the exercise was revelatory for Jenna, "Wow! I am really hard on myself!." The SPC showed Jenna how she could apply what she would say to a friend to herself, and also taught Jenna a brief self-compassion meditation. With this type of meditation the focus is on bringing forward difficult feelings (e.g., fear, worry) such that they can be soothed through self-talk that communicates understanding, warmth, and reassurance, e.g. "It's OK to feel scared, it will all work out fine, you just need to be patient" (see Germer & Neff, 2013 for a detailed clinical case illustration).

To address Jenna's distorted thinking about her sport future, the SPC encouraged her to explore "what if" scenarios. For example, "what if it were possible to compete with an elbow that is not 100%; what would that feel like." This is a technique commonly used in cognitive behavioral therapy as a way of removing psychological barriers, that is, "clearing the way" for more productive thoughts and attitudes (Giges, 2000). Engaging in this type of exercise helps move a person away

TABLE 4.1 Sample self-compassion exercise

Situation/Event	What I Say to Myself	What I Would Say to a Friend
1) _____	1) _____	1) _____
2) _____	2) _____	2) _____

from a rigid all-or-none pattern of thinking (common among those with per-fectionist tendencies) and toward a more flexible one that considers other possi-bilities (Beck, 2011). The SPC wanted Jenna to realize that her elbow did not have to be perfect in order for her to be able to compete at an elite level. To have a factual basis to work from with this particular exercise, the SPC had consulted with the AT and coach beforehand. Together, they discussed what was within the range of possibilities given Jenna's injury. While doing the exercise, the SPC encouraged Jenna to develop a very specific list of follow-up questions to ask her AT and coach. Jenna was buoyed by the prospect and admitted, "You know before we did this exercise, I didn't see the point of continuing with rehab—but now I'm kind of excited about it—not everything has to be perfect in order for me to perform well."

To help Jenna balance her school and rehabilitation responsibilities, the SPC introduced a time management strategy. It is not unusual for students, and student-athletes in particular, to feel overwhelmed by the multiple demands on their time and consequently neglect their self-care (e.g., poor diet, inadequate sleep; Etzel, 2009). Time management involves setting goals and priorities and organizing daily activities or time usage accordingly (Claessens, van Eerde, Rutte, & Roe, 2007). Although typically used with performance goals in mind, time management can also be directed to improving overall well-being. Research shows that because it fosters a greater sense of control over one's life, time management is an effective method for increasing productivity and relieving stress (Misra & McKean, 2000). Jenna was asked to create a weekly timetable in which she scheduled in class time, rehabilitation sessions, individual study time, self-compassion meditation, and time for social connections. Jenna was also encouraged to join study groups and sche-dule them into her timetable. Jenna initially found putting everything down on paper overwhelming but later admitted that it was working really well for her "I feel so organized and on top of things. I'm not as stressed as I normally am."

Having been trained in grief counseling, the SPC also explored the issue of grief with Jenna. Results from the Texas Revised Inventory of Grief (Faschingbauer, 1981) revealed that Jenna's grief symptoms were within the normal range and did not necessitate further referral. To address the profound sadness Jenna expressed over the loss of her mother, the SPC proposed an expressive letter writing exercise often recommended by bereavement therapists as a practice for processing feelings of grief (Pennebaker & Chung, 2011). Research has shown that writing about deep emotions such as grief can have psychological and health benefits. Specifically, it can promote emotional self-regulation and boost immune system functioning (Baddeley & Pennebaker, 2011). Thus, it was expected that the exercise would also have a beneficial impact on Jenna's recovery from injury. The exercise designed for Jenna involved having her write to her mother by completing sentences similar to those in Table 4.2.

The SPC explained to Jenna that the letter was for her eyes only, and that she could do it in small chunks so as to not feel overwhelmed by the exercise. Jenna was also encouraged to imagine her mother reading the letter and also what she

TABLE 4.2 Sample bereavement exercise

What I miss most about you is …
I wish I could tell you …
I wish you could see that …
I wish you were here to …

would say to her in response. Just discussing the exercise was very emotional for both the SPC and Jenna, but she welcomed the opportunity "I thought we were only going to talk about sport and my injury. It feels good to be able to talk about my mom. I really miss her."

To address the matter of Jenna's father and the impact he was having on her state of mind, the SPC facilitated, with Jenna's permission, a meeting for all three of them. The objective of the meeting was to help Jenna's father understand how he could better support his daughter. Often there is a discrepancy between what support providers think is supportive and what actually is viewed as beneficial by the recipient (Arvinen-Barrow & Pack, 2013; Bianco, 2001). The SPC wanted to create a safe environment in which Jenna could raise this discrepancy with her father, and suggest behaviors that would be more supportive.

Perspective 2:
Athletic therapist's perspective

Being well versed in the biopsychosocial model of sport injury rehabilitation (Brewer, 2007; Brewer et al., 2002), the AT knew that treatment success relied not only on developing an appropriate medical plan but also taking into account the psychosocial factors that impact rehabilitation. With Jenna, it was clear that her desire to wrestle superseded good judgment, evidenced when she ignored the on-site AT's recommendations following her initial injury. Thus, patient education about injury, the course of recovery, and the importance of adherence was a crucial component of the injury treatment plan. Since Jenna had experienced post-surgical complications, it had left both Jenna and her father skeptical about rehabilitation and health professionals in general. For the AT's plan to work, gaining their trust was imperative to treatment success. Aware of how Jenna had lied to her coach about the initial treatment recommendations, the AT was thankful to have the coach as a member of the care team as this lent itself more readily to a coordinated and successful rehabilitation plan (Clement & Arvinen-Barrow, 2013). With the coach aware of the treatment plan, Jenna would be unable to get away with lying about what she had been told.

Taking all of the above into consideration, and in consultation with the coach and the SPC, the AT devised a physical treatment plan that would serve to allay Jenna's concerns about her future in sport, foster trust in the rehabilitation process, and also tackle the isolation that typically accompanies sport injury (Evans et al.,

2012). Furthermore, she was mindful of the fact that Jenna was a high school student and therefore needed a plan that accommodated her school schedule. The rehabilitation sessions were worked into the timetable Jenna had developed with the help of the SPC.

The AT understood that before even tackling the patient education objectives with Jenna, it would be necessary to address her primary concern about being able to wrestle again competitively. Without this question being settled, it would be difficult to motivate Jenna to commit fully to her rehabilitation. As outlined in the biopsychosocial model (Brewer et al., 2002) and explained by Bianco (2007), an injured athlete's concerns will have an impact on motivation for rehabilitation, and if not properly addressed will lead to motivational deficits. The AT also appreciated that the disappointment of a failed recovery made the motivational challenge for Jenna even greater as this further exacerbated her concerns about her sporting future (Granquist & Brewer, 2013). So, prior to her first meeting with Jenna, the AT reviewed with the care team the feasibility of a return to competitive wrestling. Together, they discussed the necessary accommodations required to facilitate Jenna's recovery and re-entry into wrestling. They also identified rehabilitation milestones and planned Jenna's year-long progressive rehabilitation based on the timeline laid out by the orthopedic surgeon.

The rehabilitation plan followed the standard post-surgical protocol (e.g., Ellenbecker et al., 2009). First, the goal was to decrease pain and inflammation, increase range of motion (flexion, extension, pronation, supination of the elbow) and increase strength in uniplanes. This was followed by adding more functional exercises, increasing proprioception activities, adding close chain and open chain exercises, and increasing weight-bearing loads and sport-specific movements. This last step required specific input from the coach and together they decided Jenna could eventually focus on the footwork of a standing technique; if unable to weight bear on her arms, she could work on getting from standing to the ground on all fours, to a prone position and coming back up; weight-bearing would be introduced progressively.

Understanding that she could be an important source of support for Jenna (Clement & Shannon, 2011), in their initial session, the AT strove to show she was empathetic to Jenna's situation. She made sure Jenna knew that she did not think poorly of her for her earlier bad decisions, that she supported her desire to return to competitive wrestling, and that Jenna could trust her. "Your coach, SPC, and I want to get you back strong and ready and this is how we are going to do it." Together they reviewed the plan and the timeline, identifying key milestones along the way and the specific exercises designed to get her there. The AT explained how this timeline would inform the goals they would agree to throughout rehabilitation. Together, they discussed the concept of SMART (specific, measurable, attainable, realistic, time-based) goal-setting and agreed on short-, medium-, and long-term goals, as prescribed in the literature (Arvinen-Barrow & Hemmings, 2013; Evans & Hardy, 2002). Jenna was elated, "Really? Is it true? I can wrestle? I'm so excited!"

Having ignited Jenna's enthusiasm for the treatment plan, the AT proceeded to teach her about the elbow joint and the function of the UCL. Too often, athletes do not have a clear understanding of their injury or the rehabilitation process (Francis, Andersen, & Maley, 2000). They discussed the surgery, what likely happened that interfered with proper healing, and what needed to be done to stabilize the joint. The AT was well aware that Jenna's father was highly critical of the surgery and felt that he also could benefit from learning more about the UCL and its recovery. She also understood it was critical to get him on board with the rehabilitation plan so that he could be in a better position to support Jenna throughout the process. As mentioned earlier, parents can sometimes be misguided in their attempts to be supportive (Kanters et al., 2008). With Jenna's permission, the AT organized a joint meeting with Jenna and her father. In that meeting, she reinforced what the surgeon had said about the injury and shared with Jenna's father the clear detailed plan that Jenna would follow to lead back to her return to full contact wrestling. The AT wanted to reassure Jenna's father that his daughter was being well taken care of and would not be following in his footsteps of having to stop her sport due to injury.

To tackle Jenna's feelings of isolation, the AT, SPC, and coach worked to coordinate rehabilitation with training such that Jenna could attend team strength and conditioning sessions and practices, while doing her own individualized program. The intent was for Jenna to remain integrated and have the social support of her teammates and coach during her recovery process. Indeed, research has shown that remaining involved and integrated in the team environment is a key component of psychological recovery and readiness to return to sport (Bianco, 2007; Podlog & Eklund, 2006). The AT felt this overall approach would allow for a well-rounded treatment course for Jenna both physically and mentally, while optimizing her eventual successful return to wrestling.

Perspective 3: Wrestling coach's perspective

Jenna's coach had seen many injuries throughout his career and knew that athletes, especially the young ones, needed a great deal of support when injured. They have a tendency to catastrophize and want to throw in the towel and the coach's job is to help them put things in perspective (Rees, Mitchell, Evans, & Hardy, 2010). Jenna's coach understood that his athlete was devastated by her season-ending injury but he was a strong proponent of long-term athlete development. He believed it takes years to develop elite athletes and Jenna was no exception to that rule. For him, Jenna's injury was nothing more than a speed bump along the long road to international success and Olympic glory.

To address Jenna's concerns about her sport future, her coach sought to temper her expectations while at the same time giving her hope. He knew that having something meaningful to strive for beyond recovery was a key motivational factor for injured athletes (Podlog, Lochbaum, & Stevens, 2010). He discussed with Jenna what a realistic trajectory in wrestling looked like and explained that the average age for peak performance in Canadian women's wrestling, that is earning a world or Olympic medal, is around 27 years old (V. Zilberman, Canadian Olympic wrestling coach, personal communication, May 18, 2018). The coach reminded Jenna that she was still very young and that she had not lost out on her Olympic dream. To boost Jenna's sense of competency, the coach highlighted the many positive attributes she already possessed, and he explained that she showed a lot of physical talent on the mat and that could get her far in the sport of wrestling. He also pointed out to Jenna that she had a sharp strategic mind and the mental toughness required to carry her through any challenges she encountered. The coach wrapped up the session by sharing anecdotes of athletes who had successfully overcome injuries similar to Jenna's. The SPC had explained during one of the care team meetings that providing this type of informational support could prove inspiring to athletes, showing them that a bright future was indeed possible.

Jenna appreciated the "pep talk" from her coach but she was not entirely enthusiastic about the long drawn-out development plan. "Geez, coach, that's ages from now!" The coach understood that 27 is really far away when you are only 16, and that is was important to give Jenna more immediate goals to grab onto. This is where he elaborated on the modified training and reintegration plan that had been developed by the care team. Jenna's coach recognized that he could set the motivational climate for recovery in the same manner as he did in sport (Duda & Balaguer, 2007). He knew it was imperative to build small victories along the way to nurture Jenna's sense of competency and to keep her encouraged and motivated (Ryan & Deci, 2000). He would do so by cultivating a task-oriented recovery environment, where the focus would be on mastery of structured achievable tasks, followed by steady manageable increases in training difficulty. The coach explained to Jenna that they would use her recovery time to work on her cardiovascular endurance, muscular strength and endurance, flexibility, technique, and most importantly, her mental game. Jenna embraced the plan, "that sounds amazing, coach. I'm super psyched!"

The coach was also aware that Jenna was coping with a multitude of stressors and was grateful that these were largely addressed through her work with the SPC. To ensure Jenna did not feel isolated from the team, the coach made certain Jenna understood that even though she was injured, she was always welcome at the wrestling center. He wanted her to think of the gym as her sanctuary, a safe place where she could practice the sport she loved and just leave her problems at the door. Jenna loved this idea but she wondered how she would be able to "park her father at the door."

Recognizing the negative impact Jenna's father was having on her and the training environment in general, the coach determined that it would be necessary to address the conflict at the root of the problem – that is, the fact that Jenna's father blamed him for the injury. It was clear that they would need to talk about the injury event. Anticipating that this would be a difficult discussion for them both, the coach recruited the SPC to act as mediator. Together, they planned the best way to approach Jenna's dad. In line with conflict resolution guidelines (see Coleman, Deutch, & Marcus, 2014), they agreed that the focus had to be on acknowledging their mutual concern for Jenna's well-being in and out of sport, and planning how to work together in order to maximize Jenna's recovery and future potential.

The coach felt it was imperative that Jenna have a social support system within the team. Athletes who suffer injuries can feel disconnected because of their inability to practice their sport with their teammates (Evans et al., 2012), so it is important to keep them involved and integrated. To keep Jenna connected to her teammates, the coach, AT and the SPC arranged for her to do some of her rehabilitation during practice times. This would include her cardiovascular training, strength training, and any sport-specific exercises that did not interfere with the healing process. Once Jenna was cleared to do technique, she took part in the technical workouts with the team. These efforts would make for a much easier transition back to sport (Podlog & Dionigi, 2010) as Jenna would maintain the same schedule as if she was healthy and training with the team.

Ethical considerations and need(s) for referral

When working with a minor, it is imperative to seek parental consent before implementing any intervention (Sori & Hecker, 2015). It is also important to clarify issues of confidentiality, as there may be misunderstandings on the part of the child and the parent regarding the sharing of information. Research shows that adolescents are more likely to disclose sensitive information when confidentiality is assured, and lie about their symptoms when it is not (Gilbert, Rickert, & Aalsma, 2014). Parents, however, can be conflicted about confidentiality, supporting it on the one hand while at the same time fearing not being told important information (Duncan, Vandeleur, Derks, & Sawyer, 2011). It is, thus, imperative to educate adolescents and their parents about the protections and limits to confidentiality (e.g., necessary disclosure in the case of imminent harm). Practitioners find themselves faced with the task of protecting the child's rights and at the same time avoiding jeopardizing the functionality of the family relationship (Gilbert et al., 2014). The confidentiality discussion presents an opportunity to address these concerns and also earn the parents' trust by confirming the mutual goal of promoting the well-being of the child (Duncan et al., 2011). Given the extent of Jenna's father's involvement in her sport career, such a conversation was much needed.

Confidentiality is also a consideration where you have an interprofessional team, each bound by ethical norms and obligations appropriate to their respective disciplines. Unlike with a confidential care setting, where information is kept between the client and the practitioner, the very nature of a collaborative care setting entails that information be disclosed with third parties (Engel & Prentice, 2013). The client's permission must be sought ahead of time to avoid any potential conflict. This point was particularly salient given that Jenna's coach was on the intervention team. Injured athletes are often very concerned about the information that gets back to their coaches regarding their recovery status, particularly when experiencing plateaus or setbacks (Bianco, 2001).

It is essential that all members of the collaborative care team work within the bounds of their professional competencies (Engel & Prentice, 2013). In this particular case, involving Jenna's experience with grief, the SPC had specialized training bereavement counseling. Had this not been the case, it would have been necessary to refer Jenna to a mental health professional with the appropriate qualifications; as required by the sport psychology consultants' code of ethics (Whelan, Hill, Ginley, & Meyers, 2014).

Case update

It has been six months since the team began its intervention with Jenna, and we have seen a tremendous change in her demeanor. She has managed to regain a sense of control over her life. She is less concerned about everything having to be perfect and more oriented towards self-compassion and embracing opportunities that come her way. She is very engaged in the modified training program designed jointly by her coach and AT, and is showing a slow but steady improvement in her wrestling capabilities. As a result, she is more enthusiastic about what the future holds, and is devoting herself fully to her recovery. She is also attending practices as often as she can and as a result feeling less isolated. Jenna was able to manage her time more effectively and worked hard to finish her school year with top honors. She is also enjoying a deeper and more meaningful relationship with her father since he began his own therapy and committed to spending less time at the gym.

Conclusion

The case study presented in this chapter illustrates the fact that sport injuries are multilayered and that multiple factors must be taken into consideration when planning an intervention strategy. With Jenna, a 16-year-old high school wrestler who sustained a season-ending injury with a complicated recovery, we come to understand the combined impact of uncertainty about her future in sport, multiple stressors in her life (school, grief, overbearing father), and limited social support leave her feeling overwhelmed by her situation. Further, Jenna's case demonstrates the benefits of incorporating a team of professionals with varied competencies to address the biopsychosocial aspects of injury and rehabilitation. Composed of the school AT, the team SPC, and her sport coach, Jenna benefited from a holistic theory-driven and evidence-based treatment plan that sought to reduce her stress, improve her understanding of injury and recovery, and expand her social support network. It was hoped that in doing so, Jenna would feel more capable of confronting the challenges ahead of her, be more optimistic about the future, and be more motivated to adhere to her rehabilitation protocol. To achieve these ends, the SPC worked on equipping Jenna with strategies to manage her stress and become more positive about the future. She also helped Jenna work through her grief and become better at communicating her needs to her father. The AT worked on ensuring Jenna understood fully the principles of recovery and the need to comply fully with treatment protocols. Jenna's coach focused on helping her see the big picture and realizing that she could still be a contender in spite of her physical limitations. Together, the team was successful in setting Jenna on a positive path toward recovery, and at the same time, Jenna has acquired an array of skills sure to carry her throughout her wrestling career and beyond.

KEY POINTS

- Jenna Cousteau is a promising high school wrestler who suffered a season-ending ulnar collateral ligament tear.
- Jenna's recovery was complicated by the fact that her surgery was not entirely successful, leaving her with a longer than planned recovery period, and grave concerns about her ability to continue to excel in her sport.
- Further adding to Jenna's stress were concerns about falling behind in her studies, and feeling that she had let her father down.
- Jenna was also rather lonely; she and her father were each grieving the loss of her mother, and she did not wish to burden her teammates with her troubles.
- Informed by a biopsychosocial approach to recovery, Jenna's athletic therapist, coach, and sport psychology consultant worked as a team to create a rehabilitation plan to help her manage her grief, and access social support.
- Jenna reported that the interprofessional care team's interventions helped shift her focus from panic to enthusiasm about the future, and helped her feel "not so lost and all alone."

CRITICAL THINKING QUESTIONS

1. What are some of the important considerations when the injured athlete's coach is a member of the interprofessional care team? (Hint: think of the quality of the coach–athlete relationship).
2. What are some strategies that can be used to maximize social support and minimize the social isolation of injured athletes?
3. What are some of the challenges inherent to an interprofessional care team that must be managed in order to maximize efficacy? (Hint: think of individual personalities and experience).

RESEARCH QUESTIONS

1. What are some of the key considerations when designing psychological interventions for high school athletes?
2. Explain why it is important to take into consideration other sources of stress in an athlete's life, and not just those related to injury.

3.   Why is perfectionism problematic in recovery, and how can practicing self-compassion help?

KEY PUBLICATIONS

1.   Schwab Reese, L. M., Pittsinger, R., & Yang, J. (2012) Effectiveness of psychological intervention following sport injury. *Journal of Sport and Health Science, 1*(2), 71–79. doi: 10.1016/j.jshs.2012.06.003.

This systematic review summarizes the results of various research studies that have employed psychological interventions with competitive and recreational athletes in an injury and rehabilitation context. Interventions reviewed include: guided imagery/relaxation, goal-setting, microcounseling, acceptance and commitment therapy, and written disclosure.

2.   Podlog, L., & Dionigi, R. (2010). Coach strategies for addressing psychosocial challenges during the return to sport from injury. *Journal of Sports Sciences, 28*(11), 1197–1208. doi: 10.1080/02640414.2010.487873.

This qualitative study examines coach strategies for addressing athletes' psychosocial challenges in returning to sport following injury rehabilitation. Strategies identified include (a) coordination of a "team approach" to rehabilitation, (b) fostering open communication with athletes and treatment team members, (c) social support, (d) positive thinking and goal-setting, and (e) role models. Although the study focuses on the return-to-sport phase, many of the strategies mentioned can be applied to the rehabilitation phase as well.

References

Arvinen-Barrow, M., & Hemmings, B. (2013). Goal setting in sport injury rehabilitation. In M. Arvinen-Barrow & N. Walker (Eds.), *Psychology of sport injury and rehabilitation* (pp. 56–70). Abingdon: Routledge.

Arvinen-Barrow, M., & Pack, S. M. (2013). Social support in sport injury rehabilitation. In M. Arvinen-Barrow & N. Walker (Eds.), *Psychology of sport injury and rehabilitation* (pp. 117–131). Abingdon: Routledge.

Baddeley, J.L., & Pennebaker, J.W. (2011). The expressive writing method. In L. L'Abate & L.G. Sweeney (Eds.), *Research on writing approaches in mental health* (pp. 85-92). Bingley, UK: Emerald Group Publishing.

Baltzell, A. L. (2016). *Self-Compassion, distress tolerance and mindfulness in performance.* New York, NY: Cambridge University Press.

Beck, J.S. (2011). *Cognitive behavioral therapy: Basics and beyond* (2nd ed.). New York, NY: The Guilford Press.

Bianco, T. M. (2001). Social support and recovery from sport injury: Elite skiers share their experiences. *Research Quarterly for Exercise and Sport, 72*, 376–388. doi:10.1080/02701367.2001.10608974.

Bianco, T. M. (2007). Sport injury and the need for coach support. In D. Pargman (Ed.), *Psychological bases of sport injuries* (3rd ed., pp. 237–266). Morgantown, WV: Fitness Information Technology.

Brewer, B. W. (2007). Psychology of sport injury rehabilitation. In G. Tenenbaum & R. C. Eklund (Eds.), *Handbook of Sport Psychology* (3rd ed., pp. 404–424). New York, NY: Wiley.

Brewer, B. W. (2010). The role of psychological factors in sport injury rehabilitation outcomes. *International Review of Sport and Exercise Psychology*, 3(1), 40–61. doi:10.1080/17509840903301207.

Brewer, B. W., Andersen, M. B., & Van Raalte, J. L. (2002). Psychological aspects of sport injury rehabilitation: Toward a biopsychological approach. In D. L. Mostofsky & L. D. Zaichkowsky (Eds.), *Medical aspects of sport and exercise* (pp. 41–54). Morgantown, WV: Fitness Information Technology.

Bricker Bone, J., & Fry, M. D. (2006). The influence of injured athletes' perceptions of social support from ATCs on their beliefs about rehabilitation. *Journal of Sport Rehabilitation*, 15, 156–167.

Calabrese, J. R., Kling, M. A., & Gold, P. W. (1987). Alterations in immunocompetence during stress, bereavement, and depression: Focus on neuroendrocrine regulation. *The American Journal of Psychiatry*, 144(9), 1123–1134. doi:10.1176/ajp.144.9.1123.

Claessens, B.J.C, van Eerde, W., Rutte, C.G., & Roe, R.A. (2007). A review of the time management literature. *Personnel Review, 36*(2), 255-276. doi: 10.1108/00483480710726136.

Clement, D., & Arvinen-Barrow, M. (2013). Sport medicine team influences in psychological rehabilitation: A multidisciplinary approach. In M. Arvinen-Barrow & N. Walker (Eds.), *The psychology of sport injury and rehabilitation* (pp. 156–170). Abingdon: Routledge.

Clement, D., & Shannon, V. R. (2011). Injured athletes' perceptions about social support. *Journal of Sport Rehabilitation*, 20(4), 457–470.

Coleman, P.T, Deutch, M., & Marcus, E.C. (Eds.). (2014). *The handbook of conflict resolution: Theory and practice* (3rd ed.). San Francisco, CA: Jossey-Bass.

Cooley, E., Toray, T., & Roscoe, L. (2010). Reactions to loss scale: Assessing grief in college students. *Omega: Journal of Death and Dying*, 61(1), 25–51. doi:10.2190/OM.61.1.b.

de Oliveira, I. R. (2015). Introducing the Cognitive Distortions Questionnaire. In I. R. De Oliveira (Ed.), *Trial-based cognitive therapy: A manual for clinicians* (pp. 25–40). New York, NY: Routledge.

Dines, J. S., Camp, C., & Elattrache, N. S. (2017). Articular injuries in the athlete. In B. F. Morrey, J. Sanchez-Sotelo & M. E. Morrey (Eds.), *Morrey's the elbow and its disorders* (5th ed., pp. 637–650). Amsterdam, Netherlands: Elsevier.

Duda, J. L., & Balaguer, I. (2007). Coach-created motivational climate. In S. Jowett & D. Lavallee (Eds.), *Social psychology in sport* (pp. 117–130). Champaign, IL: Human Kinetics.

Duncan, R.E., Vandeleur, M., Derks, A., & Sawyer, S. (2011). Confidentiality with adolescents in the medical setting: What do parents think? *The Journal Of Adolescent Health, 49*(4), 428-430. doi: 10.1016/j.jadohealth.2011.02.006.

Ellenbecker, T. S., Wilk, K. E., Altchek, D. W., & Andrews, J. R. (2009). Current concepts in rehabilitation following ulnar collateral ligament reconstruction. *Sports Health*, 1(4), 301–313. doi:10.1177/1941738109338553.

Engel, J.R., & Prentice, D. (2013). The ethics of interprofessional collaboration. *Nursing Ethics, 20*(4), 426-435. doi: 10.1177/0969733012468466

Etzel, E. F. (2009). *Counseling student athletes: Issues and interventions*. Morgantown, WV: Fitness Information Technology Inc.

Evans, L., & Hardy, L. (2002). Injury rehabilitation: A goal-setting intervention study. *Research Quarterly for Exercise and Sport*, 73, 310–319. doi:10.1080/02701367.2002.10609025.

Evans, L., Hardy, L., Mitchell, I. D., & Rees, T. (2008). The development of a measure of psychological responses to injury. *Journal of Sport Rehabilitation*, 16, 21–37. doi:10.1123/jsr.17.1.21.

Evans, L., Wadey, R., Hanton, S., & Mitchell, I. D. (2012). Stressors experienced by injured athletes. *Journal of Sports Sciences*, 30(9), 917–927. doi:10.1080/02640414.2012.682078.

Faschingbauer, T. R. (1981). *Texas revised inventory of grief manual*. Houston, TX: Honeycomb Publishing.

Francis, S. R., Andersen, M. B., & Maley, P. (2000). Physiotherapists' and male professional athletes' views on psychological skills for rehabilitation. *Journal of Science & Medicine in Sport*, 3(1), 17–29. doi:10.1016/S1440-2440(00)80044-80044.

Germer, C.K, & Neff, K.D. (2013). Self-compassion in clinical practice. *Journal of Clinical Psychology*, 69(8), 856-867. doi: 10.1002/jclp.22021.

Giges, B. (2000). Removing psychological barriers: Clearing the way. In M. B. Andersen (Ed.), *Doing Sport Psychology* (pp. 17-31). Champaign, IL: Human Kinetics.

Gilbert, A.L, Rickert, V.I, & Aalsma, M.C. (2014). Clinical conversations about health: The impact of confidentiality in preventive adolescent care. *The Journal Of Adolescent Health*, 55 (5), 672-677. doi: 10.1016/j.jadohealth.2014.05.016.

Granquist, M. D., & Brewer, B. W. (2013). Psychological aspects of rehabilitation adherence. In M. Arvinen-Barrow & N. Walker (Eds.), *Psychology of sport injury and rehabilitation* (pp. 40–53). Abingdon: Routledge.

Gustafsson, H., & Lundqvist, C. (2016). Working with perfectionism in elite sport: A cognitive behavioral therapy perspective. In A. P. Hill (Ed.), *The psychology of perfectionism in sport, dance and exercise* (pp. 203–221). New York, NY: Routledge.

Hodgins, J.L, Ahmad, C.S, & Conway, J.E. (2017). The thrower's elbow. In B.F. Morrey, J. Sanchez-Sotelo & M.E. Morrey (Eds.), *Morrey's the elbow and its disorders* (5th ed., pp. 630-635). Amsterdam, Netherlands: Elsevier.

Huysmans, Z., & Clement, D. (2017). A preliminary exploration of the application of self-compassion within the context of sport injury. *Journal of Sport & Exercise Psychology*, 39(1), 56–66. doi:10.1123/jsep.2016-0144.

Jolly, C. J. (2008). Is the student-athlete population unique? And why should we care? *Communication Education, 57*(1), 145–151. doi:10.1080/03634520701613676.

Kanters, M. A., Bocarro, J., & Casper, J. (2008). Supported or pressured? An examination of agreement among parent's and children on parent's role in youth sports. *Journal of Sport Behavior*, 31(1), 64–80.

Kelc, R., Naranda, J., Kuhta, M., & Vogrin, M. (2013). The physiology of sports injuries and repair processes. In M. Hamlin, N. Draper & Y. Kathirave (Eds.), *Current issues in sports and exercise medicine* (pp. 43–86). London: Intech Publishers.

Lazarus, R.S. (2000). Cognitive-motivational-relational theory of emotion. In Y.L. Hanin (Ed.), *Emotions in sport* (pp. 39-63). Champaign, IL: Human Kinetics.

Lazarus, R. S., & Folkman, S. (1984). *Stress, appraisal, and coping*. New York, NY: Springer Publishing Company.

Leach, M.J. (2005). Rapport: A key to treatment success. *Complementary Therapies In Clinical Practice, 11*(4), 262-265. doi: 10.1016/j.ctcp.2005.05.005.

Lu, Frank J. H., & Hsu, Y. (2013). Injured athletes' rehabilitation beliefs and subjective well-being: the contribution of hope and social support. *Journal of Athletic Training, 48*(1), 92-98. doi: 10.4085/1062-6050-48.1.03.

Lu, F. J., Hsu, Y., Chan, Y., Cheen, J., & Kao, K. (2012). Assessing college student-athletes' life stress: Initial measurement development and validation. *Measurement in Physical Education & Exercise Science, 16*(4), 254–267. doi:10.1080/1091367X.2012.693371.

Miller, P. S., & Kerr, G. (2002). The athletic, academic and social experiences of intercollegiate student-athletes. *Journal of Sport Behavior*, 25(4), 346–367.

Misra, R., & McKean, M. (2000). College students' academic stress and its relation to their anxiety, time management, and leisure satisfaction. *American Journal of Health Studies, 16*(1), 41-51.

Mitchell, I. D. (2011). Social support and psychological responses in sport-injury rehabilitation.
Sport and Exercise Psychology Review, 7(2), 30–44.

Morrey, B.F., Llusá-Pérez, M., & Ballesteros-Betancourt, J.R. (2017). Anatomy of the
elbow joint. In B.F. Morrey, J. Sanchez-Sotelo & M.A. Morrey (Eds.), *Morrey's the elbow
and its disorders* (5th ed., pp. 9-32). Amsterdam, Netherlands: Elsevier.

Neff, K. D. (2011). *Self-compassion: The proven power to be kind to yourself*. New York, NY:
William Morrow Paperbacks.

Neff, K. D., Hsieh, Y., & Dejitterat, K. (2005). Self-compassion, achievement goals, and
coping with academic failure. *Self and Identity*, 4(3), 263–287. doi:10.1080/
13576500444000317.

Pennebaker, J. W., & Chung, C. K. (2011). Expressive writing: Connections to physical and
mental health. In H. S. Friedman (Ed.), *The Oxford handbook of health psychology* (pp. 417–437).
New York, NY: Oxford University Press.

Podlog, L., & Dionigi, R. (2010). Coach strategies for addressing psychosocial challenges
during the return to sport from injury. *Journal of Sports Sciences*, 28(11), 1197–1208.
doi:10.1080/02640414.2010.487873.

Podlog, L., & Eklund, R. C. (2006). A longitudinal investigation of competitive athletes'
return to sport following serious injury. *Journal of Applied Sport Psychology*, 18(1), 44–68.
doi:10.1080/10413200500471319.

Podlog, L., Lochbaum, M., & Stevens, T. (2010). Need satisfaction, well-being, and perceived return-to-sport outcomes among injured athletes. *Journal of Applied Sport Psychology*, 22(2), 167–182. doi:10.1080/10413201003664665.

Rees, T., Hardy, L., & Evans, L. (2007). Construct validity of the social support survey in sport .
Psychology of Sport & Exercise, 8(3), 355–368. doi:10.1016/j.psychsport.2006.06.005.

Rees, T., Mitchell, I., Evans, L., & Hardy, L. (2010). Stressors, social support and psychological
responses to sport injury in high- and low-performance standard participants. *Psychology of
Sport & Exercise*, 11(6), 505–512. doi:10.1016/j.psychsport.2010.07.002.

Richman, J. M., Rosenfeld, L. B., & Hardy, C. J. (1993). The Social Support Survey: An
initial validation study of a clinical measure of the social support process. *Research Social
Work Practice*, 3(3), 288–311.

Ryan, R. E., & Deci, E. L. (2000). Self-determination theory and the facilitation of intrinsic
motivation, social development, and well-being. *American Psychologist*, 55, 68–78.

Sori, C. F., & Hecker, L. L. (2015). Ethical and legal considerations when counselling children and
families. *Australian and New Zealand Journal of Family Therapy, 36*(4), 450-464. doi: 10.1002/
anzf.1126.

Tracey, J. (2003). The emotional response to the injury and rehabilitation process. *Journal of
Applied Sport Psychology*, 15(4), 279–293. doi:10.1080/714044197.

Whelan, J. P., Hill, M., Ginley, M., & Meyers, A. W. (2014). Ethics in sport and exercise psychology. In J. L. Van Raalte & B. W. Brewer (Eds.), *Exploring sport and exercise* psychology
(3rd ed., pp. 505-525). Washington, DC: American Psychological Association.

5

REACTIONS TO CONCUSSION REHABILITATION

Amy Parent, a freshman basketball player

Jill Tracey, Hayley Russell, and Melissa Paré

Key Words: 18-year-old female, freshman basketball student-athlete, athletic identity, non-adherence, coping, sport-related concussion (SRC)

Case description

Amy Parent (this name is a pseudonym and used for descriptive purposes only), is an 18-year-old basketball player in her first year of university on a basketball scholarship. Amy's priorities are simple: athletics and academics to achieve in life. Although she has had two minor shoulder injuries prior to starting university, she entered her first varsity season fit, healthy, and with great optimism. In the first game of the season, Amy sustained a concussion after taking a charge. She was knocked airborne and landed on her head and upper back. This was Amy's first major injury and she was at a loss as to how to cope. Now, Amy felt she needed to "keep it together" because she was in an unfamiliar environment, and was trying hard to fit in. Amy wanted to present herself as a hardworking and strong athlete to her team and coaches. She had worked hard to build this reputation, and felt she needed to maintain a tough exterior during her recovery. Since Amy had only played for her new coach for a couple months of pre-season training before getting injured, she wanted the coaching staff to see her as a valuable team member. She did not want them to see she was struggling with the injury (e.g., feeling depressed about not being able to train and play, lacking coping strategies to deal with her fear and anxiety). She was on a team of talented basketball players and playing time was going to be hard enough to earn, therefore the appearance of weakness was a great concern to her.

The day after sustaining her concussion, Amy visited the athletic therapist (AT) at the university. The AT informed her about the possible severity of the injury, and the potential of a lengthy rehabilitation with an uncertain timeline for return to sport. Amy had not received any prior education about concussions or the severity of the injury. She thought she would just rest for a week and then resume full practicing. She did not think she needed to check in with the AT, "what is she really going to do for me anyway? I will just take it easy for a week and be good to go."

From this point onward, Amy's experience changed as she began to realize the impact of the injury and what this could mean for her future. She was upset about not being allowed to practice and felt scared about who she was if she was not a basketball player.

Her AT and her physician instructed her to reduce screen time, which left her feeling lost and disconnected. She reacted by isolating herself in her residence room and not attending some of her rehabilitation appointments. She began to exhibit mood swings, and her teammates and friends thought some of her behavior seemed out of character for her. A key emotional trigger was waking up with a headache. Every morning she was hopeful she would feel better, but the headache symbolized being injured and that the day would be filled with pain and frustration, which led her to feel sad and hopeless. Whenever something good would happen (e.g., not having a headache, spending social time with friends, talking with her family) she was extremely optimistic. Initially, she would go to practice where she would still feel she was an athlete and be with teammates immersed in the sport environment, which made her happy. Otherwise, she spent most of the rest of the day in a dark room feeling lonely and isolated. When she did attend practices, she would be optimistic she could cope with the concussion. After practices, she would return to feeling depressed and sadness would overwhelm her. She interpreted these feelings as due to overthinking, boredom, or the effects of the concussion, often resulting in her spontaneously crying. She began taking Tylenol as a way of coping with the headaches and Ambien to try to help her sleep. She did not want her AT to know she was taking these medications so avoided going to some of her rehabilitation appointments by telling her AT she was too busy.

During the first month of her recovery, Amy saw a few healthcare providers and there was a collaborative approach to her rehabilitation. Her initial rehabilitation team included an AT, sports medicine physician, and educational assistants (EA). Education assistants typically coordinate accommodations to students' schedules, teaching learning strategies, and peer support. During this time, Amy was struggling with her reaction and emotional response both to the injury and to the unfolding reality of a potentially lengthy rehabilitation process. When the AT told Amy that concussions are complex and unique injuries to treat with no finite timeline for recovery, Amy reacted with frustration. She began to feel she was no longer a strong, fit athlete, and she questioned who she really was if she did not have basketball as the center of her life. A month post-concussion Amy was fearful of losing her identity as an athlete, worried about the length of time she may be unable to train, and was not seeing any value in attending rehabilitation. She felt increasingly lonely and the AT became quite concerned about her. Even though Amy was hiding the self-medication usage, the AT witnessed other behaviors (e.g., moodiness, avoiding contact) she was concerned about, which prompted her to cautiously confront Amy and ask if she was open to meeting with a mental performance consultant (MPC). At this point, a MPC was added to Amy's care team.

The injury

The 2017 Concussion in Sport Group (CISG) defined a sport-related concussion (SRC) as "a traumatic brain injury induced by biomechanical forces" (McCrory et al., 2017, p. 2). Sport-related concussion is a complex injury because no two present the same way. It can present in one or more of the six clinical domains: (1) somatic (headache), cognitive (feeling in a fog), and/or emotional (sadness) symptoms; (2) physical signs (loss of consciousness, nausea, neurological deficits); (3) balance impairments (gait unsteadiness); (4) behavioral changes (irritability); (5) cognitive impairments (slowed reaction times); and (6) sleep/wake disturbances (drowsiness, difficulty falling asleep). Athletes can experience disturbances ranging from one to all six domains, which makes the SRC a difficult injury to diagnose and treat for the healthcare provider and to manage for the athlete (McCrory et al., 2017). Within the first couple of weeks post-concussion, Amy was exhibiting symptoms from four of the identified six clinical domains (e.g., headache, sadness, unsteadiness, irritability, and sleep disturbances).

Key factor 1: Non-adherence

Rehabilitation non-adherence, described by Granquist and Brewer (2014) as doing too much (over-adherence) or too little (under-adherence), is quite common for injured athletes. When injured athletes deviate from the recommended program of recovery, they are said to be non-adherent. Part of Amy's reactions to rehabilitation involved trying to maintain cardiovascular fitness by cycling (over-adherence), as well as missing appointments (under-adherence). Non-adherence can slow recovery progress and may thwart attempts to return to play successfully due to an enhanced risk of further or re-injury (Frey, 2008; Granquist & Brewer, 2014).

To help Amy understand her current adherence behaviors, the practitioner could review the questions on the Rehabilitation Adherence Measure for Athletic Training (RAdMAT) developed by Granquist, Gill, and Appaneal (2010) to ascertain the degree to which Amy may be non-adherent. The RAdMAT is useful as it provides ATs an easily observable measure of rehabilitation adherence from the perspective of the practitioner. The RAdMAT is a 16-item questionnaire with three subscales (attendance, communication, attitude) where higher scores indicate greater adherence, and has demonstrated usefulness within the rehabilitation setting. The AT could then develop a plan to address non-adherence and facilitate more proactive recovery strategies.

Key factor 2: coping

Coping has been described as a "constantly changing cognitive and behavioral efforts to manage specific external and/or internal demands that are appraised as taxing or exceeding the resources of the person" (Lazarus & Folkman, 1984, p. 141). When individuals face a stressor such as sustaining an injury and facing a potentially lengthy rehabilitation, part of the response process is to assess how to manage or cope with what may be a myriad of emotions experienced throughout the rehabilitation phases (Stiller-Ostrowski & Tracey, 2014). Coping can take many forms either as adaptive or maladaptive. Adaptive coping may involve actively seeking out emotional support from a trusted person or engaging in instrumental coping by finding out information about the injury and listening to the advice from the AT. Maladaptive coping may involve withdrawing from people and isolating oneself, or engaging in potentially destructive behavior such as substance abuse (Victorson, Farmer, Burnett, Ouellete, & Barocas, 2005).

For Amy, the injury and possibly lengthy recovery was a significant stressor contributing to her emotional distress. She was using maladaptive coping in three ways: (a) avoiding telling her AT about some of her symptoms; (b) isolating herself from friends and teammates and overusing medications; and (c) spending too much time in front of a screen watching movies and doing school work, which exacerbated her headaches. Coping takes on various forms during rehabilitation and numerous researchers have demonstrated effective uses of coping intervention strategies to reduce negative or distressing psychological consequences (see Schwab Reese, Pittsinger, & Yang, 2012, for review). The review by Schwab Reese et al. revealed a consistent recommendation of the importance of coping interventions to facilitate effective rehabilitation. The identified interventions targeted at improving psychological outcomes (i.e., improving coping) would be highly valuable in assisting successful recovery and return to sport. This type of targeted intervention could be beneficial in serving athletes like Amy who have a perceived or real lack of coping mechanisms.

The Brief COPE (Carver, 1997) is a measure used in a variety of settings for assessment of coping responses. The Brief COPE is a 28-item measure assessing 14 coping strategies. The items are scored on a 4-point Likert scale (1 = I haven't been doing this at all; 4 = I've been doing this a lot). The Brief COPE is a valid and reliable measure providing researchers with an effective way to assess potentially important coping responses in a timely and efficient manner. Given Amy's level of distress and her maladaptive coping strategies demonstrated early on (e.g., overuse of medications, isolating herself); the instrument may be helpful to assess various coping responses and open a dialogue with her to discuss adaptive coping.

Key factor 3: Athletic identity

One factor significantly influencing Amy's reactions to her concussion rehabilitation was her strong sense of athletic identity. She has described herself as a person who "eats, sleeps, and breathes basketball." Athletic identity has been described as the degree to which an individual identifies with the role as an athlete (Brewer, Van Raalte, & Linder, 1993). This aspect of self-identity within the sport context forms part of an overall multidimensional self-concept. Strong athletic identity has demonstrated potential benefits, as well as costs for the athlete (Brewer et al., 1993). Some of the benefits may include a positive sense of self (McPherson, 1980) or a positive effect on performance (Werthner & Orlick, 1986). In Amy's case, she derives a positive sense of self through her involvement in basketball. She consistently describes herself as loving the game so much and often says, "I would be lost without basketball in my life." For athletes with high investment of their identity in the athlete role, difficulties can arise when they experience an injury. The difficulty has been associated with higher risk of adjustment when injured (Brewer, 1993; Stephan & Brewer, 2007). Amy's adjustment to being injured has been emotionally challenging and she expressed her frustration of feeling "worthless" indicating a significant investment in her athletic role to the detriment of awareness and acceptance of any other role. She has a strong athletic identity serving her well to motivate her to work hard and be committed to her sport; however, now she is lacking direction and purpose.

To measure Amy's athletic identity, the Athletic Identity Measurement Scale (AIMS; Brewer & Cornelius, 2001) would be appropriate to assess the degree to which she identifies with her role as an athlete. The 7-item self-report questionnaire measures the extent to which respondents agree with the statements about cognitive, affective, and behavioral, components of identification to the athlete role on a 7-point Likert scale (1 = strongly disagree; 7 = strongly agree). Higher scores on the AIMS correspond with stronger and more exclusive identification with the athlete role. Trained professionals in the use of psychometric measure such as the AIMS can use the questionnaire as a measure of identity, possibly using it in conjunction with other assessments as needed. In keeping with the importance of the multi-dimensionality of athletic identity, the measure would be an appropriate tool to help Amy understand how strongly she identities in her athletic role and where she measures with respect to the dimensions within the AIMS (i.e., social identity, exclusivity, and negative affectivity). The instrument could serve as a point for discussion about healthy balance of identity, and the positive and potential negative elements of the athletic role.

Theoretical considerations

Amy's psychosocial responses to her concussion rehabilitation can be explained through the integrated model of psychological response to sport-related concussion injury and rehabilitation (Wiese-Bjornstal, White, Russell, & Smith, 2015). In the post-concussion injury psychological response part of the model, Wiese-Bjornstal and colleagues (2015) note that when athletes experience a SRC, their personal and situational factors associated with the injury interact with their neurobiological, psychogenic, and pathophysiological responses. These factors will influence their cognitive, emotional, and behavioral responses, ultimately affecting the overall psychological recovery outcomes. For Amy, relevant personal factors affecting her reactions to her injury and rehabilitation included her lack of history of injury, characteristics of her injury, and her high symptom report. Relevant situational factors included being new to the team, trying to establish status in the team, subscribing closely to the sport ethic (Coakley, 2009) by minimizing symptom reporting, sacrificing for her sport, and maintaining her external image of being tough and committed.

The above-mentioned personal and situational factors, interacting with Amy's neurobiological, psychogenic, and pathophysiological responses subsequently influenced her cognitive appraisal of the symptoms of the SRC. In particular, Amy's symptoms included headaches, sleep disturbances, and an inability to concentrate. Amy also expressed that having a concussion was like experiencing disability – as she was unable to fulfill her role as an athlete and a student. This appraisal greatly affected her feelings and behavior surrounding the injury. In particular, Amy's appraisal of her symptoms influenced her emotions leaving her feeling sad and scared. This fear and sadness then led her to engage in maladaptive behavior (e.g., withdrawing from others).

The cognitive appraisal, emotional, and behavioral response relationship of the concussion model (Wiese-Bjornstal et al., 2015) has been well supported by research. Concussed intercollegiate athletes have exhibited higher levels of negative and depressed mood in comparison to their pre-concussion status (Mainwaring, Hutchinson, Bisschop, Comper, & Richards, 2010). Post-concussion mood disturbances can also be long-lasting, as among concussed individuals, irritability and frustration can be strong affective symptoms that emerge long after concussion occurrence, and can last longer than depressed mood (Eisenberg, Meehan, & Mannix, 2014).

Unique to the complexity of responses to concussion is the overlap of physiological impairments with psychological symptoms of responding to the injury itself. For many, it becomes difficult to delineate between feeling fatigue due to injury, and feeling fatigue due to cognitive functioning: "cognitive difficulties and slow or impaired performance on cognitive tasks depletes energy. Struggling with depression or anxiety can be fatiguing, or conversely unrelenting fatigue can contribute to depressive symptoms" (Wiese-Bjornstal et al., 2015, p. 176). This cycle of sustained fatigue (Gosselin et al., 2012) is common and can be extremely challenging to break.

Amy's responses are typical to those with SRC. Silver (2014) describes psychological cognitive appraisal of concussion symptoms as a dysfunctional feedback loop. Specifically, an athlete experiences disruptions in cognitive function post-concussion, leading to emotions such as fear and anxiety, which in turn influences subsequent cognitive functions. The above is also influenced by a continuous reciprocal interaction between cognitive appraisals, emotional, and behavioral responses ultimately affecting the concussion recovery outcomes (Wiese-Bjornstal et al., 2015). To maximize concussion recovery success, the focus of Amy's care needed to be on her appraisal of the injury, and the emotions and behaviors associated with the injury, while considering the impact of her key personal and situational factors. To ensure Amy's successful return to sport, practitioners working with her need to focus on addressing her emotional responses (termed affective symptoms and responses in the Wiese-Bjornstal et al., 2015 model). In particular, Amy experienced a variety of affective symptoms and responses, including feelings of confusion, an inability to cope, and feeling overwhelmed, all of which eventually influenced her non-adherence (behavioral symptom and response).

Interprofessional plan of care

Given the environment where the case took place, the primary rehabilitation team consisted of a physician and an athletic therapist (AT). Based on the size, structure, and available resources on campus, adopting a formal interdisciplinary team is not a formal process. In this context, an excellent primary physical care team is in place and athlete care is a top priority; however, adding formal psychological care to the team has been somewhat lacking. At the start of the concussion rehabilitation protocol, the AT had referred Amy to counseling through the campus health services department; however, Amy chose not to attend counseling.

Eight days post-concussion, with Amy's permission, the AT contacted an educational assistant (EA) at the university. Educational assistants serve to help students with varying challenges to help them reach their full academic potential, while aligning accommodations with the rehabilitation protocol. Typical focus areas are study skills and peer support. This includes adjustments to due dates and assistance with examinations (e.g., extended time to write exams, breaks from mental fatigue), or academic support sessions with the EA and peers (e.g., study hall with other students with concussions). A month post-concussion, the AT contacted a mental performance consultant (MPC) with whom she has a long-standing working relationship, asking her to assist with Amy. The primary rehabilitation team (AT and physician) and subsequently the EA was then supplemented with the MPC integrated into the team, whereby the EA and MPC formed the secondary team (Clement & Arvinen-Barrow, 2013). The MPC was in regular communication with the primary team, and following a one-on-one meeting with Amy (and with her permission), the MPC then coordinated with the AT and the EA about how to proceed addressing the psychological issues of concern. Amy was still experiencing severe post-concussive symptoms, engaging in maladaptive coping, and still under the constant care of her primary team, which is atypical to the severity of her concussion. Knowing Amy's reluctance to see a counselor, the AT and MPC agreed it could be helpful for Amy to meet with the MPC instead. The MPC has expertise working with injured athletes and understands the competitive sport environment. Pitched this way to Amy, she was agreeable and liked the idea of talking with someone with a sport and performance focus.

Based on individual competencies and expertise of the team members, the AT was tasked to address Amy's non-adherence. In particular, the AT focused on building trust and rapport through patient education (e.g., demonstrating competency thorough explanations of the injury). The AT also accompanied Amy to a couple of appointments with the physician serving as source of social support and helping explain some of the medical information provided. The AT initiated this with full support from Amy, the MPC, and the EA. The EA's role was to address Amy's maladaptive coping by incorporating social support as an intervention. The EA also ensured Amy's academic interests align with her rehabilitation protocol (e.g., offering a peer support group with others with concussions). Prior to implementation, the team consulted with Amy about the framework of the action plan to ensure she was on board and to address any questions she had. Lastly, the MPC was responsible for overseeing the development of Amy's key coping skills. The MPC also focused on Amy's sense of athletic identity, with a goal of shifting her current unidimensional identity towards a more multidimensional identity. In order for the plan of care to be successful, Amy had to be comfortable with the direction and focus, thus all professionals engaged in a team meeting with Amy where honesty and transparency of the care provided was emphasized.

Perspective 1:
The athletic therapist's perspective

The AT in this case has 12 years of experience of overseeing the care of more than 400 student-athletes, managing other full time ATs, and numerous student trainers annually. She has treated thousands of student-athletes in her career, including many with SRC. The AT has been involved with Amy since the day after sustaining her concussion and meeting her on a regular basis in the clinic with the exception of Amy's missed appointments. During their first meeting, Amy was clinically assessed by the AT, who then referred her to the physician.

During the first month post-diagnosis, Amy's treatment involved paying close attention to her symptoms and following a stepwise progression, which involved many setbacks due to the severity of the concussion, ongoing symptomology, and non-adherence to rehabilitation. Since the AT has the ability to see athletes on a weekly, even daily basis, a strong therapeutic bond was created. This is important, as a sense of trust and support built during such a vulnerable time with the athlete enhances the therapeutic relationship and facilitates a strong alliance (Tracey, 2008). This allowed the AT to be more effective in providing care from a holistic perspective. Taking this approach with Amy, the AT eventually facilitated greater adherence to the rehabilitation protocol.

As part of the patient education intervention, the AT provided Amy with examples of her non-adherence and pointed out how these actions could be hindering her progress. It was then Amy realized she needed to channel her energy into being proactive:

> I was desperate to keep physically active; but then would avoid going to rehab, so it was a vicious cycle. I would initially feel good on the bike, then get a headache and not want to see the AT for fear I would get in trouble. When she explained how this behavior might contribute to my slower healing, that was the push I needed to snap out of it and move forward.

Amy was stuck wanting to push and was steadfast in her mindset, common in competitive athletes of "more is better," instead of recognizing that rest would be more beneficial to her recovery. She viewed resting akin to quitting, which was consistent with her strong athletic identity so focused on the value of hard work and strength. The AT appealed to Amy's academic focus and approached her from an educational perspective. She talked with Amy about brain neuro-anatomy and shared current research on rest, exercise, and healing. This proved to be effective with Amy as she could see it from an academic side, and gradually adopted the data as lessons to apply to herself. The educational approach is considered foundational in the therapeutic process. Heil (1993) has noted the value of education as a cornerstone of the alliance between patient and trainer within the sports medicine team. In particular, Heil has provided numerous guidelines for education such as discussing (a) basic anatomy of the injury, (b) possible problems dealing with pain and how to cope, and (c) pros and cons for limits on physical activity depending on symptomology. Amy responded very favorably to this educational approach and it was a turning point for her adherence and overall rehabilitation.

Upon inclusion of the EA and eventually the MPC to the rehabilitation team, the AT continued ongoing concussion treatment protocols, while also paying special attention to fostering ongoing trust, patient education, and support. The expanded team offered Amy support from multiple areas of expertise. Since the treatment of SRC is changing with the development of new techniques and research, it is imperative to keep up to date with the latest techniques and protocols. Attending conferences gives healthcare providers the tools needed to provide the best care for their athletes and clients grounded in evidenced-based practice. The AT attended a large national conference while treating Amy and came back with several new evidence-based techniques to try augment the healing process. This approach also resonated with Amy, since she is interested in athletic therapy and the clinical nature of rehabilitation. Tapping into Amy's interest in the academic and clinical side was useful, as the AT noticed Amy did not miss any further appointments and began to demonstrate greater adherence. An unexpected example of the effectiveness of Amy's patient education was the AT overhearing Amy talking with other injured athletes in the clinic about the importance of attending rehabilitation and doing their prescribed exercises.

The AT not only served as an educator through the recovery process but also as a key part of the Amy's support system. This was most important during physician appointments where the AT would accompany Amy to help interpret some of the complex medical jargon. Due to her memory loss issues and ongoing symptomology, Amy was not always able to remember all of the details the physician provided or all the information she needed to provide for the physician, so the AT was helpful and provided ongoing support for Amy. Athletic trainers can be a very strong source of social support for athletes and this has been demonstrated in numerous studies (Arvinen-Barrow, Massey, & Hemmings, 2014; Arvinen-Barrow, Penny, Hemmings, & Corr, 2010; Russell & Tracey, 2011; Tracey, 2008).

Through sustained interaction with Amy, the AT discussed her injury and rehabilitation process and possible detrimental effects of non-adherence. Amy began to see how her attitude, behaviors, and attributions within her control were affecting her healing process. The AT facilitated Amy's sense of autonomy throughout her rehabilitation by using a collaborative approach. For example, the AT gave options of exercises allowing Amy to choose the specific exercise and having open dialogue as to why certain exercises are appropriate. This amplified Amy's feeling of having some control and autonomy over her rehabilitation program as she noted, "it was easier to buy into what she [AT] was asking me to do. I finally saw the reason behind her madness" and it fit with her motivation to heal and return to sport.

Perspective 2:
The educational assistant's perspective

Amy's EA has worked at the university's Accessible Learning Center (ALC) for ten years helping students with temporary or permanent disabilities be successful students. As per her role, the EA has the ability to coordinate with the primary care team to ensure athletes' academic interests align with their rehabilitation protocol. This includes coordinating with professors to allow extension for assignments and assistance with examinations (e.g., splitting exams into sections across two days to reduce mental fatigue). The EA and Amy worked together to attain the proper work-rest balance through the strategy of scheduling short time segments to do schoolwork with breaks for rest. Amy learned how to prioritize her tasks and recognize her limits in terms of her cognitive ability while still recovering from her SRC. In the case of concussions, these services are critical, due to the cognitive impairments (e.g., difficulty concentrating) and the need for cognitive rest (e.g., not attending classes; Kasamatsu, Cleary, Bennett, Howard, & McLeod, 2016).

As directed by her physician, Amy was unable to attend classes for six weeks, which made completing course work difficult to manage, as she was required to learn the material on her own. The AT connected Amy with the EA eight days post-concussion, after being removed from classes as per physician recommendation, with a goal to build a learning strategy to manage her course load within the confines of her rehabilitation protocol. During their first meeting, the EA connected with Amy's professors to inform them of the situation and request adjustments and flexibility to deadlines as necessary throughout the semester. The EA then proceeded to inquire about Amy's perceptions of her strengths academically. A simple question of "What do you think you can manage academically?" elicited a range of responses in Amy, which the EA then compared to her prescribed SRC treatment protocol. Amy believed she could "push through" the symptoms and was able to teach herself the missed curriculum on her own. After listening to Amy's perspective, the EA worked with her to develop a learning strategy to empower Amy in her own learning, while also adhering to the rehabilitation protocol. Once the accommodations were in place, which happened within the first couple of visits over the first month of working with the EA, Amy said she felt tremendous relief. "I am so relieved. Now I can just focus on healing."

The implemented learning strategy consisted of providing Amy with a note-taker for all of her classes, alternate deadlines for assignments, and the use of "chunking" when completing course work. For examinations, Amy was provided aids such as extra time, enlarged font, writing in a quiet room, and the ability to take breaks as needed. The use of a note-taker allowed Amy not to attend classes (as instructed by her doctor) without the fear or added stress of falling behind in the class. Her class notes were printed on an enlarged font by the Accessible Learning Center (ALC) to reduce the amount of screen time Amy was exposed to on a daily basis, and Amy could review the material and continue her studies and keep up with assignments (with adjusted due dates). All of her assignments were strategically spaced throughout the semester to encourage the use of "chunking." Chunking is the concept of separating course work into smaller segments to prevent provoking symptoms, as well as to facilitate productive study sessions by maximizing concentration and information retention. This strategy is used in educational settings and is a well-documented technique to reduce cognitive load (Munyofu et al., 2007). Chunking parameters are individualized to each person based on their own threshold for symptoms, attention span, and the subject medium (hardcopy or online). For Amy, she was able to chunk her problem based course work (e.g., calculus and chemistry) in 30-minute intervals and her reading and writing based course work (e.g., health policy) into 20-minute intervals before symptoms appeared or focus was lost. As long as Amy used the chunking method, she was able to use it as a coping method to manage the emotional responses she felt about falling behind in classes. This method allows for a balance between schoolwork and cognitive rest, which is necessary for a full recovery (McGrath, 2010).

The EA also introduced Amy to the Academic Support Klub (ASK). This type of peer support group was adapted from work done with spinal cord injury patients to help students with academic support connect with other peers and de-stigmatize the need to ask for help (Divanoglou & Georgiou, 2017). The group met weekly in a quiet room for students to do their course work and provided peer tutors in a variety of subjects. The majority of the students using this service were also using the chunking method. A break section was provided where students could rest before starting their next segment of course work. It was common in the break section for students to meet new people and have conversations about the reason they require an EA and coping strategies they have learned throughout their university career. During her time at ASK, Amy met several other student-athletes who were rehabilitating from a concussion. They bonded over sharing their experiences of frustration and sadness about being away from sport and the difficulty of managing symptoms, but also shared positive coping strategies they have found work for them. This developed into not only academic support, but also a sense of social support with fellow student-athletes who knew what Amy was going through.

Perspective 3:
The mental performance consultant's perspective

At the time when Amy met with the MPC, a month had passed from her concussion onset. Amy was struggling with ongoing symptoms, and the uncertainty of the recovery timeline contributed to her feelings of frustration: "what's the point if

I am not playing anymore." When first meeting with the MPC, Amy was habitually isolating herself from her teammates and had missed several rehabilitation appointments.

During the initial meeting the MPC listened intently to Amy's story of her experience thus far dealing with her concussion. The MPC used an educational and growth-based framework incorporating a Life Development Intervention model (LDI; Danish & D'Augelli, 1983; Hodge, Danish, & Martin, 2013). Since LDI has an emphasis on self-directed change and being goal-directed, this fit well with Amy's personality. Additionally, her competitive sport background and tendency to be goal-oriented and future-focused complemented this approach.

Through the process of listening and gathering information during the first meeting, the MPC noted numerous comments indicating an exclusive athletic identity. Based on her observations, the MPC then outlined an intervention plan for Amy that included four key mental skills (see Table 5.1).

Since Amy had mentioned she enjoys journaling and drawing, the MPC encouraged Amy to continue to write about her experiences. The journaling, originally done as a form of expressive writing, eventually morphed into a form of graphical representations of her emotions, symptoms, experiences, and overall mood. Some of the drawings featured Amy doing a multitude of activities such as reading, working a part-time job at the library, and coaching young children. Seeing the variety of roles she enjoyed depicted graphically helped Amy to see herself beyond her role as a basketball player. During one of her sessions with the MPC, Amy expressed that the combination of journaling and drawing was very relaxing. "I find that journaling and drawing makes me feel at ease. When I read my journal entries, it is like ... I see myself from a distance and start connecting the dots. For example, how I have only seen myself as an athlete." The MPC encouraged Amy to keep journaling and drawing to explore her likes and other activities outsider of basketball. Amy began to see there was more to her than her image of a basketball player, and realized other roles in her life provide her with tremendous fulfillment and sense of purpose. One day she explained: It is amazing what drawing can do ... I kind of let my mind just take over and draw what it wants. And I surprise myself ... drawing so many different things that are not related to basketball."

Journaling as a therapeutic strategy is an established tool in healthcare. For example, Bolton and Wright (2004) noted the use of therapeutic writing demonstrated

TABLE 5.1 Key mental skills

Intervention	Desired outcome or target
Journaling and Drawing	Outlet to express feelings, exploring identity
Relaxation with Imagery	Coping with SRC, increasing adherence
Cognitive Restructuring	Increasing self-awareness, exploring identity, eliminating negative self-talk

utility for the versatility of it as a process for personal, explorative and expressive writing. Similarly, expressive writing within a cognitive-behavioral framework has been described as a method to express "emotions, self-regulation, reframing and dealing more effectively with negative feelings" (Lowe, 2006, p. 60). In a study of patients with chronic pain, the participants described the writing process as enlightening, and it allowed them to see new and helpful perspectives of their pain experiences (Furnes & Dysvik, 2012).

To help Amy cope with her SRC related pains, and increase her confidence in her rehabilitation, the MPC taught Amy relaxation with visual imagery whereby she visualized herself dribbling up the court and shooting free throws. Coupled with relaxation, this type of performance imagery (Arvinen-Barrow, Clement, & Hemmings, 2013) during rehabilitation has been beneficial in enhancing overall coping skills and improving adherence to rehabilitation (Wesch et al., 2011). Careful consideration was placed on the imagery types, vividness, and accuracy, to ensure Amy was comfortable with the imagery script, and that the images were positive and reflective of the desired intervention outcome. This is particularly important, as athletes who consider negative visual metaphors, as Amy did, can be successfully guided to redirect their thinking to positive images (Durden, 2017). Durden also noted the benefit of imaging the sport as useful for creating a sense of motivation to return to sport and this resonated strongly with Amy. Eventually, Amy transferred her relaxation and imagery skills to her shooting practices (once she was cleared by the AT to do so), and found she was able to image the shot more clearly. This is consistent with Durden (2017), who stated that use of relaxation prior to imaging is a facilitator to more vivid images.

Lastly, the MPC helped Amy restructure the negative self-talk she had been engaging in during her rehabilitation. Cognitive restructuring and positive self-talk has been demonstrated to be beneficial for rehabilitation by numerous researchers (Latinjak, Zourbanos, López-Ros, & Hatzigeorgiadis, 2014; Van Raalte, Vincent, & Brewer, 2017). Together the MPC and Amy explored some of the statements Amy was commonly using to describe her situation (e.g., feelings of uselessness, fearful of losing fitness, and the coach not wanting her to be a part of the team). During the process, Amy began to recognize how common negative self-statements such as "not being able to train makes me feel useless and unfit" were contributing to her emotional distress, and how her self-talk affected her healing process. Once Amy became aware of some of her self-defeating statements, she and the MPC worked on reframing her inner dialogue focusing on positive statements related to her possible contributions to the team involving non-court activities (e.g., aiding with video of games, assisting the coach at practice, coordinating social events for the team). With the support of her MPC, Amy also had an honest conversation with her coach sharing her fears of losing her spot on the team. This was a pivotal part of the reframing, as it reassured Amy that her coach believed in her, and assured Amy would be welcome back to the team when she was ready.

Case update

After recovering from her concussion, seven months later, Amy has found a new inner strength, confidence, and determination that is evident to everyone around her. This has allowed her to find new perspective in the challenges she faces in everyday life. Amy returned to playing basketball and enjoyed a successful season with the team. She recognized the physical and psychological challenges of recovering from a concussion, and was appreciative of the new mental skills she had developed during rehabilitation. She is now regularly using the same skills in her sport and life as a whole, and is constantly buying new journals. Her experience has inspired her to help others experiencing similar hardships and she is now motivated to parlay her experiences into a new and meaningful role by becoming an athletic therapist.

Conclusion

Freshman basketball player Amy sustained a severe concussion two minutes into her first intercollegiate game. The injury was a pivotal moment in her life as it called into question her identity as an athlete, her struggle to adhere to rehabilitation, and challenged her coping skills. The case highlights the complex nature of concussion and the challenge of an uncertain timeline for recovery, with a focus on Amy's reactions to rehabilitation. Amy's reactions to rehabilitation were addressed through the framework of the sport-concussion adapted model (Wiese-Bjornstal et al., 2015). The AT worked with Amy to address her non-adherence through building trust, patient education, and support. The EA addressed Amy's coping skills through targeted learning strategies and peer support. The MPC worked with Amy to develop coping skills and shift her unidimensional athletic identity into a more multidimensional one. Amy was able take advantage of available resources by positively reframing her injury, which helped her navigate through her rehabilitation. The case sheds light on the uniqueness of SRC, the need and benefit for psychological intervention, and the importance and value of an interprofessional plan of care.

KEY POINTS

- Amy, a freshman basketball player sustained a severe concussion two minutes into her first game of her varsity career.
- Amy's reactions to her injury and symptomology, coupled with her exclusive athletic identity, made it difficult for her to cope and manage being a student-athlete resulting in non-adherence issues.
- A team approach was used to address Amy's concerns. The AT addressed non-adherence through patient education and support (e.g., explaining brain neuro-anatomy). The EA addressed coping skills through targeted learning strategies (e.g., chunking academic work) and peer support (e.g.,

group study skills sessions). The MPC worked with Amy to develop coping skills (e.g., goal setting) and reduce the unidimensionality of her athletic identity (e.g., drawing demonstrating other interests).

• Amy recognized the challenges of recovering from a concussion and working collaboratively with the AT, EA, and MPC allowed her to adequately address her psychological needs and develop key mental skills and enhance her sense of confidence and positive mindset for rehabilitation and performance.

CRITICAL THINKING QUESTIONS

1. In what ways did Amy's cognitive-affective reactions to her concussion influence her behaviors (e.g., coping, rehabilitation adherence)?
2. What might be the biopsychosocial consequences of non-adherence and how might an AT address these in a rehabilitation setting?
3. For those working with competitive athletes, how can we facilitate discussion about both the benefits and detriments of a unidimensional athletic identity in order to explore a more balanced sense of self?

RESEARCH QUESTIONS

1. Do student-athletes with concussions who participate in the Academic Support Klub (ASK) report less psychological distress post-concussion?
2. Given that concussion research still lacks longitudinal studies fully exploring the dynamic nature of concussion rehabilitation, the cyclic nature of responses, and the role of post-concussion issues on athlete coping, what are the experiences of concussed individuals with lengthy and uncertain timelines for recovery?
3. Given the multidimensional nature and complexity of concussion management, to what extent do factors such as involvement of an interprofessional care team influence the rehabilitation outcomes (e.g., efficacy of treatment plan, reduced emotional distress)?

KEY PUBLICATIONS

1. Brewer, B. W., Cornelius, A. E., Stephan, Y., & Van Raalte, J. L. (2010). Self-protective changes in athletic identity following anterior ligament reconstruction. *Psychology of Sport & Exercise, 11*(1), 1–5. doi: 10.1016/j. psychsport.2009.09.005.

This article examines self-protective changes in athletic identity (AI) following anterior cruciate ligament reconstruction among 108 individuals, most of whom were involved in either competitive or recreational sport. Participants completed the AIMS (Brewer & Cornelius, 2001) to assess the extent to which they identify in the athlete role. Over a 24-month period post-surgery AI decreased, particularly among those who experienced slower progress in rehabilitation. Decreasing AI as a strategy to preserve self-esteem may serve a self-protective need. Those who demonstrated a reduced AI may be responding to a perceived threat to their self-image due to rehabilitation challenges including slower than anticipated recovery time.

2.   Wiese-Bjornstal, D. M., White, A. C., Russell, H. C., & Smith, A. M. (2015). Psychology of sport concussions. *Kinesiology Review, 4,* 169–189. doi: 10.1123/kr.2015-0012.

This review adapts the integrated model of psychological response to sport injury and rehabilitation process (Wiese-Bjornstal, Smith, Shaffer, & Morrey, 1998) to a concussion-specific model. The concussion-specific model summarizes the roles of psychological, psychiatric, and psychosocial factors influencing concussion risk, response, and outcomes. In order to minimize risk of concussions and promote recovery from concussions, the authors suggest targeting athlete cognitions, affect, behaviors, and social influences surrounding concussions outlined in the paper.

References

Arvinen-Barrow, M., Clement, D., & Hemmings, B. (2013). Imagery in sport injury rehabilitation. In M. Arvinen-Barrow & N. Walker (Eds.), *Psychology of sport injury and rehabilitation* (pp. 71–85). Abingdon:Routledge.

Arvinen-Barrow, M., Massey, W. V., & Hemmings, B. (2014). Role of sport medicine professionals in addressing psychosocial aspects of sport-injury rehabilitation: Professional athletes' views. *Journal of Athletic Training,* 49(6), 764–772. doi:10.4085/1062-6050-49.3.44.

Arvinen-Barrow, M., Penny, G., Hemmings, B., & Corr, S. (2010). UK chartered physiotherapists' personal experiences in using psychological interventions with injured athletes: An interpretative phenomenological analysis. *Psychology of Sport & Exercise,* 11(1), 58–66. doi:10.1016/j.psychsport.2009.05.004.

Bolton, G., & Wright, J. K. (2004). Conclusions and looking forward. In G. Bolton, S. Howlett, C. Lago & J. K. Wright (Eds.), *Writing cures: Introductory handbook of writing in counselling and psychotherapy* (pp. 228–231). New York, NY: Brunner-Routledge.

Brewer, B. W. (1993). Self-identity and specific vulnerability to depressed mood. *Journal of Personality,* 61(3), 343–364. doi:10.1111/j.1467-6494.1993.tb00284.x.

Brewer, B. W., & Cornelius, A. E. (2001). Norms and factorial invariance of the Athletic Identity Measurement Scale. *Academic Athletic Journal,* 15, 103–113.

Brewer, B. W., Van Raalte, J. L., & Linder, D. E. (1993). Athletic identity: Hercules' muscles or Achilles' heel? *International Journal of Sport Psychology,* 24(2), 237–254.

Carver, C. S. (1997). You want to measure coping but your protocol's too long: Consider the Brief COPE. *International Journal of Behavioral Medicine,* 4, 92–100.

Clement, D., & Arvinen-Barrow, M. (2013). Sport medicine team influences in psychological rehabilitation: A multidisciplinary approach. In M. Arvinen-Barrow & N. Walker (Eds.), *The psychology of sport injury and rehabilitation* (pp. 156–170). Abingdon:Routledge.

Coakley, J. J. (2009). *Sport in society* (10th ed.). Boston, MA: Irwin McGraw-Hill.

Danish, S. J., & D'Augelli, A. R. (1983). *Helping skills II: Life development intervention.* New York, NY: Human Sciences.

Divanoglou, A., & Georgiou, M. (2017). Perceived effectiveness and mechanisms of community peer-based programmes for spinal cord injuries: A systematic review of qualitative findings. *Spinal Cord*, 55, 225–234. doi:10.1038/sc.2016.147.

Durden, M. (2017). Utilizing imagery to enhance injury rehabilitation. *The Sport Journal*, 19, 1–5. http://thesportjournal.org/article/utilizing-imagery-to-enhance-injury-rehabilitation/#post/0.

Eisenberg, M. A., Meehan, W. P., & Mannix, R. (2014). Duration and course of post-concussive symptoms. *Pediatrics*, 133(6), 999–1006.

Frey, M. (2008). The other side of adherence: Injured athletes who are too motivated. *Athletic Therapy Today*, 13(3), 13–14.

Furnes, B., & Dysvik, E. (2012). Therapeutic writing and chronic: Experiences of therapeutic writing in a cognitive behavioral programme for people with chronic pain. *Journal of Clinical Nursing*, 21(23–24), 3372–3381. doi:10.1111/j.1365-2702.2012.04268.x.

Gosselin, N., Chen, J. K., Bottari, C., Petrides, M., Jubault, T., Tinawi, S., ... Ptito, A. (2012). The influence of pain on cerebral functioning after mild traumatic brain injury. *Journal of Neurotrauma*, 29(17), 2625–2634. doi:10.1089/neu.2012.2312.

Granquist, M. D., & Brewer, B. W. (2014). Psychosocial aspects of rehabilitation. In M. D. Granquist, J. J. Hamson-Utley, L. Kenow & J. Stiller-Ostrowski (Eds.), *Psychosocial strategies for athletic training* (pp. 187–208). Philadelphia, PA: F. A. Davis.

Granquist, M. D., Gill, D. L., & Appaneal, R. N. (2010). Development of a measure of rehabilitation adherence for athletic training. *Journal of Sport Rehabilitation*, 19(3), 249–267. doi:10.1123/jsr.19.3.249.

Heil, J. (1993). *Psychology of sport injury*. Champaign, IL: Human Kinetics.

Hodge, K., Danish, S. J., & Martin, J. (2013). Developing a conceptual framework for life skills interventions. *The Counseling Psychologist*, 41(8), 1125–1152. doi:10.1177/0011000012462073.

Kasamatsu, T., Cleary, M., Bennett, J., Howard, K., & McLeod, T. V. (2016). Examining academic support after concussion for the adolescent student-athlete: Perspectives of the athletic trainer. *Journal of Athletic Training*, 51(2), 153–161. doi:10.4085/1062-6050-51.4.02.

Latinjak, A. T., Zourbanos, N., López-Ros, V., & Hatzigeorgiadis, A. (2014). Goal-directed and undirected self-talk: Exploring a new perspective for the study of athletes' self-talk. *Psychology of Sport & Exercise*, 15(5), 548–558. doi:10.1016/j.psychsport.2014.05.007.

Lazarus, R. S., & Folkman, S. (1984). *Stress, appraisal, and coping*. New York, NY: Springer Publishing Company.

Lowe, G. (2006). Health-related effects of creative and expressive writing. *Health Education*, 106(1), 60–70. doi:10.1108/09654280610637201.

McCrory, P., Meeuwisse, W., Dvorak, J., Aubry, M., Bailes, J., Broglio, S., ... Vos, P. E. (2017). Consensus statement on concussion in sport – the 5th international conference on concussion in sport held in Berlin, October 2016. *British Journal of Sports Medicine*, 51(11), 838–847. doi:10.1136/bjsports-2017-097699.

McGrath, N. (2010). Supporting the student-athlete's return to the classroom after a sport-related concussion. *Journal of Athletic Training*, 45(5), 492–498. doi:10.4085/1062-6050-45.5.492.

McPherson, B. D. (1980). Retirement from professional sport: The process and problems of occupational and psychological adjustment. *Sociological Symposium*, 30, 126–143.

Mainwaring, L. M., Hutchinson, M., Bisschop, S. M., Comper, P., & Richards, D. W. (2010). Emotional response to sport concussion compared to ACL injury. *Brain Injury*, 24(4), 589–597. doi:10.3109/02699051003610508.

Munyofu, M., Swain, W. J., Ausman, B. D., Lin, H., Kidwai, K., & Dwyer, F. (2007). The effect of different chunking strategies in complementing animated instruction. *Learning, Media and Technology*, 32(4), 407–419. doi:10.1080/17439880701690109.

Russell, H., & Tracey, J. (2011). What do injured athletes want from their health care professionals? *International Journal of Athletic Therapy & Training*, 16(5), 18–21. doi:10.1123/ijatt.16.5.18.

Schwab Reese, L., Pittsinger, R., & Yang, J. (2012). Effectiveness of psychological intervention following sport injury. *Journal of Sport and Health Sciences*, 1(2), 71–79. doi:10.1016/j.jshs.2012.06.003.

Silver, J. M. (2014). Neuropsychiatry of persistent symptoms after concussion. *Psychiatric Clinics*, 37(1), 91–102. doi:10.1016/j.psc.2013.11.001.

Stephan, Y., & Brewer, B. W. (2007). Perceived determinants of identification with the athlete role among elite competitors. *Journal of Applied Sport Psychology*, 19(1), 67–79.

Stiller-Ostrowski, J. L., & Tracey, J. (2014). Emotional responses to injury. In M. D. Granquist, J. J. Hamson-Utley, L. J. Kenow & J. L. Stiller-Ostrowski (Eds.), *Psychosocial strategies for athletic training*. Philadelphia, PA: F.A. Davis.

Tracey, J. (2008). Inside the clinic: Health professionals' role in their clients' psychological rehabilitation. *Journal of Sport Rehabilitation*, 17(4), 413–431.

Van Raalte, J. L., Vincent, A., & Brewer, B. W. (2017). Self-talk interventions for athletes: A theoretically grounded approach. *Journal of Sport Psychology in Action*, 8(3), 141–151. doi:10.1080/21520704.2016.1233921.

Victorson, D., Farmer, L., Burnett, K., Ouellete, A., & Barocas, J. (2005). Maladaptive coping strategies and injury-related distress following traumatic physical injury. *Rehabilitation Psychology*, 50(4), 408–415. doi:10.1037/0090-5550.50.4.408.

Werthner, P., & Orlick, T. (1986). Retirement experiences of successful Olympic athletes. *International Journal of Sport Psychology*, 17, 337–363.

Wesch, N., Hall, C. R., Prapavessis, H., Maddison, R., Bassett, S. F., Foley, L., … Forwell, L. (2011). Self-efficacy, imagery use, and adherence during injury rehabilitation. *Scandinavian Journal of Medicine & Science in Sports*, 22(5), 695–673. doi:10.1111/j.1600-0838.2011.01304.

Wiese-Bjornstal, D. M., Smith, A. M., Shaffer, S. M., & Morrey, M. A. (1998). An integrated model of response to sport injury: Psychological and sociological dynamics. *Journal of Applied Sport Psychology*, 10(1), 46–69. doi:10.1080/10413209808406377.

Wiese-Bjornstal, D. M., White, A. C., Russell, H. C., & Smith, A. M. (2015). Psychology of sport concussions. *Kinesiology Review*, 5, 169–189. doi:10.1123/kr.2015-0012.

6

REACTIONS TO SPORT INJURY REHABILITATION

Jaimee Jacobsen, a junior collegiate volleyball player

Dana K. Voelker, Ashley Coker-Cranney, Allison Hetrick, and Nettie Puglisi Freshour

Key Words: 20-year-old female, junior collegiate volleyball player, body image concerns, sport-related body pressures, deviant overconformity, perfectionism, Achilles tendon rupture

Case description

Jaimee Jacobsen, affectionately called "JJ" since childhood (this name is a pseudonym and used for descriptive purposes only) is a 20-year-old female collegiate volleyball player in her junior year. JJ has a history of body image concerns that emerged during high school due to growing pressures to maintain a lean and toned physique considered ideal for female volleyball players. JJ was exposed to high school locker room talk where, in addition to chatter about schoolwork, friends, and crushes, her teammates criticized their own bodies and teased each other about their "huge" butts and thighs.

Upon entering a high-level college program, pressures to perform increased, and JJ's body image concerns intensified. Beliefs that "looking good" in volleyball spandex would attract spectators to their games were common. JJ sought to not only be a better volleyball player, but to also "look the part." In secret, she weighed herself three to four times a week. JJ also significantly reduced her carbohydrate consumption, which was only noticeable to her coaches and teammates while on the road. However, to her coaches and teammates, her highly selective eating habits appeared to reflect a "disciplined" approach to nutrition and "dedication" to being a high-level athlete versus a significant cause for concern.

In her junior year, at a point of fatigue during a mid-season game, JJ lunged to avoid a mis-hit and ruptured her Achilles tendon. JJ sat on the ground as the athletic trainer (AT) was called to the court during the stoppage. JJ confidently stated that she was "fine" and that "someone just hit [her] ankle." The AT conducted a quick on-court assessment and helped her off to the athletic training room. Lying down on the athletic training table, JJ strained to see the injury at the back of her ankle. Seeing the visible deformity of her injury for the first time, JJ's eyes widened as she stared in disbelief. Clearly distressed, she began crying as she described how "gross" and unsightly her ankle appeared.

JJ was seen by the orthopedic surgeon the next day and scheduled for surgery. She was informed that she would be non- and partial-weight bearing for approximately six weeks and that it would take 6 to 12 months to return to sport; JJ was immediately distraught with the news of such a long recovery time. Prevented from her normal training routine, her main fears were gaining weight and losing her sense of self as an athlete. Six weeks of restriction from cardio workouts and up to one year out of volleyball seemed like an eternity. With a "whatever it takes" attitude, JJ believed that if she worked hard enough, she could prevent weight gain during rehabilitation and significantly reduce her recovery time.

After surgery, JJ became concerned by the appearance of scars as well as atrophy surrounding the injured area, claiming that her leg was turning to "cottage cheese." She was placed in a heavy splint and given crutches; JJ thought of exercises to perform using the splint as extra weight. Two days after surgery, as nausea from the painkillers subsided, she began a routine of four-way hip exercises and all the core and upper extremity exercises she knew. She also eliminated carbohydrates and began consuming less in general to "compensate" for the absence of her normal exercise routine. When JJ's friends and teammates noticed her "lack of appetite," she stated the pain medication made her nauseous, which gave her a plausible excuse to eat much less. Over the course of rehabilitation, JJ snuck in extra reps, convinced that "more was better."

JJ continued to attend games and assumed responsibilities as a student coach on the sideline. After a close loss, one of her coaches mentioned in passing, "Well, we could have used you out there, huh?" JJ became concerned that her absence had been a big loss to the team and knew her coaches eagerly anticipated her return. In attempts to provide support, JJ's teammates often asked about her progress and when they might expect her to participate in practice again. JJ assured her coaches and teammates that she was making good progress, despite objective indications that her "extra hard work" was extending her timeline.

At three months post-surgery, JJ was returned to the weight room under the supervision of the AT. Driven to please her coaches and teammates and regain her status on the team, JJ used the fitness center at her apartment to burn more calories when she felt she was "not pushed hard enough" by her AT. JJ began experiencing significant, consistent pain that puzzled her medical staff. As the medical staff regressed the exercise protocol, JJ pushed harder. She requested more pain medication and iced her ankle in the evening so she could exercise more during the day. When the medical staff instructed her to slow down because the injury was not healing well, JJ felt like a failure.

The injury

The Achilles tendon ruptures when the tendon is fully extended and the attached muscles are then forcefully contracted (Gruber, Giza, Zachazewski, & Mendelbaum, 2013). Athletes typically describe the sensation as getting kicked or hit in the back of the ankle or stepping in a hole. As outlined in Gruber et al. (2013), the athlete has immediate deformity and loss of function, is unable to flex the foot downward, and thus has difficulty walking. Surgical repair is necessary, and the athlete is non- or partial-weight bearing for up to six weeks. Early rehabilitation includes light strengthening and range of motion exercises. Later exercises involve more intense strength, range of motion, and balance training. Running progressions typically begin around three months post-surgery. Typical return to play is 6–12 months following early motion protocols (Gruber et al., 2013).

Key factor 1: Sport-related body pressures

Body pressures, commonly known as "weight pressures" in the academic literature, involve perceived coercion to change or maintain one's body weight, shape, size, or appearance. Female athletes not only experience pressures from the broader sociocultural environment, such as family, peers, and the media, but also from the sport environment, such as coaches, teammates, appearance expectations, and required form-fitting or revealing athletic attire (Reel, Petrie, SooHoo, & Anderson, 2013). A plethora of cross-sectional, qualitative, and preliminary longitudinal research supports relationships between sport-related body pressures, internalization of body ideals (i.e., adopting external pressures as one's own), body dissatisfaction, negative affect (e.g., worry, sadness), and disordered eating (Krentz & Warschburger, 2013; Reel et al., 2013; Voelker & Reel, 2015).

Coaches are among the most frequently cited sources of sport-related body pressures reported by female athletes (Kong & Harris, 2015). Although coaches may not intend to be harmful, their comments can become a form of negative pressure for female athletes to, often unrealistically, change their bodies (Muscat & Long, 2008). In addition to the coach, tight spandex required in women's volleyball has been identified as a source of body pressure, specifically in collegiate players (Steinfeldt, Zakrajsek, Bodey, Middendorf, & Martin, 2013). JJ was exposed early to body-negative "locker room talk" with teammates and, more than likely, sexual objectification in form-fitting athletic attire. Although it is unclear from the case whether JJ received negative or derogatory comments from coaches about her body, her self-weighing and restrictive eating behaviors largely went unnoticed because they were performed in secret and interpreted as "discipline" and "dedication" in the sport context; however, these behaviors precipitated the increasingly serious concerns that arose post-injury.

Given the complexity in detection, using a formal instrument could be valuable to understanding how female athletes may be affected by their sport environment relative to their bodies and allow qualified helping professionals to target educational programming. The Weight Pressures in Sport-Females (WPS-F; Reel et al., 2013), for example, is an 11-item measure, shortened from an original 20 items (Reel, SooHoo, Petrie, Greenleaf, & Carter, 2010), that examines pressures experienced uniquely from the sport environment with regard to one's body weight, appearance, and performance on a 6-point Likert scale (1 = never; 6 = always). Two subscales, coach and sport pressure about weight and pressures regarding appearance and performance, are assessed in the 11-item version. The WPS-F has been shown to be reliable and valid with female collegiate athletes. The WPS-F creators indicate that, from a time perspective, the qualified practitioner may choose the abridged 11-item version, but could consider the original 20-item version to assess a broader scope of sport-related body pressures and develop educational programming.

Key factor 2: Deviant overconformity

In addition to sport-related body pressures, athletes are typically expected to conform to the sport ethic – strive for distinction, play through pain/injury, sacrifice for the game and the team, and accept no obstacles in pursuit of excellence (Hughes & Coakley, 1991). Athletes are often rewarded socially for their commitment to the sport ethic, through affiliation, status, and recognition, which validates their athletic identities (Coakley, 2009). Because injury is often a significant obstacle and may threaten athletic identity, some athletes resort to deviant overconformity – behaviors they believe demonstrate their commitment to the sport ethic, which will reaffirm their identity as an athlete and renew social approval. Athletes who overconform may over-adhere to their rehabilitation protocol, train despite pain or injury, and use performance-enhancing substances (Coker-Cranney, Watson, Bernstein, Voelker, & Coakley, 2018; Hilliard, Blom, Hankemeier, & Bolin, 2017; Podlog et al., 2013). Disordered eating behaviors are another form of deviant overconformity. Coaches and peers are instrumental in shaping team and sport culture and may reinforce expectations to complete extra training and restrict diets to control body weight, shape, size, and appearance (Johnston & Carroll, 1998). Consequently, some athletes learn that their ability to regulate their weight is a symbol of elite status and athletic identity characterized by self-discipline, focus, power, and control (Petersson, Ekstrom, & Berg, 2013).

In JJ's case, efforts to control her body weight, shape, size, and appearance were perhaps reflective of her strong desires to maintain her athletic identity, renew and prolong her athletic participation, and demonstrate her unwavering commitment to the expectations of her athlete role. Reinforcement from coaches, perceived pressure from teammates, and early experiences that heightened her body awareness led JJ to believe that her continued involvement in volleyball was contingent upon her willingness to demonstrate her commitment to being an athlete. She then demonstrated her commitment by ignoring her body's need for sufficient rest, continuing to physically stress her body through contraindicated exercise, minimizing the seriousness of her injuries and rehabilitation status, managing pain with prolonged use of prescribed pain relievers, and restricting her dietary intake. Currently, assessing athlete behaviors as deviant overconformity is dependent upon the practitioner's interview skills. No universal measure of deviant overconformity exists at present. Therefore, the practitioner must rely on a conceptual understanding of this construct in combination with participant disclosure of the motives that drive their overconforming behaviors.

Key factor 3: Perfectionism

Relatedly, personality traits, like perfectionism, play a role in this case. Perfectionism is a multidimensional construct characterized by perfectionistic strivings (i.e., motivation to achieve rigorous standards) and perfectionistic concerns (i.e., worry over mistakes, fear of negative evaluation from others, and negative responses to perceived failures; Hill, 2016). Athletes experience perfectionism uniquely depending on personal characteristics and the situation (Flett & Hewitt, 2016). For example, perfectionism may be functional, particularly during times of steady progress, in which an athlete effectively strives to reach goals for herself, coaches, and teammates. However, in situations, like injury, in which those goals are threatened, negative cognitive reactions may result, including harsh self-criticism and excessive preoccupation with mistakes (Flett & Hewitt, 2014).

JJ indeed demonstrates perfectionism, characterized by strivings and concerns over achieving a specific body ideal, improving as an athlete, and satisfying, or even exceeding, the expectations of others related to appearance and performance. JJ's perfectionism is likely to have fueled many of her successes, including excelling to college-level sport. Conversely, as JJ's injury posed a threat to her appearance and performance goals, she reacted with self-deprecation (e.g., describing her leg as "cottage cheese"), anxiety and worry (e.g., concern over the appearance of scars), and pushed her body's limits to avoid perceived failure (e.g., sneaking extra reps and eliminating carbohydrates in an attempt to expeditiously return to play in pre-injury physical shape). Her perfectionistic strivings and concerns became a driver of her unhealthy, overconforming behavior. In JJ's competitive sport context, the dangers of her perfectionism were easily masked; self-criticism, worry over mistakes, avoiding failure, and reaching high performance standards with an "at-all-costs" mentality were normative. Thus, even unhealthy over-striving went undetected by her teammates and coaches.

Several assessment tools for perfectionism exist for use by a qualified practitioner, although it is critical to consider the intended population, limitations, and usages for each. As an example, Burgess, Frost, and DiBartolo (2016) developed an eight-item version of the original and widely used Frost Multidimensional Perfectionism Scale (F-MPS-Brief; Frost, Marten, Lahart, & Rosenblate, 1990). This measure includes two dimensions – perfectionistic striving and evaluative concerns – assessed on a 5-point Likert scale (1 = strongly disagree; 5 = strongly agree). Preliminary reliability and validity data supports its utility, and this measure is recommended when a short, yet robust, measure is appropriate. However, examination of the measure's performance specifically with athletes is needed.

Theoretical framework

To conceptualize JJ's case, the integrated model of psychological response to sport injury and rehabilitation process (Wiese-Bjornstal, Smith, Shaffer, & Morrey, 1998) can be a useful framework. The model purports that an athlete's emotional and behavioral responses to injury, and ultimate recovery outcomes, are shaped by her cognitive appraisals, which are influenced by a range of personal and situational factors. These cognitive appraisals are proposed to influence an athlete's emotional responses (e.g., fear of uncertainty, frustration), behavioral responses (e.g., effort and intensity of rehabilitation), and physical and psychological recovery outcomes (e.g., healing, return to play).

Beginning with personal and situational factors, JJ is a highly motivated perfectionist with a strong athletic identity in a sport culture that rewards achievement believed to be the result of hard work and sacrifice. She was socialized to believe that determination and discipline earns the respect and appreciation of her coaches, which would facilitate her future in sport. She also valued her connection with her teammates, which was strengthened through shared experiences, including pressure to attract an audience with their bodies and physically demanding training schedules. JJ competed in a high-level college program, was considered a major contributor to her team, and was in the drudge of mid-season.

Consequently, JJ viewed her injury as a threat, an enemy to overcome, and was motivated to return to sport as quickly as possible. Her history told her that to beat an opponent, she needed to work harder and that she could expect success because she was better than most. In psychologically disconnecting herself from the injury to conquer it, JJ saw her body as a machine that could be manipulated to a serve a specific purpose. She made drastic, even if unhealthy, changes to her eating and exercise to ensure her body could train, compete, and "look good" in volleyball attire. Her commitment to the sport ethic propelled her efforts to shorten the rehabilitation timeline, and she felt guilty and shameful when her progress slowed. These emotional responses prompted her to further engage in overconforming behaviors – training beyond her rehabilitation protocol, using medication to manage prolonged pain, and restricting her diet – because she believed that doing so would allow her to heal quicker, return to sport faster, and succeed. The dynamic interplay between JJ's cognitive appraisals, emotional responses, and behavioral responses led to an extended rehabilitation and potential longer-term consequences.

Interprofessional plan of care

Working in a high-level college program, the AT, the certified mental performance consultant (CMPC), and the sports dietitian had pre-existing working relationships with JJ, her team, and the coaches. These relationships would likely have facilitated insight into JJ's environment, perfectionistic strivings, concern over mistakes, and strong athletic identity pre-injury. Although the extent of her health-compromising behavior may have been unknown to practitioners prior to the injury, establishing early relationships with athletes, like JJ, expedites the ability of practitioners to respond appropriately to concerns within their own scope of practice as they arise, and especially in response to a critical incident, like athletic injury. Further, strong rapport with JJ's coaches would allow each of these helping professionals to assist the coaching staff in providing JJ with effective and appropriate support pre- and post-injury. Examples include prohibiting comments related to JJ's body weight, shape, size, or appearance and advising the coaches to encourage JJ to take her time for a safe, versus faster, recovery.

After the injury, instruments like the Emotional Response of Athletes to Injury-Sports Medicine Professional form (ERAIQ-SMP; Smith, 1996) would be useful in assessing JJ's needs over the course of rehabilitation. Its purpose makes the ERAIQ-SMP easily administered by the practitioner with the most contact with the athlete. The ERAIQ-SMP is designed to gather information from athletes at intake related to the nature of the injury, athlete goals and motivation, athletic identity, social support, stressors, emotional responses, and rehabilitation adherence. Although it is unnecessary to re-administer the full questionnaire to an athlete several times across the rehabilitation protocol, using specific items to measure progress on targeted areas of improvement can provide feedback to the interdisciplinary team and the athlete to guide future interventions. In JJ's case, information from this assessment over time, combined with field observations and informal interviews, would reveal rehabilitation overadherence, deviant overconformity, and body image and eating concerns. Consequently, consultation with and referral to a licensed mental health professional and physician who specialize in athletes and eating pathology must be made. Caring confrontation techniques are generally recommended in referral conversations (see also Voelker & Schlitzer-Tierney, 2016). This approach requires the referring practitioner to meet with the client in a confidential setting, communicate their genuine care and concern for the client's overall health and safe return to play, and specify observable concerns (e.g., "I noticed you have been doing additional reps beyond what the AT suggests. May I ask you more about that?"). The practitioner must then listen empathically. Successful referrals often include offers to assist in setting up the appointment and athlete follow-through (e.g., "In order to be of most help and support to you, I need to connect you with the right expertise. Let's call for an appointment together. I can go with you the first time if that would help"). Communication and coordination between helping professionals overseeing JJ's care are vital for effective treatment, although there are specific guidelines that must be followed to do so ethically and legally (See Ethical Considerations and Need(s) for Referral section).

Perspective 1: The athletic trainer's perspective

>Within the interdisciplinary team, it is the AT's responsibility to prevent, recognize, and refer any number of physical and psychological needs of the athletes in

their care (National Athletic Trainers' Association, 2011). A season-ending injury can be the first time an athlete's body has failed them physically, which is a confusing, emotional, and stressful experience. Close observation of JJ's emotional and behavioral responses throughout rehabilitation would be critical given the combination of her perfectionist personality and weight and appearance concerns; together these factors would place her at risk for overadherence to the rehabilitation protocol.

In this case, the AT would facilitate the treatment process by serving as the "eyes and ears" on the ground. Due to the unique setting with which ATs interact with athletes, they are in an ideal position to garner critical information that may not otherwise be observed by other professionals in a supportive role (Clement & Shannon, 2011). For example, attending team meals on campus and during road trips allows the AT to observe eating habits versus solely relying on athlete self-report. Athletes also often hang out and engage in long, personal conversations in the athletic training rooms with ATs. This dialogue can often provide insight into the team culture, attitudes, and behaviors that may also be a factor in the athlete's treatment.

For instance, as someone with strong motivation to rehabilitate her injury, JJ would be likely to spend a lot of time in the athletic training room, which could be used as an opportunity for conversation and rapport building. It is during this time that the AT would likely learn more about her motives and struggles. Specifically, the tremendous pressure JJ placed on herself was mistaken for competitiveness. In truth, she presented similarly to those with addictive characteristics as observed in her obsessive preoccupation with weight and appearance and her insistence on completing additional exercise despite its contraindications. JJ's approach to pain and fear was confrontational in nature such that she viewed her injury as a temporary, inconvenient annoyance and disruption to her life (Leeuw et al., 2007). With a no pain, no gain mentality, she pushed the limits of her protocol. Additionally, JJ's request for more pain medication would be concerning to the AT; acute inflammatory symptoms typically last four to six days, and significant continued pain would indicate potential complications, such as infection or over-activity (Kisner, Colby, & Borstad, 2018).

Educating the athlete is imperative to the rehabilitation process (Christakou & Lavallee, 2009). Post-injury the AT should discuss the nature of the injury, surgical procedure, post-operation expectations (e.g., pain treatment), ambulation on campus, personal hygiene management (e.g., showering), early rehabilitation exercises, and how to minimize scarring. For JJ, it would be important to assist her in reframing her interpretation of scars from a symbol of negativity (e.g., ugliness) to optimism (e.g., evidence of meeting a challenge and overcoming it). Discussing setbacks would also be crucial. Successful return to play is contingent, in part, on psychological readiness. In addition to building confidence and fostering motivation, athletes should have realistic expectations (Podlog, Banham, Wadey, & Hannon, 2015) and the AT must remain honest and supportive when discussing those expectations to maintain a trusting relationship.

As athletes relay concerns, they should be met with energetic, individualized, and solution-based recommendations (Christakou & Lavallee, 2009). Specifically, the AT and JJ should work collaboratively to identify solutions that foster her autonomy in the rehabilitation plan while maintaining an optimal healing environment for the injured tissue. This could be accomplished by modifying activity and allowing JJ to choose some of the exercises and conditioning from an approved list. Having a sense of some control during the recovery process would help empower JJ to improve compliance with the program. To meet JJ's need for relatedness and decrease the sense of isolation from the team, the AT could modify some activities to allow JJ to participate in team workouts with a modified plan, as deemed appropriate from the treatment team. It would be important for JJ's concerns to be continually revisited to ensure her safety. For example, upon learning about the extra exercise at her apartment fitness center, confronting JJ would be necessary, but must be done with compassion by demonstrating care, asking questions, and ultimately opening the lines of communication relative to this behavior.

In addition to observation, information gathering, and treatment modification, the AT must often coordinate athlete care. Among the AT's many roles is to assist with the logistics of referral and treatment adherence (Bonci et al., 2008), such as appointment-tracking and timely communication with the treatment team regarding injury recovery. Further, following JJ's documented consent for providers to communicate confidential treatment matters (see Ethical Considerations and Need(s) for Referral Section), the AT may be tasked with reinforcing the efforts of other professionals working with JJ. For example, the AT could support the sports dietitian's approach by encouraging JJ to hydrate during and refuel at the end of each rehabilitation session to promote healing and more efficient and effective recovery. The AT could also be instrumental in supporting the CMPC's work by reinforcing and assisting JJ in reframing her thoughts. For example, if JJ reported, "I'll never get back to the court," the AT would have an opportunity to interject in ways that would help JJ disconnect herself from her negative thinking such as, "You're having *the thought* that you'll never get back to the court, but you are not your thoughts." Such reinforcements could lead to additional conversations, such as about JJ's mood and outlook towards recovery, that would offer a better understanding of her progress.

Perspective 2:
Certified mental performance consultant's perspective

Importantly, athletes with suspected eating pathologies should receive treatment from licensed, specially trained mental health professionals. Consequently, the focus of JJ's certified mental performance consultant (CMPC) would be on performance issues tied to her injury rehabilitation and overconforming behaviors. Although there may be some overlap between potential clinical concerns and performance-related issues, legally and ethically, the CMPC must maintain competency boundaries (Etzel &

Skvarla, 2017) and take advantage of their referral network which includes an appropriately trained licensed mental health professional and physician.

JJ reported her body image concerns arose during high school and magnified as body pressures increased over the duration of her sport participation. Her tendency towards doing more likely started much earlier, as she learned that success was garnered from working harder and being better than her opponents. Identifying where, when, and who reinforced the more-is-better, perfectionistic mentality JJ adopted would be of paramount importance. Specifically, JJ reported self-weighing and cutting carbohydrates in response to perceived body pressures. When these behaviors were acknowledged by her coaches as indicative of her dedication and discipline, JJ's inclination to increase the frequency and intensity of her behaviors grew. Messages she received in her youth – that sport success requires sacrifice, that more is better, and that determination is dependent upon behaviors off the court – were all confirmed as coaches and teammates noticed and approved her efforts. When she became injured, JJ did what she learned up to that point – do more.

From a sport psychology perspective, this thinking is important as it would directly affect JJ's engagement in health-compromising behaviors. In light of her injury, JJ found herself in a place where doing more was ineffective; in fact, it was prolonging her return to play, which disrupted her appraisals of athletic success, as well as injury. Given her resistance to accept feedback from her medical staff and choosing to pursue her own agenda, working with, rather than against her, would be critical. One helpful approach is motivational interviewing (see Markland, Ryan, Tobin, & Rollnick, 2005; Rollnick, Miller, & Butler, 2007) where a collaborative relationship is nurtured to roll with client resistance, develop discrepancy, and support client autonomy. Through the course of this approach, JJ would meet all her basic psychological needs: autonomy would be reached through working collaboratively; relatedness would be addressed by expressing empathy; and competence would be demonstrated by celebrating successful approximations of adaptive behavior until she returned to sport.

Concepts and methods from Acceptance and Commitment Therapy (ACT; Hayes, 2016) would also be useful in helping JJ to approach injury rehabilitation more productively. According to ACT, suffering occurs when clients avoid aversive experiences, entangle their sense of self with their circumstances, treat thoughts as reality, lose track of their values, lose contact with the present moment, and fail to engage in steps toward meaningful pursuits. The goal is to build psychological flexibility through experiential activities, whereby clients can change their relationship with their thoughts and experiences to help them live more fulfilling and meaningful lives. Acceptance and commitment therapy has been successfully used with injured athletes in as few as four sessions; using an educational ACT framework helped injured athletes to build acceptance of their thoughts and emotions, commitment to adaptive rehabilitation behaviors, and certainty in return-to-play transitions (Mahoney & Hanrahan, 2011).

To address JJ's tendency to do more, centering exercises could be used to help her maintain contact with the present moment. JJ was uncomfortable with the idea of sitting idly and avoided this by *doing something* like restricting her diet or exercising. However, as long as she dedicated energy to preventing discomfort, she could not spend it on opportunities that brought her closer to a healthy return to play. Additionally, helping her build acceptance of her circumstances, and to see them for what they are, could make her less likely to avoid the unpleasant feelings she associated with her injury and her body. By helping her understand that thoughts are not reality, but rather momentary events that occur in her own head, she could strip them of their power. Simply asking her to notice her thought patterns, and add to them the phrase, "I am having the thought that …" (a thought diffusion strategy), could remind her that her thoughts are temporary, and do not reflect absolute reality. By being more self-compassionate and less critical, she may be more open to feedback from her sports medicine team, more mindful of engaging in practices that inch her closer to healthy return to play. Addressing JJ's presenting concerns from an ACT perspective and using a motivational interviewing approach, she could be empowered to make powerful strides toward recovery and a fulfilling athletic career.

Perspective 3: The sports dietitian's perspective

Given JJ's history and current dietary restriction, the sports dietitian should assess for Relative Energy Deficiency in Sports (RED-S), which involves an imbalance between energy consumption and energy expenditure (Mountjoy et al., 2018). Insufficient energy to support body functions involved in health and performance can result in a range of health risks, such as menstrual dysfunction, declines in bone density, and weakened immunity (Mountjoy et al., 2014). The RED-S Clinical Assessment Tool (CAT) can be used by qualified practitioners to assess if an individual is consuming the necessary number of calories, per body weight, to perform basic body functions (Mountjoy et al., 2015). This measure would be helpful in tracking whether JJ consumed a variety of foods and balanced her intake with her current physical activity and rehabilitation exercise. Weekly follow-up meetings and discussions would be the best option towards safe healing and return to sport in this case.

JJ's vulnerable state relative to concerns about her body would necessitate that the sports dietitian empathetically discuss with her the body changes that may occur during injury rehabilitation and the importance of allowing the body time to heal while fueling it properly. Nutrition goals during athletic injury are focused on healing, rebuilding, and maintaining lean mass for return to play (Tipton, 2010). Because JJ's level of activity would likely fluctuate over the course of injury rehabilitation, the sports dietitian would work with her to adjust her energy consumption appropriately. JJ's specific needs would be met by following the general dietary recommendations for athletes that include consumption of 6–10g of carbohydrates/KG of body weight and 1.2–1.7g of protein/KG of body weight while ensuring 20–35% of total intake comprises healthy fat (Rodriguez,

DiMarco, & Langley, 2009). Educating JJ on her basic needs according to her basal metabolic rate, which accounts for age, height, weight, gender, and lean mass, would serve as the baseline for her caloric requirements. JJ and her sports dietitian would explore how her body could break down muscle for energy (hindering her healing) and store fat if she neglected to consume the appropriate nutrients. Through empathetic, open-minded exploration, JJ could gain increased understanding that carbohydrates and protein contain the same number of calories per gram and begin to appreciate the need for additional protein and a minimum level of carbohydrates to promote healing and recovery.

Notably, rather than giving JJ a specific number of calories to achieve and a prescriptive plan that she is likely to fixate on, the sports dietitian would focus on achieving dietary balance with an emphasis on health while challenging notions of "good" and "bad" foods in her dietary goals (Rodriguez et al., 2009). Using a 24-hour food recall as the basis for discussion, the sports dietitian and JJ would work together to identify times in her daily routine that she could add nutrient-dense meals and snacks to aid in the recovery process. Information on certain foods that can aid in recovery and get her back to participation (e.g., those high in anti-oxidants that help decrease inflammation) would be explored through various activities and collaborative sessions. After learning JJ was drastically cutting her calories, especially carbohydrates, the sports dietitian would need to work with her to slowly add them back in, particularly before and after rehabilitation sessions, using foods JJ felt comfortable experimenting with. During this process, it would be critically important to create an environment in which JJ felt safe and comfortable. Thus, the approaches discussed must be accompanied by nutrition counseling to help JJ reframe any negativity related to her dietary consumption and reinforce notions that food, including carbohydrates, are healthy for proper healing (Mittnacht & Bulik, 2014). Further, JJ would be encouraged to weigh herself only in the presence of the sports dietitian. Weighing herself in a safe, supervised setting would allow the sports dietitian to help JJ appropriately interpret any weight fluctuation, reduce anxiety associated with this practice, and deemphasize the need to weigh herself excessively.

Ethical considerations and need(s) for referral

Numerous ethical and legal issues are inherently tied to the principled care of athletes and those with co-morbid clinical psychological concerns (Etzel & Skvarla, 2017). In JJ's case, ethical considerations include those related to competence and confidentiality. Every provider in the treatment team must be sufficiently competent to be involved in the process of (a) assessing JJ's presenting concerns, (b) crafting collaborative interventions with JJ, (c) engaging in regular follow-up on intervention and recovery, and (d) making timely, appropriate referrals to providers who specialize in psychological concerns that are beyond the team members' own scope of practice. Because competence is largely self-determined based on education, training, and supervised experience, treatment team members must make regular, honest assessments of their current ability to help athletes like JJ, including judgment of whether they are qualified to administer specific assessments. They must police their own awareness, knowledge base, work, and work outcomes with clients. Attending a weekend workshop, reading some books about the psychology of injury and disordered eating, or having access to online information about treatment is insufficient to deem oneself competent.

With the client's permission to do so, regular consultation with treatment team members and other expert providers is essential to good ethical practice and maintaining an appropriate scope of work. It should be noted, though, that client confidentiality is an additional concern when working in interdisciplinary teams. Boundaries of what information the client consents to share between professionals (i.e., Releases of Information) should be established at the outset of the treatment team's formation and updated as needed (Moncier, 2014). Professionals in a supportive role, like the AT, CMPC, and sports dietitian, should have regular contact with athletes to do good work. The AT may see athletes at every practice or game, the CMPC may meet with the team regularly in addition to individual sessions, and the sports dietitian may interact with athletes periodically throughout the day at fuel stations or training tables. These supportive personnel are vital conduits to other helping professionals who may only see athletes as needed (i.e., when an athlete presents with signs and symptoms of clinical concern or when an athlete requires surgery). Prompt detection and referral of clinical concerns are best executed when referral networks are established a priori and when first responders are educated on the signs and symptoms of potential clinical disturbance.

For the AT, CMPC, and sports dietitian in this case, recognizing the aspects of JJ's concerns that rest beyond the boundaries of their expertise (i.e., the signs and symptoms of a possible clinical eating disorder diagnosis) is a vital ethical responsibility to protecting her welfare. Critically, while interprofessional communication is key to maintaining quality care, making effective referrals, and ensuring that messaging to JJ remains consistent between practitioners, these helping professionals are also ethically required to protect her right to confidentiality by honoring the limits of her Release of Information.

Case update

One year post-injury, JJ has returned to play for her senior year. Upon resuming her regular sport training, JJ's concerns about body weight and appearance have lessened. However, her relationship with food, exercise, and her body is improving as she continues her work with the sports dietitian, CMPC, and a licensed mental health professional. Although she is still demonstrating some difficulty challenging her whatever-it-takes and more-is-better attitudes, JJ continues to entertain the possibility that such attitudes are not only detrimental to her current sport performance, but her quality of life. Importantly, her work is additionally focused on effectively transitioning out of sport, building a healthy body image, and setting expectations for role fulfillment in retirement.

Conclusion

JJ's case is a demonstration of the dynamic interplay between personal and situational factors that can complicate successful recovery from injury. High levels of perfectionism, a strong athletic identity, and early body pressure experiences informed JJ's adverse response to athletic injury, including negative cognitive appraisals, emotional responses, overconforming behaviors, and undesirable rehabilitation outcomes. Successful navigation of JJ's return to play requires attention to physical (e.g., nutrition, healing), psychological (e.g., perfectionism, body image), and social factors (e.g., core beliefs related to performance enhancement and overconformity). Thus, treatment team members with a variety of specialties are needed to optimize her recovery outcomes. Key team members included the AT to address physical issues, the CMPC to address mental performance issues, the sports dietitian to address nutritional issues, as well as referrals to a licensed mental health professional to address clinical body image concerns and eating pathology and a physician to monitor health status. Each treatment team member serves to support and reinforce the work of others while remaining cognizant of the ethical limitations of their training and practice.

KEY POINTS

- Response to injury involves a dynamic interplay between personal and situational factors that affect the way athletes think, feel, and behave, which ultimately influence injury recovery outcomes. Addressing each provides the most comprehensive approach to facilitate successful return to sport.
- Pressures from the sport environment to achieve a specific body ideal are associated with body image concerns, negative affect, and disordered eating, all of which may intensify following athletic injury and complicate the injury rehabilitation process.
- Athletes with a strong athletic identity, perfectionism, and who have been socialized to believe that more is better are susceptible to overconforming behaviors, including those related to diet, overtraining, and overadherence to injury rehabilitation protocols.
- Delineating professional competencies and workloads can be a complex process, but is required to provide appropriate recommendations for injured athletes with new or pre-existing body image and eating concerns. Communication between practitioners is vital to addressing athletes' needs holistically, while maintaining ethical integrity.

CRITICAL THINKING QUESTIONS

1.   The focus of this case was on ways JJ's injury exacerbated her body image and eating concerns. How might JJ's body image and eating concerns have *contributed* to her injury?
2.   This case investigated the provision of necessary treatment for JJ throughout her injury rehabilitation in which body pressures and concerning eating and exercise behaviors compromised the process. Although the emphasis was on treatment, what might be done to address JJ's broader sport environment to help prevent these eating and exercise concerns in the first place?
3.   The perspectives of three professionals were described in this case – the AT, CMPC, and sports dietitian. Referrals to a licensed mental health professional and physician, ideally who specialize in athletes and eating disorders, were also discussed. Who else may play a role in JJ's recovery and what might those individuals do to support her?

RESEARCH QUESTIONS

1.   What personal and situational factors (e.g., personality characteristics, overconformity, body pressures) predict rehabilitation overadherance in athletes?
2.   Describe the experiences of athletes coping with body image concerns during injury recovery.
3.   What are the challenges and supports to successful treatment of injured athletes with body image and eating concerns?

KEY PUBLICATIONS

1.   Coker-Cranney, A. M., Watson, J. C., Bernstein, M., Voelker, D. K., & Coakley, J. (2018). How far is too far? Understanding identity and overconformity in collegiate wrestlers. *Qualitative Research in Sport, Exercise and Health, 10*(1), 92–116. doi: 10.1080/2159676X.2017.1372798.

This study uses life story and semi-structured interviews to investigate identity and overconformity in collegiate wresters. Findings from interviews with three wrestlers indicated that athletic identity stems from early experiences with family members, coaches, and teammates. During those early experiences, the wrestlers learned how the athlete role is defined, the importance of the athlete role in their lives, and the expectations of those who strive to be recognized as athletes. As the wrestlers continued participation, and were increasingly socialized into their athlete role, they were exposed to and experimented with a range of behaviors to meet expectations. Those who identified strongly with the athlete role and endeavored to prolong their participation in wrestling willfully engaged in health-compromising behaviors including disordered eating, dysfunctional exercise, performance-enhancing substance use, use of prescription drugs without a prescription, and playing injured. As one wrestler stated, "Nothing is too crazy. You can never go too far" (p. 107), indicating the deeply held sub-cultural beliefs about what is required for athletes to meet expectations, continue participation, and distinguish themselves.

2.   Mahoney, J., & Hanrahan, S. (2011). A brief educational intervention using acceptance and commitment therapy: Four injured athletes' experiences. *Journal of Clinical Sport Psychology*, 5, 252–273. doi: 10.1123/jcsp.5.3.252.

The authors of this study implemented an educational Acceptance and Commitment Therapy (ACT) program for four injured athletes recovering from anterior cruciate ligament surgery. The program consisted of four weekly one-on-one meetings grounded in ACT principles. Focus areas included cognitive defusion (i.e., separating self from thoughts), mindfulness (i.e., non-judgmental present awareness), acceptance (i.e., willingness to experience life as-is, rather than was or could/should be), and values (i.e., clarifying guiding principles/goals). Athletes completed measures of sport injury anxiety, acceptance, and mindfulness before and after the intervention. They were interviewed at the conclusion of the program to solicit feedback. Findings indicated the participants tended to avoid unpleasant experiences at the start of the program, but generally became more open and accepting of unpleasant experiences towards the end. Participants reported cognitive defusion and mindfulness were the most useful strategies toward developing acceptance and willingly committing to value-driven behavior. Researchers concluded future programs would benefit from more sessions that include all principles of ACT. In sum, this study shows acceptance and mindfulness approaches to injured athletes may provide benefits related to rehabilitation adherence and successful return to play.

References

Bonci, C. M., Bonci, L. J., Granger, L. R., Johnson, C. L., Malina, R. M., Milne, L. W., … Vanderbunt, E. M. (2008). National Athletic Trainers' Association position statement: Preventing, detecting, and managing disordered eating in athletes. *Journal of Athletic Training*, 43(1), 80–108. doi:10.4085/1062-6050-43.1.80.
Burgess, A. M., Frost, R. O., & DiBartolo, P. M. (2016). Development and validation of the Frost Multidimensional Perfectionism Scale – brief. *Journal of Psychoeducational Assessment*, 34(7), 620–633. doi:10.1177/0734282916651359.
Christakou, A., & Lavallee, D. (2009). Rehabilitation from sports injuries: From theory to practice. *Perspectives in Public Health*, 129(3), 120–126. doi:10.1177/1466424008094802.
Clement, D., & Shannon, V. R. (2011). Injured athletes' perceptions about social support. *Journal of Sport Rehabilitation*, 20(4), 457–470.
Coakley, J. J. (2009). Deviance in sports: is it out of control? In J. J. Coakley (Ed.), *Sports in society: Issues and controversies* (pp. 152–193). New York, NY: McGraw-Hill.
Coker-Cranney, A. M., Watson, J. C., Bernstein, M., Voelker, D. K., & Coakley, J. (2018). How far is too far? Understanding identity and overconformity in collegiate wrestlers. *Qualitative Research in Sport, Exercise and Health*, 10(1), 92–116 doi:10.1080/2159676X.2017.1372798.

Etzel, E. F., & Skvarla, L. A. (2017). Ethical considerations in sport and performance psychology. In O. Braddick (Ed.), *Oxford research encyclopedia of psychology*. Oxford: Oxford University Press. doi:10.1093/acrefore/9780190236557.013.141.

Flett, G. L., & Hewitt, P. L. (2014). "The perils of perfectionism in sports" revisted: Toward a broader understanding of the pressure to be perfect and its impact on athletes and dancers. *International Journal of Sport Psychology*, 45, 395–407.

Flett, G. L., & Hewitt, P. L. (2016). Reflections on perfectionism and the pressure to be perfect in athletes, dancers and exercisers. In A. P. Hill (Ed.), *The psychology of perfectionism in sport, dance and exercise* (pp. 296–319). New York, NY: Routledge.

Frost, R. O., Marten, P., Lahart, C., & Rosenblate, R. (1990). The dimensions of perfectionism. *Cognitive Therapy and Research*, 14, 449–468. doi:10.1007/BF01172967.

Gruber, J., Giza, E., Zachazewski, J., & Mendelbaum, B. R. (2013). Achilles tendon repair and rehabilitation. In L. Maxey & J. Magnusson (Eds.), *Rehabilitation for the post surgical orthopedic patient* (pp. 554–557). St. Louis, MO: Elsevier Mosby.

Hayes, S. C. (2016). Acceptance and commitment therapy, relational frame theory, and the third wave of behavioral and cognitive therapies. *Behavior Therapy*, 47(6), 869–885. doi:10.1016/j.beth.2016.11.006.

Hill, A. P. (2016). Conceptualizing perfectionism: An overview and unresolved issues. In A. P. Hill (Ed.), *The psychology of perfectionism in sport, dance and exercise* (pp. 3–30). New York, NY: Routledge.

Hilliard, R. C., Blom, L. C., Hankemeier, D., & Bolin, J. (2017). Exploring the relationship between athletic identity and beliefs about rehabilitation overadherence in college athletes. *Journal of Sport Rehabilitation*, 26(3), 208–220. doi:10.1123/jsr.2015-0134.

Hughes, R., & Coakley, J. (1991). Positive deviance among athletes: The implications of overconformity to the sport ethic. *Sociology of Sport Journal*, 8(4), 307–325.

Johnston, L. H., & Carroll, D. (1998). The context of emotional responses to athletic injury: A qualitative analysis. *Journal of Sport Rehabilitation*, 7(3), 206–220. doi:10.1123/jsr.7.3.206.

Kisner, C., Colby, L. A., & Borstad, J. (2018). *Therapeutic exercise: Foundations and techniques*. Philadelphia, PA: F. A. Davis.

Kong, P., & Harris, L. M. (2015). The sporting body: Body image and eating disorder symptomatology among female athletes from leanness focused and nonleanness focused sports. *The Journal of Psychology: Interdisciplinary and Applied*, 149(2), 141–160. doi: 10.1080/00223980.2013.846291.

Krentz, E. M., & Warschburger, P. (2013). A longitudinal investigation of sports related risk factors for disordered eating in aesthetic sports. *Scandinavian Journal of Medicine & Science in Sports*, 23(3), 303–310. doi:10.1111/j.1600-0838.2011.01380.x.

Leeuw, M., Goossens, M. E., Linton, S. J., Crombez, G., Boersma, K., & Vlaeyen, J. W. (2007). The fear-avoidance model of musculoskeletal pain: Current state of scientific evidence. *Journal of Behavioral Medicine*, 30(1), 77–94. doi:10.1007/s10865-10006-9085-9080.

Mahoney, J., & Hanrahan, S. J. (2011). A brief educational intervention using acceptance and commitment therapy: Four injured athletes' experiences. *Journal of Clinical Sport Psychology*, 5, 252–273. doi: 10.1123/jcsp.5.3.252.

Markland, D., Ryan, R. M., Tobin, V. J., & Rollnick, S. (2005). Motivational interviewing and self-determination theory. *Journal of Social & Clinical Psychology*, 24(6), 811–831. doi:10.152/jscp.2005.24.6.811.

Mittnacht, A. M., & Bulik, C. M. (2014). Best nutrition counseling practices for the treatment of anorexia nervosa: A Delphi study. *International Journal of Eating Disorders*, 48(1), 111–122. doi:10.1002/eat.22319.

Moncier, J. C. (2014). Sports medicine: The ethics of working as part of a university medical team. In E. F. Etzel & J. C. Watson II (Eds.), *Ethical issues in sport, exercise, and performance psychology* (pp. 99–110). Mogantown, WV: Fitness Information Technology.

Mountjoy, M., Sundgot-Borgen, J., Burke, L., Carter, S., Constantini, N., Lebrun, C., … Ljungqvist, A. (2014). The IOC consensus statement: Beyond the female athlete triad – relative energy deficiency in sport (RED-S). *British Journal of Sports Medicine*, 48(7), 491–497. doi:10.1136/bjsports-2014-093502.

Mountjoy, M., Sundgot-Borgen, J., Burke, L. M., Carter, S., Constantini, N., Lebrun, C., … Ackerman, K. E. (2015). Relative energy deficiency in sport (RED-S) clinical assessment tool (CAT). *British Journal of Sports Medicine*, 49(7), 421–423. doi:10.1136/bjsports-2014-094559.

Mountjoy, M., Sundgot-Borgen, J. K., Burke, L. M., Ackerman, K. E., Blauwet, C., Constantini, N., … Budgett, R. (2018). IOC consensus statement on relative energy deficiency in sport (RED-S): 2018 update. *British Journal of Sports Medicine*, 52(11), 687–697. doi:10.1136/bjsports-2018-099193.

Muscat, A. C., & Long, B. C. (2008). Critical comments about body shape and weight: Disordered eating of female athletes and sport participants. *Journal of Applied Sport Psychology*, 20(1), 1–24. doi:10.1080/10413200701784833.

National Athletic Trainers' Association. (2011). *Athletic training educational competencies* (5th ed.). Dallas, TX: National Athletic Trainers' Association.

Petersson, S., Ekstrom, M. P., & Berg, C. M. (2013). Practices of weight regulation among elite athletes in combat sports: A matter of mental advantage? *Journal of Athletic Training*, 48(1), 99–108. doi:10.4085/1062-6050-48.1.04.

Podlog, L., Banham, S. M., Wadey, R., & Hannon, J. C. (2015). Psychological readiness to return to competitive sport following injury: A qualitative study. *The Sport Psychologist*, 29(1), 1–14. doi:10.1123/tsp.2014-0063.

Podlog, L., Gao, Z., Kenow, L. J., Kleinert, J., Granquist, M. D., Newton, M., & Hannon, J. (2013). Injury rehabilitation overadherence: Preliminary scale validation and relationships with athletic identity and self-presentation concerns. *Journal of Athletic Training*, 38, 372–381. doi: 10.4085/1062-6050-48.2.20.

Reel, J. J., Petrie, T. A., SooHoo, S., & Anderson, C. M. (2013). Weight pressures in sport: Examining the factor structure and incremental validity of the weight pressures in sport – females. *Eating Behaviors*, 14(2), 137–144 doi:10.1016/j.eatbeh.2013.01.0.

Reel, J. J., SooHoo, S., Petrie, T. A., Greenleaf, C., & Carter, J. E. (2010). Slimming down for sport: Developing a weight pressures in sport measure for female athletes. *Journal of Clinical Sport Psychology*, 4(2), 99–111. doi:10.1123/jcsp.4.2.99.

Rodriguez, N. R., DiMarco, N. M., & Langley, S. (2009). Position of the American Dietetic Association, Dietitians of Canada, and the American College of Sports Medicine: Nutrition and athletic performance. *Journal of the American Dietetic Association*, 109, 509–527. doi:10.1016/j.jada.2009.01.005.

Rollnick, S., Miller, W. R., & Butler, C. C. (2007). *Motivational interviewing in health care: Helping patients change behavior.* New York, NY: Guilford Press.

Smith, A. M. (1996). Psychological impact of injuries in athletes. *Sports Medicine*, 22, 391–405. doi: 10.2165/00007256-199622060-00006.

Steinfeldt, J. A., Zakrajsek, R. A., Bodey, K. J., Middendorf, K. G., & Martin, S. B. (2013). Role of uniforms in the body image of female college volleyball players. *The Counseling Psychologist*, 41(5), 791–819. doi:10.1177/0011000012457218.

Tipton, K. D. (2010). Nutrition for acute exercise-induced injuries. *Annals of Nutrition and Metabolism*, 57(Suppl 2), 43–53. doi:10.1159/000322703.

Voelker, D. K., & Reel, J. J. (2015). An inductive thematic analysis of female competitive figure skaters' experiences of weight pressure in sport. *Journal of Clinical Sport Psychology*, 9(4), 297–316. doi:10.1123/jcsp.2015-0012.

Voelker, D. K., & Schlitzer-Tierney, A. (Eds.). (2016). Eating disorders in sport: Detection and referral guidelines for the AASP-certified consultant. https://appliedsportpsych.org/site/assets/files/1113/aaspedsig-detection_referralguidelines-final.pdf.

Wiese-Bjornstal, D. M., Smith, A. M., Shaffer, S. M., & Morrey, M. A. (1998). An integrated model of response to sport injury: Psychological and sociological dynamics. *Journal of Applied Sport Psychology*, 10(1), 46–69. doi:10.1080/10413209808406377.

7

REACTIONS TO MUSIC PERFORMANCE INJURY REHABILITATION

Brandon Jackson, a freshman music performance major

Jessica Ford, Russ Johnson, Damien Clement, and Monna Arvinen-Barrow

Key Words: 18-year-old male, music performance major, cognitive and somatic anxiety, re-injury anxiety, over-adherence, rotator cuff tendonitis

Case description

Brandon Jackson (this name is a pseudonym and used for descriptive purposes only) is an 18-year-old freshman music performance major attending college on a full music scholarship. A month in, Brandon was excelling in his college's orchestra. His clarinet and orchestra professors were also acknowledging and reinforcing his improvements. As a Type A personality, he enjoyed the challenge of continuing to master the clarinet, and it would not be uncommon for him to spend a great deal of time practicing, often remaining in the basement of the music hall until three or four in the morning. As a result of these long sessions, Brandon noticed a subtle nagging right shoulder pain that seemed to worsen with extended clarinet play. For the next few weeks he continued to play through the pain, taking breaks as needed, as in his mind it was "no big deal." His shoulder pain, though, grew progressively worse and intolerable, and Brandon, with the help of some Internet searches, began to self-medicate with ice and various anti-inflammatory medications just to get through orchestra rehearsal sessions. After dealing with this situation for about a month or so, Brandon finally gave in and visited the health clinic on campus. He got a referral to a sports medicine doctor in the area, who, after an MRI, diagnosed him with rotator cuff tendonitis. He was required to take time off from playing the clarinet, and he was referred to physical therapy for flexibility and strengthening exercises.

Brandon reluctantly began attending physical therapy sessions, which he felt were a waste of time:

I just don't see the point in all of this. It's just a little bit of pain which goes away after I rest. The doctor told me it's rotator cuff tendonitis, what is that? My physical therapist (PT) doesn't understand how important it is for me to practice. He just wants me to do these stupid exercises, which I am not really sure I am doing correctly anyway.

Brandon thought to himself, I am a dedicated, motivated and high-achieving individual and I am willing to do "whatever it takes" to return to orchestra. Brandon, thus, began doing two to three times as many of his prescribed exercises at home. He reasoned that the more he did the faster he would heal and be back to full functioning. Brandon decided not to tell his PT of his "more is better approach" as it seemed to be working, to a certain extent. His pain would increase at times but then, with a little bit of rest, he would feel fine. Those "fine days" seemed to coincide with his physical therapy sessions, so to his PT he was showing improvement, and based on Brandon's feedback and performance during these sessions, the PT soon cleared him for a modified return to play the clarinet while still coming in for weekly sessions.

During the first rehearsal back, Brandon was seemingly going through the motions, and he took frequent breaks in fear of further aggravating his injury. He also found himself trembling while playing and his heart was beating out of his chest. Brandon thought these reactions were unusual but he did not think too much of them. However, he did notice that every so often, worrying thoughts began to creep into his mind:

What if I never get back to how I used to play? What if I never get my orchestra seat back from Lindsey? I wonder if I am doing too much outside of physical therapy? I don't seem to be recovering well ... I should tell my PT that I am doubling up on home exercises, but what if he gets mad?

Brandon's thoughts surrounding his predicament had started to translate into other domains; he was unable to focus on his day-to-day tasks, and his thoughts were consumed with fears of failure as a musician and his ability to make it at the collegiate level. His clarinet professor recognized that something was "off" with Brandon. Given the positive relationship the clarinet professor has with her students, she pulled Brandon aside for a chat after one of their practice sessions. During this conversation, Brandon started crying and told the clarinet professor what was going on. Brandon's clarinet professor recommended that he see a licensed psychologist due to his pervasive anxieties surrounding his injuries. She also wondered if Brandon needed to further consult his PT, given that his symptoms were not getting much better.

The injury

Rotator cuff tendonitis is an inflammation of both the tendons and the lubrication mechanism (bursa) surrounding the shoulder (Starkey & Brown, 2015). The injury, in Brandon's case, was caused by the repetitive overuse of his shoulder because of his persistent clarinet playing. Rotator cuff tendonitis often presents with a slow onset of symptoms, typically beginning with pain after activity, progressing to pain during activity, culminating with constant pain during activities of daily living (Starkey & Brown, 2015). After the initial inflammation phase, the rehabilitation for rotator cuff tendonitis focuses on increasing the flexibility and strength of the muscular structure surrounding the rotator cuff, shoulder, and scapular (McConville & Iannotti, 1999). The estimated time for Brandon's return to the orchestra at this stage of his injury is approximately six to eight weeks (McConville & Iannotti, 1999).

Key factor 1: Cognitive and somatic anxiety

In a music context, cognitive anxiety is characterized as mental worry often associated with negative self-talk, an increased internal responsiveness to the reactions of others (e.g., judges, audience members), and fears about the implications of a bad performance (Wallace & Alden, 1997), whereas somatic anxiety concerns the physical manifestations of anxiety, such as increased heart rate and sweating, to name a few (Kenny, 2006). Brandon's cognitive anxiety is evidenced by his internalized thoughts and worries about whether or not he would return to his pre-injury level of play, ruminating doubts about his abilities to play at the college level, and his fear of failure as a musician. In contrast, Brandon's somatic anxiety presents itself as his heart beating rapidly and his hands trembling.

When returning to play following an injury, cognitive and somatic anxiety are important factors to consider because anxiety is said to be the most debilitating psychological factor related to performance (Martens, Vealey, & Burton, 1990), and is seen as "the primary threat to the psychological well-being of musicians" (Osborne, Greene, & Immel, 2014, p. 2). In Brandon's case, the prevalence of cognitive and somatic anxiety is evidenced both in music and in his life. He is demonstrating an inability to focus on his day-to-day tasks, he is occupied with recurrent thoughts of failure, and he is unable to play his instrument effectively due to his increased heart rate and trembling hands. To assess Brandon's cognitive and somatic anxiety, we recommend the use of Kenny Music Performance Anxiety Inventory (K-MPAI; Chang-Arana, Kenny, & Burga-León, 2017). This is a 40-item questionnaire evaluating anxiety within the context of a music performance. All items are scored on a 7-point Likert scale (0 = strongly agree; 6 = strongly disagree).

Key factor 2: Re-injury anxiety

In addition to general symptoms of cognitive and somatic anxiety, Brandon is also experiencing specific anxieties related to re-injuring himself. Although no explicit definition of re-injury anxiety exists, based on previous literature (Walker, Thatcher, & Lavallee, 2010), it can be defined as an individual's cognitive and somatic responses to hypothetical thoughts or feelings of re-injuring oneself. Re-injury anxiety can present itself as reoccurring worrying thoughts during rehabilitation activities and on return to training and competing (Podlog, Dimmock, & Miller, 2011), as well as feelings of nausea, tension, and increased sweating (Walker, 2006). It can also present itself as holding back efforts and hesitating to perform maximally during a performance (Wadey, Podlog, Hall, Hamson-Utley, & Hicks-Little, 2014). Re-injury anxiety increases the likelihood of a secondary injury due to compensatory physical actions taken while returning back to play (Podlog et al., 2011). In Brandon's case, if left unaddressed, re-injury anxiety can impede his ability to perform optimally as a musician in the orchestra (Paull & Harrison, 1997), and coping with injury may threaten his identity as a musician (Zaza, Charles, & Muszynski, 1998). It has also been found that re-injury anxiety is subject to increase when performers are put in the same positions/situations that caused the initial injury (Wadey et al., 2014), which in Brandon's case, appears to be unavoidable as he is playing the same instrument in the orchestra.

To assess Brandon's re-injury anxiety, we recommend using the Re-injury Anxiety Inventory (RIAI; Walker et al., 2010). The RIAI is a 28-item measure that assesses rehabilitation re-injury anxiety and re-entry into competition re-injury anxiety on a 4-point Likert scale (0 = not at all; 3 = very much so). Although not musician population specific, the measure could be modified to Brandon's case by replacing the word *competition* with *orchestra*.

Key factor 3: Over-adherence

Typically defined as "the extent to which an individual completes behaviors as part of a treatment regimen designed to facilitate recovery from injury" (Granquist & Brewer, 2013, p. 42), adherence appears to be another contributing factor affecting Brandon's injury rehabilitation process. In Brandon's case, it is clear that he is doing too much outside of the rehabilitation, and he is failing to disclose this information to his PT. While patients who adhere to their physical therapy tend to have better overall recovery outcomes (Vasey, 1990), over-adherence can be harmful (Granquist & Brewer, 2013). Doing activities and behaviors that exceed the recommended guidelines can be detrimental to recovery, particularly as they are likely to place extra stressors on the body before it has had the appropriate time to heal effectively (Hilliard, Blom, Hankemeier, & Bolin, 2017).

In Brandon's case, it is imperative to identify what is causing him to over-adhere. Some of the potential barriers to physical therapy adherence include general inconvenience, perceived lack of time, feelings of low self-efficacy and helplessness, and lack of social/family support (for a review, see Jack, McLean, Moffett, & Gardiner, 2010). Other identified barriers for over-adherence include perceived inability to fit exercise into daily routine, pain or discomfort while completing the prescribed exercises, lack of motivation to complete exercises, lack of positive feedback given by the physical therapist, feeling as though the prescribed exercises are not helping, and a perceived lack of autonomy in the recovery process (Sluijs, Kok, & van der Zee, 1993). It is also known that performers who identify themselves predominantly through their performance domain, and are overzealous to meet recovery goals, are more likely to exhibit over-adherence (Podlog et al., 2013). Similarly, personality traits such as trait anxiety, neuroticism, and conscientiousness have been associated with over-adherence behaviors (Podlog et al., 2013), all of which are evident in Brandon's case.

Given that adherence to treatment is central to successful recovery from injury (Clement, Granquist, & Arvinen-Barrow, 2013) and over-adherence has been found to have the opposite effect (Granquist & Brewer, 2013), understanding Brandon's key reasons for over-adherence is important. This could be done by asking Brandon to complete an activity log for a few days, listing all physical therapy related home exercises, clarinet playing, and other life activities that involve the use of his injured arm and shoulder. This could then be used as a foundation for a one-on-one conversation with Brandon to identify the extent of his over-adherence and any underlying reasons for it.

Theoretical considerations

Brandon's responses to his injury can be explained through the sport anxiety model (Smith & Smoll, 1990). The model proposes that when placed in a potentially stressful performance related situation, the person will cognitively appraise the situation, and these appraisals have a bidirectional relationship with physiological arousal. This psychophysiological relationship is influenced by the person's general anxiety and their existing coping skills, and depending on the stress response, a range of cognitive, behavioral, and physiological task-relevant and/or irrelevant responses will in turn influence the upcoming performance either positively or negatively (Smith & Smoll, 1990). That performance will then, in turn, influence any subsequent performance situations, consequently impacting any subsequent cognitive appraisals and physiological arousals of such situations (for more details of the model, please see Smith & Smoll, 1990).

In Brandon's case, when initially faced with an injury, he appraises it as "no big deal" and continued to play, even staying up late to practice at night. These appraisals were influenced by factors such as a Type A personality, being a freshman on a scholarship, and his decision to self-medicate the pain as a coping strategy. Initially, he sees no performance decrements as a consequence of his behavior, thus reinforcing the subsequent appraisals of "I know what I am doing, and this is going well." However, as the injury appears to worsen, Brandon gets more anxious, and feels that his PT does not understand how important practice is for him. To cope with his increased anxieties, Brandon appraises the prescribed exercises as unhelpful to his recovery, ignores his PT's advice, and over-adheres to his rehabilitation in the hopes of returning back to the orchestra in a timely manner. In other words, Brandon's task-relevant response is his determination to return to the orchestra. However, given his worries of being a failure as a musician and not being able to return back to his pre-injury level of performance, and his anger towards others musicians who covered his position in the orchestra while he was injured, Brandon's dominant behavioral response to his situation is over-adherence to physical therapy and continuing to play his clarinet against his PT's advice.

Interprofessional plan of care

The clarinet professor, upon noticing something was "off" with Brandon, encouraged him to find a licensed psychologist, and to consult with his PT to ensure a safe re-entry to orchestra. Brandon was hesitant, as he felt ashamed to admit to the PT that he was over-adhering, so the clarinet professor decided to contact the PT on Brandon's behalf with permission. Since she knew Brandon had expressed some doubts about the PT, the clarinet professor also reached out to an athletic trainer (AT) she knew personally for some advice. Turns out the AT worked in a private clinic that accepted Brandon's insurance, knew the PT in question, and worked closely with a licensed psychologist who specialized in working with range of performers. The next day, when the clarinet professor met with Brandon, she shared this information with Brandon who indicated that he would like to set up appointments with both the AT and the licensed psychologist so he could get back to the orchestra soon. With Brandon's permission, the clarinet professor set an initial meeting between all of the professionals involved in the case: the PT, the AT, the licensed psychologist, and herself. This was followed by a meeting with Brandon to discuss the overall plan of action for his care. During the initial meeting, the PT relayed pertinent information about Brandon's prognosis to the AT. This information was used to inform future physical and psychosocial interventions used by the AT and the licensed psychologist. Consistent with the recommended processes of setting up a care team (Clement & Arvinen-Barrow, 2013), the team identified the licensed psychologist as the case manager for Brandon, meaning that they would act as the main communicator between all parties involved.

Perspective 1: The licensed psychologist perspective

During the initial session with the licensed psychologist, Brandon indicated that he was "excited to meet and work through his concerns." Brandon disclosed the history of his rotator cuff tendonitis, and noted:

> My hands start to shake when I start to play my clarinet. I think I get nervous because I don't want to make a mistake, mainly because I want my seat back from Lindsey, but also because I don't want to get hurt and go through all of this again.

Brandon said that he also "starts to get sweaty palms, breathe heavy, and feel nauseous" before every rehearsal, which adversely influenced his play and exacerbated his fears about his place in the orchestra and his ability to play well in the future. Brandon further commented:

> it's like a circle I can't get out of. I start to get nervous about playing well, my body starts reacting to the nerves, and then my mind starts thinking about all

the other things that can now go wrong because my body is reacting badly. That's why I stop playing and take breaks.

With the information provided by Brandon and the members of his care team, the psychologist determined that the key concern to address was Brandon's cognitive, somatic, and re-injury anxiety. As such, across a series of sessions, the psychologist implemented interventions to target the anxiety, such as (a) cognitive restructuring, (b) relaxation techniques, and (c) encouraging Brandon to participate in non-music activities.

Although few studies have addressed cognitive restructuring interventions within a music domain (Hoffman & Hanrahan, 2012), there is evidence to suggest that acknowledging maladaptive thought patterns can be helpful in decreasing cognitive anxiety (Hoffman & Hanrahan, 2012). The first phase of treatment therefore concerned identifying Brandon's maladaptive thought patterns. The psychologist educated Brandon on how, at times, thoughts can be dysfunctional and therefore unhelpful to recovery. This was followed by education on how identifying and reframing maladaptive thoughts into more realistic and rational thoughts can have a positive effect on Brandon's feelings and behaviors, and consequently his rehabilitation, recovery, and return to the orchestra.

By using appropriate questioning, the psychologist first worked with Brandon to identify some of the maladaptive thoughts he had disclosed during earlier sessions. To reframe Brandon's thoughts, the psychologist asked him to complete a "thought record" (Beck, 1976) in which he would first think about a performance situation, then write down his thoughts surrounding the performance. Next, Brandon would provide evidence that supports and refutes such thoughts, followed by rewriting a more balanced, realistic appraisal of the performance (see Table 7.1). The psychologist ensured that Brandon's "thought record" would target his maladaptive cognitions related to his re-injury anxiety, including "I'll never getting better" and "I don't seem to recover well."

The next aspect of the clinical treatment was concerned with Brandon's somatic manifestations of anxiety. The psychologist taught Brandon a basic relaxation exercise that could be reinforced by both the AT and the clarinet professor as part of Brandon's plan of care. The exercise was centered around diaphragmatic

TABLE 7.1 Sample thought record exercise

Maladaptive thought	Facts that support the thought	Facts that refute the thought	New, more realistic thought
e.g., I'll never get better.	e.g., My shoulder still hurts. I am not playing like I used to.	e.g., I am making small improvements every day. Other people have had this injury and they eventually recovered.	e.g., If I stick to my recovery plan, I will get better with time.

breathing (i.e., controlled "belly" breathing), which has been shown to decrease physical symptoms associated with anxiety in a music performance (Wells, Outhred, Heathers, Quintana, & Kemp, 2012). Researchers (e.g., Cupal & Brewer, 2001) have also suggested that relaxation training is a heavily supported intervention for re-injury anxiety, as it reduces muscle tension and allows the participant to feel in control of their body. Before a rehearsal or during breaks in performance, Brandon was instructed to sit comfortably in a chair, fold his hands on his belly, and breathe in slowly and calmly through the stomach. He was instructed that his hands should move up and down when he breathes. Brandon was to then exhale slowly to a count of "five," and to repeat the breathing repetitions as many times as needed. This relaxation exercise, when coupled with his "thought record," aimed to adequately target Brandon's presenting somatic anxiety concerns.

The final aspect of clinical psychology treatment addressed Brandon's identity. Brandon appeared to be in the beginning stages of exhibiting threats to his identity as a musician, as evidenced by the transferability of his anxiety and related behaviors to other aspects of his life outside of music performance (e.g., being unable to focus on his day-to-day tasks), and an intense focus on his craft. To address this, Brandon worked with the psychologist to identify aspects of his self-concept that existed beyond him being a musician. This strategy further aimed to quell his anxiety and over-adherence, as Brandon was able to put less pressure on himself to return from rehabilitation quickly, stating, "I feel like I have more to offer than just being a clarinet player. I do not have to rush getting back, or over-practice, and risk further hurting myself."

Perspective 2: The athletic trainer's perspective

Following his initial diagnosis, Brandon was referred to physical therapy, but did not "fully buy into" the rehabilitation, eventually resorting to ignoring his rehabilitation plan and hiding his extensive clarinet practice routines from his PT. Consequently, when the injury symptoms persisted and Brandon had exhibited increased signs of anxiety, his clarinet professor reached out to an AT, who was a friend of hers, since Brandon had expressed doubt about his initial PT. Following the initial care team meetings, the AT felt that he needed to incorporate three core concepts into Brandon's, now second, rehabilitation program. More specifically, the AT wanted to (a) understand what Brandon's expectations of the injury rehabilitation process were, (b) educate Brandon about his injury and subsequent rehabilitation program, and (c) create systematic goals to minimize the chances of Brandon engaging in over-adherence.

Research has shown that individuals often enter rehabilitation with expectations of what the process would be like and these expectations typically influence the outcome of the process (Hardin, Subich, & Holvey, 1988). Brandon's first rehabilitation experience had been less than ideal, and as such, understanding his expectations were now vitally important before starting the second rehabilitation program. The AT asked Brandon to complete the Expectations about Athletic Training Questionnaire (EAAT; Clement et al., 2012), and found out that Brandon had low expectations of personal commitment, did not believe the AT would provide facilitative conditions for his recovery, and was not realistic regarding his expectations. Using these results, the AT then spent additional time with Brandon during their first treatment session with a goal of getting to know Brandon better, and establishing a robust and trusting foundation for their professional relationship. In particular, the AT paid specific attention to understanding Brandon's history and relationship with music and playing clarinet. Among the questions asked were (a) how he became interested in playing the clarinet, (b) how long he had been playing the instrument, (c) why he enjoyed it so much, (d) what not playing the clarinet meant to him, and (e) "Could you show me how you play so I can understand your mechanics during this activity better?" Spending this additional time getting to know Brandon appeared to have been beneficial, since at the end of the first session Brandon stated: "thanks for showing interest in me and my music. At first, I thought you were just someone who deals with athletes who have injuries, but you are not that at all. I am glad I was able to teach you about the clarinet."

The AT then educated Brandon about the rotator cuff, its pathology, and his upcoming rehabilitation program. According to Sabo (2013), "patient education is a key component of rehabilitation, especially with regard to injury type, healing timeframes, and how prescribed exercises" (p. 15) relate to performance. The more educated patients are about their rehabilitation program, the more confident they are about completing the process (Taylor & Taylor, 1997). As part of the education, the AT used a "model" of the shoulder which displayed the origins and insertions of the various muscles associated with rotator cuff. He also used sections of an anatomy and physiology textbook to help explain how the shoulder is a "poorly vascularized area," which delays the healing process and results in a six to eight week timeframe to return. As part of the education process, the AT also introduced Brandon to Bobby, a junior tennis player who was in the final stages of her own rotator cuff tendonitis rehabilitation. Bobby told Brandon how at first the rehabilitation was painful and how she did not want to do it. She also said that once she truly started to listen to the AT and followed the rehabilitation instructions, the pain started to decrease. Bobby also discussed how at times there would be setbacks, like increased pain and inflammation, particularly when she was trying too much too soon. By letting the AT know about these setbacks in an honest manner, Bobby now felt that she was very close to full recovery and felt confident about getting back to the tennis court. Using peer modeling as described above, "clearly and unequivocally demonstrates that injuries heal and athletes successfully return to sport" (Taylor & Taylor, 1997, p. 256).

The final strategy to help safeguard against over-adherence was the implementation and inclusion of systematic goal-setting into Brandon's rehabilitation program. Goal-setting is one of the most commonly utilized psychological skills in the injury rehabilitation setting (Covassin, Beidler, Ostrowski, & Wallace, 2015). Using the recommended goal-setting procedures (see Arvinen-Barrow & Hemmings, 2013; Wade, 2009), the AT and Brandon worked together to establish an appropriate outcome goal for his rehabilitation, measurable performance goals, and detailed daily process goals. Brandon's outcome goal was to return to playing the clarinet pain-free in eight weeks. This was broken down to a number of performance goals (e.g., increase his passive shoulder forward flexion by 10 degrees range of motion in comparison to previous week) and specific process goals (e.g., complete a hugging motion around a cylindrical object with the shoulder internally rotated to 45 degrees, for 10 seconds at time for a minute in duration, to strengthen the serratus anterior muscle).

Perspective 3:
The clarinet professor's perspective

Although the clarinet professor set up Brandon's initial care team, it was agreed that she would step down as the care coordinator, based on her competencies and role. Instead, the clarinet professor would (a) provide Brandon with emotional and technical support in returning to playing the clarinet, (b) help Brandon adjust his expectations for return to play, and (c) consider Brandon's placement within the orchestra so that he felt that he was a valued member of the orchestra while also effectively managing his anxiety.

Supported by the theory of self-efficacy (Bandura, 1977), the clarinet professor provided Brandon emotional and technical support. She did this in number of different ways, including reminding Brandon of his past performance accomplishments, encouraging Brandon to complete his relaxation exercises (e.g., eliciting effective physiological arousal) while at orchestra practice prompting Brandon to explore vicarious experiences (e.g., reminding Brandon of Bobby's recovery journey), and providing verbal persuasion by acknowledging any progress made. The clarinet professor made every effort not to compare Brandon's progress to those of others in the orchestra section. She also encouraged Brandon to focus on the "process" of recovery rather than the "outcome" of returning, and did not elicit any additional pressure for Brandon to get healthy quicker than the care team anticipated. Lastly, the clarinet professor frequently "checked in" on Brandon via text message as a source of emotional support, and followed up on Brandon's progress with the licensed psychologist and the AT to ensure that they were all on the same page with his recovery.

Ethical considerations and need(s) for referral

When discussing Brandon's case, the care team should maintain confidentiality and non-maleficence to ensure that they are adhering to the existing standards of professional practice in their respective fields (American Psychological Association, 2017; National Athletic Trainers' Association, 2018). Regardless of role, the primary concern of the care team must be the duty to the patient. The ethical code of conduct for both the American Psychological Association and the National Athletic Trainers' Association each suggest that practitioners should not misrepresent their skills and training, and must operate within their boundaries of competence (American Psychological Association, 2017; National Athletic Trainers' Association, 2018). For example, in Brandon's case, clinical mental health concerns (e.g., anxiety) must be addressed by a licensed psychologist, physical health concerns (e.g., shoulder injury) must be addressed by the AT, and technical concerns (e.g., clarinet performance expectations) must be addressed by the clarinet professor. Given the nature of their relationship, the clarinet professor would also need to recognize her boundaries of competency when handling Brandon's psychological and physical concerns. In this case, stepping down as the care coordinator for Brandon's recovery demonstrated the clarinet professor's acknowledgment of her professional boundaries.

Case update

Brandon responded well to his treatment plan, and now, two months from his first meeting with the licensed psychologist and the AT, he is fully participating in the orchestra without rotator cuff pain. Brandon is also more cognizant of his overuse tendencies, and finds the breathing exercises very beneficial in coping with the demands of orchestra, school, and life in general. He is slowly gaining awareness of his maladaptive thoughts, and finds that they are becoming more and more infrequent. Additionally, Brandon also found activities outside of music and is now an active member of a local gym.

Conclusion

This chapter focused on Brandon Jackson, an 18-year-old freshman music performance major who suffered from rotator cuff tendonitis from playing the clarinet. Initially, Brandon delayed his medical care until his pain became unmanageable. The early phases of his rehabilitation were less than optimal, Brandon over-adhered, and returned back to modified orchestra practice too soon. This amplified his psychosocial responses to his injury, namely cognitive, somatic, and re-injury anxiety. It was at this stage when his clarinet professor noted a change in Brandon, and made a referral to a licensed psychologist and an AT. Brandon's anxieties were addressed through cognitive restructuring, relaxation, and identity-oriented exercises. The AT worked with Brandon to re-conceptualize his flawed expectations of treatment and recovery, provided psychoeducation about the injury, and set manageable goals to curtail treatment over-adherence. Finally, the clarinet professor provided emotional and technical support throughout Brandon's recovery. After two months, Brandon responded well to his treatment plan and he is fully participating in the orchestra without rotator cuff pain or debilitating music performance anxiety.

KEY POINTS

- Brandon Jackson, a freshman music performance major who plays the clarinet, suffered a rotator cuff tendonitis injury.
- As his shoulder pain grew worse, Brandon was referred to a PT for flexibility and strengthening exercises, and he was required to take time off from playing. Reluctant to adhere to the treatment and wanting to get better fast, Brandon began overdoing the prescribed exercises at home, and his shoulder did not improve.
- After eventually being cleared for modified play, Brandon starting exhibiting signs of cognitive (e.g., worrying thoughts), somatic (e.g., heart racing), and re-injury (e.g., fear of being unable to return) anxiety. The clarinet professor referred Brandon to an AT for additional work on the shoulder and a licensed psychologist for the anxiety.
- An interdisciplinary approach was used to address Brandon's concerns. Specifically, the licensed psychologist dealt with Brandon's anxiety (e.g., cognitive restructuring, relaxation exercises, identity), while the AT worked with Brandon to adjust his treatment expectations and set appropriate treatment goals. The clarinet professor provided emotional and technical support throughout Brandon's recovery process.
- Brandon reported that his care team helped him to deal with his anxiety more effectively, enabled him to play without pain, and gave him the tools to help prevent overuse injuries in the future.

CRITICAL THINKING QUESTIONS

1. Brandon's personality, to a certain extent, played a role in the development of his injury. What are some coping strategies he could have employed preemptively to better manage his situation?
2. The collegiate orchestra environment is very competitive, and as such, individuals like Brandon feel the need to continue playing despite injuries. What could the clarinet professor and others involved in collegiate orchestras do to better cultivate an environment where students do not feel the pressure to push through injuries?
3. Given its prevalence within the musician population, how can orchestras or music programs foster a team-based approach to address the interdisciplinary nature of anxiety?

RESEARCH QUESTIONS

1. Identify prominent macro-system and micro-system characteristics that may impact a musician's over-adherence to rehabilitation.

2. Describe the ways in which musicians' experiences of anxiety differ from athletes' experiences of anxiety. How might these differences inform treatment?
3. One of the main causes of music performance anxiety is "pressure from self" (Kenny, Driscoll, & Ackermann, 2014). In what ways can a musician's self-concept and their personal expectations influence maladaptive behaviors?

KEY PUBLICATIONS

1. Spahn, C. (2015). Treatment and prevention of music performance anxiety. In E. Altenmüller, S. Finger & F. Boller (Eds.). *Progress in brain research* (pp. 129–140). Amsterdam, the Netherlands: Elsevier.

The aim of this chapter is to demonstrate the prevalence and multimodal nature of music performance anxiety, its theoretical underpinnings, various treatment approaches, and strategies for overall prevention. Readers can choose from a variety of theoretical frameworks for treatment suggestions. The ways in which music instruction and the music performance environment inform music performance anxiety is addressed, which illuminates pedagogical implications for instructors, students, and practitioners.

2. Pecen, E., Collins, D., & MacNamara, Á. (2016). Music of the night: Performance practitioner considerations for enhancement work in music. *Sport, Exercise, and Performance Psychology, 5*(4), 377–395. doi:10.1037/spy0000067.

Given the increasing number of sport psychologists working with musicians, the purpose of this paper is to acknowledge the nuanced differences that practitioners must consider when working in a music performance domain (e.g., resources and support, sociocultural variances) as opposed to sport. The paper addresses prevalent issues, implications for the psychologist, practitioner suggestions, and pertinent resources for providing an evidence-based, holistic form of treatment for musicians.

References

American Psychological Association. (2017). Ethical principles of psychologists and code of conduct. Retrieved September 6, 2018, from www.apa.org/ethics/code/.

Arvinen-Barrow, M., & Hemmings, B. (2013). Goal setting in sport injury rehabilitation. In M. Arvinen-Barrow & N. Walker (Eds.), *Psychology of sport injury and rehabilitation* (pp. 56–70). Abingdon: Routledge.

Bandura, A. (1977). Self-efficacy: Towards a unifying theory of behavior change. *Psychological Reviews, 84*, 191–215. doi:10.1037/0033–295X.84.2.191.

Beck, A. (1976). *Cognitive therapy and the emotional disorders.* Harmondsworth: Penguin.

Chang-Arana, Á. M., Kenny, D. T., & Burga-León, A. A. (2017). Validation of the Kenny Music Performance Anxiety Inventory (K-MPAI): A cross-cultural confirmation of its factorial structure. *Psychology of Music, 46*(4), 551–567. doi:10.1177/0305735617717618.

Clement, D., & Arvinen-Barrow, M. (2013). Sport medicine team influences in psychological rehabilitation: A multidisciplinary approach. In M. Arvinen-Barrow & N. Walker (Eds.), *The psychology of sport injury and rehabilitation* (pp. 156–170). Abingdon: Routledge.

Clement, D., Granquist, M. D., & Arvinen-Barrow, M. (2013). Psychosocial aspects of athletic injuries as perceived by athletic trainers. *Journal of Athletic Training*, 48(4), 512–521. doi:10.4085/1062-6050-49.3.52.

Clement, D., Hamson-Utley, J., Arvinen-Barrow, M., Kamphoff, C., Zakrajsek, R. A., & Martin, S. B. (2012). College athletes' expectations about injury rehabilitation with an athletic trainer. *International Journal of Athletic Therapy & Training*, 17(4), 18–27. doi:10.1123/ijatt.17.4.18.

Covassin, T., Beidler, E., Ostrowski, J., & Wallace, J. (2015). Psychosocial aspects of rehabilitation in sports. *Clinics in Sports Medicine*, 34(2), 199–212. doi:10.1016/j.csm.2014.12.004.

Cupal, D. D., & Brewer, B. W. (2001). Effects of relaxation and guided imagery on knee strength, re-injury anxiety, and pain following anterior cruciate ligament reconstruction. *Rehabilitation Psychology*, 46(1), 28–43. doi:10.1037/0090-5550.46.1.28.

Granquist, M. D., & Brewer, B. W. (2013). Psychological aspects of rehabilitation adherence. In M. Arvinen-Barrow & N. Walker (Eds.), *Psychology of sport injury and rehabilitation* (pp. 40–53). Abingdon and New York, NY: Routledge.

Hardin, S. I., Subich, L. M., & Holvey, J. M. (1988). Expectancies for counseling in relation to premature termination. *Journal of Counseling Psychology*, 35(1), 37–40. doi:10.1037/0022-0167.35.1.37.

Hilliard, B. C., Blom, L., Hankemeier, D., & Bolin, J. (2017). Exploring the relationship between athletic identity and beliefs about rehabilitation overadherence in college athletes. *Journal of Sport Rehabilitation*, 26(3), 208–220. doi:10.1123/jsr.2015-0134.

Hoffman, S. L., & Hanrahan, S. J. (2012). Mental skills for musicians: Managing music performance anxiety and enhancing performance. *Sport, Exercise, and Performance Psychology*, 1(1), 17–28. doi:10.1037/a0025409.

Jack, K., McLean, S. M., Moffett, J. K., & Gardiner, E. (2010). Barriers to treatment adherence in physiotherapy outpatient clinics: A systematic review. *Manual Therapy*, 15(3), 220–228. doi:10.1016/j.math.2009.12.004.

Kenny, D. T. (2006). Music performance anxiety: Origins, phenomenology, assessment and treatment. *Journal of Music Research*, 31, 51–64.

Kenny, D. T., Driscoll, T., & Ackermann, B. (2014). Psychological well-being in professional orchestral musicians in Australia: A descriptive population study. *Psychology of Music*, 42(2), 210–232. doi:10.1177/0305735612463950.

McConville, O., & Iannotti, J. P. (1999). Partial-thickness tears of the rotator cuff: Evaluation and management. *Journal of the American Academy of Orthopedic Surgeons*, 7(1), 32–40.

Martens, R., Vealey, R. S., & Burton, D. (1990). *Competitive anxiety in sport*. Champaign, IL: Human Kinetics.

National Athletic Trainers' Association. (2018). Code of ethics. Retrieved September 6, 2018, from www.nata.org/membership/about-membership/member-resources/code-of-ethics.

Osborne, M. S., Greene, D. J., & Immel, D. T. (2014). Managing performance anxiety and improving mental skills in conservatoire students through performance psychology training: A pilot study. *Psychology of Well-Being*, 4(1), 2–17. doi:10.1186/s13612-13014-0018-0013.

Paull, B., & Harrison, C. (1997). *The athletic musician: A guide to playing without pain*. Lanham, MD: Scarecrow Press.

Podlog, L., Dimmock, J. A., & Miller, J. (2011). A review of return to sport concerns following injury rehabilitation: Practitioner strategies for enhancing recovery outcomes. *Physical Therapy in Sport*, 12(1), 36–42. doi:10.1016/j.ptsp.2010.07.005.

Podlog, L., Gao, Z., Kenow, L., Kleinert, J., Granquist, M. D., Newton, M., & Hannon, J. (2013). Injury rehabilitation overadherence: Preliminary scale validation and relationships with athletic identity and self-presentation concerns. *Journal of Athletic Training*, 48(3), 372–381. doi:10.4085/1062-6050-48.2.20.

Sabo, M. (2013). Physical therapy rehabilitation strategies for dancers: A qualitative study. *Journal of Dance Medicine & Science*, 17(1), 11–18. doi:10.12678/1089-313X.17.1.11.

Sluijs, E. M., Kok, G. J., & van der Zee, J. (1993). Correlates of exercise compliance in physical therapy. *Physical Therapy*, 73(11), 771–782. doi:10.1093/ptj/73.11.771.

Smith, R. E., & Smoll, F. L. (1990). Sport performance anxiety. In H. Leitenberg (Ed.), *Handbook of social and evaluation anxiety* (pp. 417–454). Boston, MA: Springer.

Starkey, C., & Brown, S. D. (2015). *Examination of orthopedic & athletic injuries* (4th ed.). Philadelphia, PA: F. A. Davis Company.

Taylor, J., & Taylor, S. (1997). *Psychological approaches to sports injury rehabilitation*. Gaithersburg, MD: Aspen.

Vasey, L. M. (1990). DNAs and DNCTs - Why do patients fail to begin or to complete a course of physiotherapy treatment? *Physiotherapy*, 76(9), 575–578. doi:10.1016/S0031-9406(10)63052-0.

Wade, D. T. (2009). Goal setting in rehabilitation: An overview of what, why and how. *Clinical Rehabilitation*, 23(4), 291–296. doi:10.1177/0269215509103551.

Wadey, R., Podlog, L., Hall, M., Hamson-Utley, J. J., Hicks-Little, C., & Hammer, C. (2014). Reinjury anxiety, coping, and return-to-sport outcomes: A multiple mediation analysis. *Rehabilitation Psychology*, 59(3), 256–266. doi:10.1037/a0037032.

Walker, N. (2006). The meaning of sports injury and re-injury anxiety assessment and intervention (Doctoral dissertation). University of Wales, Aberystwyth.

Walker, N., Thatcher, J., & Lavallee, D. (2010). A preliminary development of the re-injury anxiety inventory (RIAI). *Physical Therapy in Sport*, 11(1), 23–29. doi:10.1016/j.ptsp.2009.09.003.

Wallace, S. T., & Alden, L. E. (1997). Social phobia and positive social events: The price of success. *Journal of Abnormal Psychology*, 106(3), 416–424. doi:10.1037/0021-843X.106.3.416.

Wells, R., Outhred, T., Heathers, J. A., Quintana, D. S., & Kemp, A. H. (2012). Matter over mind: A randomised-controlled trial of single-session biofeedback training on performance anxiety and heart rate variability in musicians. *Plos One*, 7(10), e46597. doi:10.1371/journal.pone.0046597.

Zaza, C., Charles, C., & Muszynski, A. (1998). The meaning of playing-related musculoskeletal disorders to classical musicians. *Social Science & Medicine*, 47(12), 2013–2023. doi:10.1016/S0277-9536(98)00307-00304.

8

REACTIONS TO RETURN TO DUTY

Kyra Johnson, a first lieutenant, U.S. Army

Leslie Podlog, William Brown, and Jessica Tidswell

Key Words: 23-year-old female, Army first lieutenant, return-to-duty (RTD) concerns, lack of confidence, external locus of control, isolation, loss of identity, tibia bone stress injury

Case description

Kyra Johnson (this name is a pseudonym used for descriptive purposes only) is a first lieutenant (1LT) and Medical Platoon Leader in the United States Army. Unfortunately, magnetic resonance imaging (MRI) revealed that Kyra incurred a grade II anterior tibia bone stress injury following an intensive training program designed to prepare her for the Expert Medical Field Badge (EFMB). The EFMB is a special badge that is given to a soldier following successful completion of a comprehensive test of physical and tactical acumen (e.g., weapons capabilities, land navigation, evacuation skills). After undertaking an arduous 12-week rehabilitation program, Kyra had mixed thoughts and emotions about her ability to resume her job as Medical Platoon Leader. On one hand, she was excited about the prospect of testing her physical prowess, taking command of her platoon, and resuming her chosen military path. On the other hand, Kyra had significant worries about re-injury and experienced apprehension that she still had "what it took" to perform demanding physical tasks in pressurized environments. She reported a lack of control over her body's ability to cope with increased training loads and to reach important career milestones. She also desperately wanted to demonstrate her leadership skills, something that was of admitted concern. In sum, Kyra experienced numerous apprehensions about her return to duty (RTD).

In her initial week back on duty, Kyra began reintegrating into her unit, but this proved difficult. The injury had resulted in a decrease in her fitness level and she was unable to keep up with the physical training. She also felt fatigued and "out of shape." Kyra's fitness levels and physical activity restrictions – as outlined in her RTD program – prevented her from participating in many of the platoon's weekly training exercises. For instance, during the initial weeks of her return, Kyra was not allowed to attempt the ruck march with 40 pounds of gear. Because of her training restrictions, Kyra's executive officer (XO), a highly fit soldier, was responsible for leading the platoon. To make matters worse, her platoon embarked on a two-week field training exercise, in which Kyra did not participate. Instead, she stayed with the rear detachment at the company headquarters on post. Kyra felt very isolated and detached from her platoon during those two weeks. Upon her platoon's return, she heard many soldiers talking about the great training experience and how the XO performed exceptionally well, motivating the unit and accomplishing the entire training objective. Hearing these stories further undermined Kyra's confidence in her ability to lead her platoon. The fact that Kyra was the only female Medical Platoon Leader only added to her pressure to perform well.

Over the course of the next month, Kyra experienced limited success in increasing her training volume and assuming greater leadership responsibilities. Unfortunately, as her physical training volume increased her symptoms began to reappear. Following a 2-mile timed run, Kyra felt searing pain in her shin and thought to herself, "Why is this happening again? I thought I was finished with all this nonsense. Is my body ever going to heal?" After her commander noticed Kyra wincing following the run, he ordered her to revisit the nurse practitioner (NP) for further evaluation, a directive Kyra reluctantly followed. Kyra indicated to her NP that she no longer felt a sense of control over her body, which she once characterized as "invincible." In speaking with her NP, Kyra, visibly frustrated, referred to her shin as her "weak link." During their meeting, the NP informed Kyra that she would likely be unable to make a second attempt at the upcoming EFMB, scheduled to occur at another installation. The NP also referred Kyra to the physical therapist (PT) for additional rehabilitation sessions. The PT indicated that Kyra would need to undergo 6 weeks of additional physical therapy. The news further undermined Kyra's already depleted confidence in her physical capabilities, her leadership aspirations, and her sense of "self" as a tough female soldier. Given her obvious negative emotional state, the NP suggested that Kyra also meet with a sport psychologist with expertise in the psychology of return to performance following injury.

The injury

A grade II anterior tibia bone stress injury is a common overuse injury among athletes and military personnel (Lee, 2011). It is typically caused by repetitive and submaximal loading of the bone with insufficient rest time for recovery (Mattila, Niva, Kiuru, & Pihlajamäki, 2007). In Kyra's case, the injury was determined to be the result of fatigue, which occurred following a rapid increase in training volume exceeding her body's ability to repair itself. Soldiers and athletes with anterior grade 2 stress injuries often describe focal pain in their shins during weight bearing exercises such as running or jumping, which decreases with rest (Astur et al., 2016; Knapik, Reynolds, & Hoedebecke, 2017). Although the injury did not require surgery it necessitated a brief period of non-weight bearing activity followed by a slow return to daily ambulation. Kyra participated in a 12-week rehabilitation program prior to her initial RTD.

Key factor 1: A lack of confidence in return-to-duty capabilities

Although Kyra was excited about the prospect of testing her physical capabilities and returning to lead her platoon, her injury had a detrimental impact on her confidence in her overall skills as a soldier and unit leader. In particular, a lack of confidence in executing demanding physical tasks within her unit (e.g., leading from the front), apprehensions about meeting senior officers' performance expectations, and feelings of vulnerability associated with re-injury risk were articulated. Such concerns were exacerbated upon Kyra's RTD, as she experienced injury flare-ups and had to remain on post during the two-week field training exercise.

Evidence suggests that these concerns are commonplace among high-performance individuals (Ardern et al., 2014; Feller & Webster, 2013; Reel et al., 2018) and may be particularly relevant during the return to participation phase. For instance, qualitative interviews with Australian coaches (Podlog & Eklund, 2007a) and high-performance athletes (Podlog & Eklund, 2006) revealed that a lack of confidence in one's ability to avoid re-injury, regain competitive fitness, reach pre-injury levels, stay "ahead of" competitors, and maintain one's spot on the team were all commonplace. Evidence suggests that athletes' lack of confidence upon their return to sport diminishes the likelihood of an eventual return and can have negative implications for post-injury performances (Ardern et al., 2014; Podlog & Eklund, 2006). Military specific research has also shown that lack of confidence in coping with injury demands and low expectations about graduating have been predictive of attrition among basic training recruits (Booth-Kewley, Larson, & Highfill-McRoy, 2009; Larson, Booth-Kewley, & Ryan, 2002; Lee, 2011; Morgan & Bibb, 2011). The above findings suggest that reduced confidence in one's physical and performance competencies may be prevalent among returning athletes and those in physical performance domains.

To assess Kyra's lack of confidence in her RTD capabilities, practitioners can use the Injury-Psychological Readiness to Return to Sport (I-PRRS; Glazer, 2009). It is a six-item measure used to capture individual's confidence to perform sport-specific activities following an injury on a Likert scale (0 = no confidence at all; 50 = moderate confidence; to 100 = complete confidence). The total score is calculated by summing the six items, dividing the sum by ten, thus resulting in a score out of 60.

Key factor 2: External locus of control

Kyra's case also reveals a lack of control over her body's healing abilities, career trajectory, and pressures to RTD. These factors suggest locus of control as a key factor
influencing the quality and effectiveness of Kyra's RTD. Kyra felt that her body's
inability to cope with progressive increases in training volume and uncertainties about
her career trajectory were negatively impacting her ability to assume full duties upon
RTD. These appraisals are not surprising, as injured military service members have also
demonstrated a lack of control and feelings of uncertainty regarding the time course of
recovery (Hauret et al., 2004). Appraisals of uncertainty and the importance of
reinforcing an internal locus of control have been highlighted in various sport injury
studies (e.g., Carson & Polman, 2017; Laubach, Brewer, Van Raalte, & Petitpas, 1996;
Murphy, Foreman, Simpson, Molloy, & Molley, 1999). For example, Murphy et al.
found that an internal locus of control among injured athletes was positively associated
with physical therapist ratings of athletes' rehabilitation adherence (i.e., time spent in
recovery-related behaviors, $r = .59$).

Locus of control can be assessed using the Sports Rehabilitation Locus of
Control Scale (SRLC; Murphy, Foreman, Simpson, Molloy, & Molley, 1999). The
scale includes three subscales rated on a 6-point Likert scale (0 = strongly disagree;
5 = strongly agree). Although not military specific, the wording in the measure
can be easily modified for Kyra by changing items where the terms "return to
match fitness" appear with "return to duty fitness."

Key factor 3: Feelings of isolation and loss of a soldier identity

A final factor affecting Kyra's RTD is related to her feelings of isolation and lack of
a "soldier" identity. The Army as an institution inculcates the concept of *esprit de
corps* — common feelings of pride, enthusiasm, and regard for the honor of the
group – and this concept carries through from basic through advanced training.
Kyra's feelings of isolation and loss of identity are consistent with existing research.
In military settings, it has been found that Navy recruits at risk for depression (i.e.,
a clinical mental health diagnosis experienced by injured service members) may also
experience a lack of belonging to their unit, loneliness, and feelings of insecure
attachment (Koren, Norman, Cohen, Berman, & Klein, 2005; Williams et al.,
2004). Kyra's feelings are also consistent with those of high-performance athletes
(Podlog & Eklund, 2006) and ballet dancers (Reel et al., 2018). For example,
Podlog and Eklund (2006) found that elite athletes indicated feelings of isolation
from their sport and training partners during their competitive absence. Similarly,
Reel et al. (2018) revealed that professional ballet dancers experienced feelings of
alienation from their training group and extensive concerns regarding their identity
as dancers while injured until they returned back to rigorous workouts and
performances.

Feelings of isolation can be assessed using the UCLA Loneliness Scale (Version 3;
Russell, 1996). The 20-item measure is scored on a 4-point Likert scale (1 = never;

4 = always). Identity concerns could be assessed using the Athletic Identity Measurement Scale (AIMS; Brewer, Van Raalte, & Linder, 1993). The AIMS is a seven-item questionnaire measuring the degree to which someone identifies themselves with the athlete role. All seven items are scored on a 7-point Likert scale (1 = strongly disagree; 7 = strongly agree). Although not military specific, the items can be easily adapted to Kyra's situation. For example, the item "most of my friends are athletes" can be modified to "most of my friends are service members." Similarly, the item "I would be very depressed if I were injured and could not compete in sport" could be modified to "I would be very depressed if I were injured and could not complete my duties."

Theoretical considerations

Kyra's psychological responses to her RTD can be explained through the Basic Psychological Needs Theory (BPNT), a sub-theory of the larger Self-Determination Theory (Ryan & Deci, 2000). According to BPNT, all individuals, regardless of gender, culture or ethnic background, have three basic psychological needs for competence, autonomy, and relatedness (Ryan & Deci, 2000). In Kyra's case, her sense of competence was affected as a result of her perceived decreased physical ability, worries about injury flare-ups, and apprehensions regarding her leadership capabilities (i.e., a perceived ability or proficiency in interactions with the environment and in pursuit of particular tasks; Ryan & Deci, 2002). Kyra's sense of autonomy (i.e., a perceived sense of control and the feeling that one self-endorses one's actions or is volitional in choosing particular courses of action; Ryan & Deci, 2002) was also affected as Kyra felt a lack of control over her body, her ability to achieve career objectives and milestones, and her perceptions of external pressures to RTD. Lastly, Kyra's case also suggests lack of relatedness (i.e., perceived sense of connectedness to a community or a group, and believing that one's membership within the group is valued by other members; Baumeister & Leary, 1995). In particular, Kyra's feelings of isolation and a loss of identity as a "soldier" were indicative of a lack of connection with fellow unit members.

The BPNT also assumes that environments that support individuals' feelings of competence, autonomy, and relatedness will have beneficial implications for personal motivation, well-being, persistence, and overall task performance (Ryan & Deci, 2000). As such, it is likely that addressing these key factors should yield beneficial consequences and assist Kyra in her RTD. Support for the above contentions has been found in the sport injury literature. Several reviews of the sport injury literature indicate the relevance of competence, autonomy and relatedness concerns among returning athletes (Ardern, Taylor, Feller, & Webster, 2013; Podlog, Dimmock, & Miller, 2011; Podlog & Eklund, 2007b). Similarly, numerous studies support the benefits of need satisfaction in facilitating adaptive health, well-being, and performance outcomes (Banack, Sabiston, & Bloom, 2011; Podlog, Heil, & Schulte, 2014; Podlog, Lochbaum, & Stevens, 2010). For example, in a study of 204 formerly injured competitive athletes from Canada, Australia, and the

United States, researchers found that when needs for competence and autonomy were satisfied during rehabilitation, the athletes experienced greater positive emotions, which in turn facilitated a positive return-to-sport outcome (Podlog et al., 2010). Moreover, athletes who believed their relatedness needs were satisfied, experienced greater self-esteem and vitality, both of which helped to reduce athletes' return-to-sport concerns (e.g., re-injury anxiety) following the return to competition (Podlog et al., 2010).

Interprofessional plan of care

In Kyra's case, the NP coordinated her comprehensive RTD plan. Given the nature of Kyra's concerns, both the NP and PT felt that the inclusion of a sport psychology consultant (SPC) would provide additional expertise to her care, which was beyond their professional training and competencies. The NP had established a solid working relationship with the SPC, and had made previous referrals of soldiers. The NP and PT agreed that it would be beneficial for Kyra to meet with the SPC individually, so the SPC could gain a first-hand account of Kyra's prominent concerns and challenges. A team meeting between the NP, PT, and SPC followed this initial one-on-one meeting. The aim of the team meeting was to ensure consistent understanding of Kyra's salient concerns and to delineate key service provider roles.

During the team meeting, the three practitioners agreed that the BPNT frame-work focused on enhancing Kyra's perceptions of personal competence, autonomy, and relatedness would be useful in alleviating her concerns and facilitating her RTD. Based on the team members' respective competencies, it was decided that the SPC would be best suited to address isolation and identity issues (relatedness concerns), the PT would focus on confidence issues pertaining to physical function and re-injury apprehensions (competence concerns), and the NP would address issues of external control and pressures to RTD (autonomy concerns). The three practitioners were also careful to select strategies that had shown clinical efficacy and/or an empirical evidence-base. During the practitioner meeting it was agreed that before any implementation of the plan, Kyra would be consulted to ensure she was comfortable with the approach and delineation of tasks outlined. Kyra's comfortableness and acceptance of the plan was deemed critical to the success of such efforts moving forward.

Perspective 1: The sport psychology consultant's perspective

In working with Kyra, the SPC adopted a client-centered approach, used a range of active listening skills, and showed empathetic regard (Waumsley & Katz, 2013). At the outset of Kyra's first session with the SPC, she indicated, "it's nice to be able to talk to someone who isn't in the military. I don't always feel like I can be entirely open with members of my unit or my superior officers." During the initial session, Kyra reaffirmed concerns regarding separation from her training unit, and identity worries. Characterizing such beliefs were statements such as "My body just isn't doing what it should and so I keep missing opportunities to be part of training exercises. I just don't feel like a valuable member of the platoon"; "I don't see an end in sight to this injury. Maybe I'm just not mentally or physically cut out for this [being a soldier]. I'm really starting to wonder if I'm really the solider I thought I was"; "Missing the field training exercise was hard, especially hearing all the comments and stories about it. I thought I would be way more engaged with my platoon than I have been"; and "I'm sure my XO and superior officers think I'm trying to take the easy way out. Maybe they are right … Maybe I'm just 'soft.'"

The SPC felt that the key issue underlying Kyra's feelings of isolation and identity concerns related to her ongoing negative self-talk. Specifically, her self-talk focused on personal shortcomings and deficiencies, questioning of her abilities, and harsh self-criticism, all quite common among injured performers and athletes (Johnson, 2000). To address Kyra's maladaptive inner dialogue, the SPC encouraged Kyra to think about the ways in which her negative thoughts might be influencing her emotions (including feelings of isolation), and subsequent behaviors. Part of this process was a writing exercise guided by questions such as (1) "What has been most difficult for you about your injury?"; (2) "What are the things you miss the most about being with your unit?"; (3) "Describe the impact of your injury on your energy levels?"; (4) "What impact do your emotions have on injury-related behaviors (e.g., rehabilitation compliance)?"; and (5) "What are the thoughts that come to mind when you lay down to sleep?"

The above exercise helped Kyra raise her awareness of her self-dialogue. In discussing Kyra's written reflections during the second session, Kyra admitted that her recurrent negative thoughts were having a detrimental impact on her emotions (i.e., frustration, disappointment, guilt, sadness), her energy levels, effort in training, and interactions with her unit. The SPC suggested that Kyra might benefit from a more 'self-compassionate' or 'kinder' inner dialogue (Neff & McGehee, 2010) and emphasized that being compassionate with oneself did not imply a lack of personal accountability. Instead, self-compassion is an acknowledgment that being overly hard on oneself would likely result in a spiral of negative thoughts (e.g., self-perceptions), emotions (anger, guilt, frustration, sadness) and behaviors (reduced rehabilitation effort and performance on skill tasks). Kyra acknowledged that a full recovery would require engaging in more adaptive behaviors (e.g., backing off her training when she felt pain) and that altering her self-talk would be an important starting point. Towards this end, the SPC suggested Kyra complete a "thought shifting" exercise, in which she identified negative self-talk, and used a key word (e.g., "stop") to help her shift from the negative thought to a more self-compassionate one (Chase, Magyar, & Drake, 2005).

To further address Kyra's sense of relatedness, during the third session, the SPC asked Kyra if she would be willing to meet with a fellow soldier who had successfully returned to duty following a prolonged bone stress injury recovery. Researchers (e.g., Flint, 2007; Podlog & Eklund, 2006) have found that having a

TABLE 8.1 Sample thought shifting exercise

Negative Self-Statements		Self-Compassionate Thoughts
1) _____STOP shift to →		1)_____
2) _____STOP shift to →		2)_____
3) _____STOP shift to →		3)_____
4) _____STOP shift to →		4)_____
5) _____STOP shift to →		5)_____

role model during injury rehabilitation can be beneficial. In this case, the SPC was hoping that an injured role model would help normalize Kyra's experiences and concerns, give her a sense that she was not alone in her doubts, and help her accept limitations rather than seeing them as a sign of incapability or "softness." Kyra agreed to the meeting and appreciated the personal support offered by the SPC in setting it up. Kyra was also given a task to complete. In meeting with the role model, Kyra was to find out information on the following:

1.   What challenges did they experience?
2.   To what extent did the injury impact how they viewed themselves as a person or soldier?
3.   How did they cope with injury challenges?
4.   In what ways were other individuals helpful or unhelpful?
5.   Were there any benefits to having had an injury?
6.   If they could offer Kyra one or two pieces of advice what would they be?

During the fourth (final) session, Kyra indicated that her time with the role model was extremely beneficial. In particular, she felt that knowing others had experienced similar concerns was reassuring, and that it was possible to overcome her current challenges. The role model had also provided some helpful ideas about managing feelings of isolation and identity concerns, including spending more time with friends, keeping busy, seeking needed support, and reminding herself that she was valuable regardless of whether she was injured or not. Kyra also indicated a greater awareness of how her negative self-talk was creating an unhelpful spiral of negative emotions, feelings of inadequacy, and diminished effort, all of which were hurting her RTD efforts. Equipped with a stronger support network and a strategy to address her negative self-talk, Kyra indicated reduced feelings of isolation and a greater belief in achieving her long-term goals as a service member.

Perspective 2: The physical therapist's perspective

Despite undergoing a 12-week rehabilitation program, Kyra's symptoms reappeared after RTD. Consequently, the NP indicated a need for follow-up evaluation and rehabilitation with the PT. Upon Kyra's return to the rehabilitation clinic, the PT was aware of the need to address Kyra's physical symptoms, and to rebuild Kyra's confidence in her physical capabilities (i.e. sense of competence), the rehabilitation program itself, and in the PT's abilities. To achieve these aims, the PT decided to integrate three key components into the rehabilitation and RTD plan: (1) specific, measureable, achievable, realistic, and time bound (SMART) goals; (2) group rehabilitation sessions; and (3) assessment of Kyra's confidence in her abilities prior to any further RTD.

Since goal-setting is a key factor in successful injury rehabilitation (Evans & Hardy, 2002), the PT and Kyra collaboratively worked to develop SMART (specific, measureable, achievable, realistic and time bound) goals for Kyra (Arvinen-Barrow & Hemmings, 2013). In Kyra's case, her rehabilitation outcome goal was "to return to duty and lead my platoon." The final goals consisted of time bound short- and medium-term physical and performance goals: (1) to be able to run at a 9:00/mile pace for 20 minutes without stopping and without pain; (2) to complete the 12-mile ruck march with 40 pounds of gear; and (3) to return to unrestricted active duty as Medical Platoon Leader. Setting SMART goals helped Kyra, a highly goal-oriented and driven woman, focus on small achievable benchmarks en-route to her goal of unrestricted RTD. Attaining and having the ability to track her goals appeared to be instrumental in facilitating Kyra's confidence beliefs.

The PT also encouraged Kyra to rehabilitate in a group environment with the aim of boosting her confidence in her physical abilities, model effective recovery behaviors, and to provide peer support. This was achieved by coordinating two group rehabilitation sessions per week with other injured service members. The group sessions allowed Kyra to interact with and observe other soldiers undergoing rehabilitation. Over time, Kyra started to feel that it was "okay" to be injured and not with her unit. Interactions with other soldiers about their successes and challenges enabled Kyra to see that being a "good soldier" did not have to be defined by always being with her platoon and leading from the front. She also became more aware that she had many "good" qualities despite her body not cooperating the way she wanted. She started to believe in herself and appreciated the value of the rehabilitation process, and as a result, achieved success in her rehabilitation. As her symptoms faded, Kyra became more positive during PT sessions and had an enhanced outlook on her injury prognosis and RTD.

To assess Kyra's confidence in her readiness to make an unrestricted RTD, the PT used the Injury-Psychological Readiness to Return to Sport scale (I-PRRS; Glazer, 2009) as it can reliably capture confidence perceptions and reveal areas of concern that the individual is not articulating in discussions with their PT. The scale was administered on two occasions during Kyra's re-entry to the rehabilitation unit – once at the half-way point of her six-week program and upon clearance for an unrestricted RTD. Kyra reported increased scores from 48/60 to 56/60 (with 60 being the highest confidence possible), indicating that she felt elevated confidence and was psychologically ready for RTD. In the final days of physical therapy, Kyra appeared confident, strong, and happy.

Perspective 3: The nurse practitioners' perspective

When Kyra's injury symptoms resurfaced following RTD, she was ordered to revisit the NP for further evaluation. Based on the meeting with Kyra, it became evident that she was experiencing a lack of confidence in her ability to RTD, presented with an external sense of control, feelings of isolation, and loss of a soldier identity. This was articulated by Kyra in number of ways: "My body won't heal like I need it to. I just don't feel like I'm in control of my destiny"; "It doesn't matter what I do, I just don't see myself achieving my career goals"; "I know my commanding officers see me as injury prone. I'm sure they thought I'd be fully recovered by now. I can tell they're questioning my toughness and leadership capabilities"; and "I see the disappointment in their [commanders] eyes when they look at me."

Based on the interprofessional plan of care, the NP focused her efforts on autonomy support strategies. The NP was ideally suited to utilize such strategies given her: (1) substantial military experience with 20 years of service; (2) familiarity with military pressures and expectations to display "grit" and to push through pain and injury; (3) medical knowledge of bone stress injuries; and (4) attendance at various workshops focused on autonomy supportive communication.

To help Kyra regain her sense of autonomy, the NP conducted three different exercises. In the first exercise, the NP asked Kyra to reflect on her injury recovery/ RTD expectations (Heil, 1993). Kyra and the NP discussed how gaining awareness of expectations and their sources could be helpful in building internal energy, direction, and enhanced self-confidence. Equally, understanding how expectations from others that reflected their personal interests or that led Kyra to experience feelings of guilt and self-doubt (i.e., controlled expectations) could be counterproductive. The NP asked Kyra to complete Table 8.2 by doing the following: (1) identify important injury/ RTD expectations; (2) consider where her RTD expectations came from; (3) consider whether her RTD expectations were autonomous (emanating from within) or controlled (emanating from external sources); (4) contemplate whether the expectation was "lifting her up" or "weighing her down"; and finally (5) whether the expectation was worth keeping or getting rid of. Kyra was encouraged to return back to this chart to remind herself of which expectations were helpful and which were unhelpful.

TABLE 8.2 Sample managing expectations exercise

Injury-Related Expectations	*Source of Expectations*	*Source – Autonomous or Controlled?*	*Expectations – Weighing you Down or Lifting you up?*	*Keep Expectation*	*Get Rid of Expectation*
1) _____	1) _____	1) _____	1) _____	1) _____	1) _____
2) _____	2) _____	2) _____	1) _____	2) _____	2) _____
3) _____	3) _____	3) _____	3) _____	3) _____	3) _____
4) _____	4) _____	4) _____	4) _____	4) _____	4) _____

In the second exercise, the NP asked Kyra to identify factors impacting her recovery progression and RTD that she perceived as either controllable or non-controllable. The NP endorsed the benefits of Kyra embracing factors under her control, particularly during instances or periods where Kyra was prone to engaging in repetitive (circular) thinking or worrying thoughts beyond her control. To complete exercise two, the NP asked Kyra to fill in Table 8.3.

As a third and final exercise designed to promote a sense of autonomy, the NP asked Kyra to complete the Sports Rehabilitation Locus of Control Scale (SRLC; Murphy, Foreman, Simpson, Molloy, & Molloy, 1999). The NP felt that completion of the scale would help elicit further discussion regarding factors under Kyra's control. The SRLC was administered on two occasions – once at the mid-point of Kyra's re-entry into the rehabilitation unit and on a second occasion when Kyra was medically cleared to resume an unrestricted RTD. Comparison of Kyra's questionnaire responses at the two time points revealed that Kyra felt a greater internal locus of control by the time she was medically cleared to make an unrestricted RTD. Kyra suggested that she felt as though the exercises gave her some simple tools to refocus her thoughts and energies on realistic expectations and controllable factors. She remarked that in "unloading unrealistic expectations" she felt a greater sense of control over her ability to meet future challenges and that she had renewed confidence and motivation in achieving her career aspirations.

Ethical considerations and need(s) for referral

Within the Army, the primary care manager (PCM), typically but not always an NP, is the conduit to effective care and coordination of ancillary services for service members. As such, communication between the NP and subspecialty services is critical to ensure that service members are progressing in their recovery as expected. Given the severe nature of Kyra's injury and her psychosocial challenges, the NP referred Kyra to a civilian SPC colleague that the NP had worked with previously. The inclusion of the SPC to the rehabilitation team ensured a coordinated effort in addressing Kyra's physical and psychosocial RTD challenges. Although treatment team members discussed Kyra's plan of care, specific comments made to the SPC were kept confidential, in line with ethical and professional standards pertinent to the profession.

TABLE 8.3 Sample identifying controllable and uncontrollable factors influencing RTD exercise

IDENTIFYING FACTORS	
Factors under your Control	Factors NOT under your Control
1._____	1._____
2._____	2._____
3._____	3._____
4._____	4._____
5._____	5._____

Case update

Six months after her unrestricted RTD, Kyra appeared to be thriving, both physically and psychologically. With the benefit of hindsight, Kyra indicated that her second stint in rehabilitation was crucially important in enabling her to make a complete recovery and to RTD without further physical limitations or complications. Kyra successfully completed her second attempt at the Expert Medical Field test earning her EFMB Badge. Earning the badge was not only a huge psychological triumph but it was instrumental in Kyra's promotion to the rank of captain. Kyra also indicated that the strategies provided by her SPC, PT and NP (i.e., thought shifting, SMART goals, managing expectations) were invaluable in enabling her to handle new challenges at work and in her personal life.

Conclusion

Kyra, a first lieutenant (1LT) and Medical Platoon Leader described in this case study suffered a grade 2 anterior bone stress injury and as a consequence, underwent a 12-week rehabilitation program. Despite her physical activity restrictions upon RTD, Kyra's physical injury symptoms worsened and she experienced a variety of psychosocial concerns, which, upon interprofessional team consultation, were addressed using strategies that enhanced her sense of relatedness, competence, and autonomy (Ryan & Deci, 2000). The SPC addressed Kyra's relatedness-based concerns by using self-talk interventions and employing peer support. The PT worked with Kyra to develop her sense of competence by setting SMART goals, organizing group rehabilitation sessions, and assessing Kyra's confidence in her abilities prior to any further RTD. Finally, the NP implemented strategies targeting Kyra's sense of autonomy through the use of an exercise aimed to identify and manage RTD expectations, and to change Kyra's perceived locus of control. Kyra reported that the collective efforts of her rehabilitation team helped address her psychosocial needs and gave her greater hope in the prospect of achieving a promising and fruitful military career.

KEY POINTS

- Kyra, a first lieutenant (1LT) and Medical Platoon Leader suffered a grade 2 anterior tibia bone stress injury.
- Despite Kyra's physical activity restrictions upon RTD, her injury symptoms intensified during training exercises.
- Following her RTD, Kyra experienced a range of psychosocial concerns pertaining to her sense of competence (e.g., diminished confidence in executing physical tasks, and leadership abilities), autonomy (lack of control over her body, external locus of control), and relatedness (feelings of isolation and loss of "soldier" identity).

- A team approach was used to address Kyra's concerns. Specifically, the SPC dealt with Kyra's relatedness concerns (e.g., role modelling), while the PT worked with Kyra to enhance her sense of competence (e.g., SMART goal-setting, group rehabilitation). Additionally, the NP implemented strategies targeting autonomy perceptions by encouraging Kyra to reflect on her current expectations and where those expectations emanated from, and to focus on factors under her control.
- Kyra reported that the collective efforts of her rehabilitation team helped address her psychological needs and gave her greater hope in the prospect of achieving her career aspirations.

CRITICAL THINKING QUESTIONS

1. How did Kyra's thoughts and emotions impact her rehabilitation/RTD behaviors (e.g., rehabilitation adherence)?
2. Based on details in the scenario, what inferences can you draw about the socio-cultural dynamics surrounding injury within the Army environment? How might this have influenced the nature or extent of Kyra's injury and RTD concerns?
3. Each practitioner employed several strategies when addressing Kyra's psychological needs. Can you think of any alternate strategies that might be effective in addressing Kyra's injury and RTD concerns? Why might such interventions be effective?

RESEARCH QUESTIONS

1. To what extent do psychosocial factors such as motives to return to duty, re-injury anxieties, and confidence beliefs predict RTD outcomes (e.g., return vs. non-return, post-injury performance, performance anxiety)?
2. Describe the experiences of female soldiers attempting a return to duty following bone stress injuries?
3. To what extent do environmental supports for soldiers' psychological needs (competence, autonomy, and relatedness) impact RTD outcomes (e.g., re-injury anxieties, post-injury performance, performance anxiety)?

KEY PUBLICATIONS

1. Podlog, L., & Brown, W. J. (2016). Self-determination theory: A framework for enhancing patient-centered care. *The Journal for Nurse Practitioners, 12*, 359–362. doi: 10.1016/j.nurpra.2016.04.022.

This paper underscores the relevance of self-determination theory (SDT) as a framework for conceptualizing and applying patient-centered care within the

United States Army Medical Department (AMEDD). Historically, patient-practitioner communication within AMEDD settings has involved controlling language and hierarchical presentation of information. The aim of this report was to examine the value of SDT constructs and research in advancing patient-centered care in AMEDD settings. The report included a review of research on patient-centered care and health outcomes as well as a discussion of SDT principles and strategies for promoting patient-centered care.

2.   Bianco, T. (2001). Social support and recovery from sport injury: Elite skiers share their experiences. *Research Quarterly for Exercise and Sport, 72*, 376–388. doi: 10.1080/02701367.2001.10608974.

This qualitative study involves ten Canadian and U.S. National Team skiers who suffered season-ending injuries. Participants described challenges and stresses associated with injury rehabilitation and return to sport following injury. The skiers also articulated the importance of social support from various sources (coaches, physiotherapists, teammates) in facilitating their recovery. In particular, skiers reported benefiting from several types of social support, namely emotional, informational and tangible support. These forms of support were instrumental in reducing athlete distress and maintaining motivation through the various phases of injury recovery.

References

Ardern, C. L., Österberg, A., Tagesson, S., Gauffin, H., Webster, K. E., & Kvist, J. (2014). The impact of psychological readiness to return to sport and recreational activities after anterior cruciate ligament reconstruction. *British Journal of Sports Medicine*, 48(22), 1613–1650. doi:10.1136/bjsports-2014-093842.

Ardern, C. L., Taylor, N. F., Feller, J. A., & Webster, K. E. (2013). A systematic review of the psychological factors associated with returning to sport following injury. *British Journal of Sports Medicine*, 47(17), 1120–1126. doi:10.1136/bjsports-2012-091203.

Arvinen-Barrow, M., & Hemmings, B. (2013). Goal setting in sport injury rehabilitation. In M. Arvinen-Barrow & N. Walker (Eds.), *Psychology of sport injury and rehabilitation* (pp. 56–70). Abingdon: Routledge.

Astur, D. C., Zanatta, F., Arliani, G. G., Moraes, E. R., de Castro Pochini, A., & Ejnisman, B. (2016). Stress fractures: Definition, diagnosis and treatment [Fraturas por estresse: Definição, diagnóstico e tratamento]. *Revista Brasileira de Ortopedia (English Edition)*, 51(1), 3–10. doi:10.1016/j.rboe.2015.12.008.

Banack, H. R., Sabiston, C. M., & Bloom, G. A. (2011). Coach autonomy support, basic need satisfaction, and intrinsic motivation of paralympic athletes. *Research Quarterly for Exercise and Sport*, 82(4), 722–730. doi:10.5641/027013611X13275192111989.

Baumeister, R. F., & Leary, M. R. (1995). The need to belong: Desire for interpersonal attachments as a fundamental human motivation. *Psychological Bulletin*, 117(3), 497–529. doi:10.1037/0033-2909.117.3.497.

Booth-Kewley, S., Larson, G. E., & Highfill-McRoy, R. M. (2009). Psychosocial predictors of return to duty among Marine recruits with musculoskeletal injuries. *Military Medicine*, 174(2), 139–152. doi:10.7205/MILMED-D-01-2708.

Brewer, B. W., Van Raalte, J. L., & Linder, D. E. (1993). Athletic identity: Hercules' muscles or Achilles' heel? *International Journal of Sport Psychology*, 24(2), 237–254.

Carson, F., & Polman, R. C. J. (2017). Self-determined motivation in rehabilitating professional rugby union players. *BMC Sports Science, Medicine and Rehabilitation*, 9(2), 1–11. doi:10.1186/s13102-13016-0065-0066.

Chase, M. A., Magyar, T. M., & Drake, B. M. (2005). Fear of injury in gymnastics: Self-efficacy and psychological strategies to keep on tumbling. *Journal of Sports Sciences, 23*(5), 465–475. doi:10.1080/02640410400021427.

Evans, L., & Hardy, L. (2002). Injury rehabilitation: A goal-setting intervention study. *Research Quarterly for Exercise and Sport*, 73, 310–319. doi:10.1080/02701367.2002.10609025.

Feller, J., & Webster, K. E. (2013). Return to sport following anterior cruciate ligament reconstruction. *International Orthopaedics*, 37(2), 285–290. doi:10.1007/s00264-00012-1690-1697.

Flint, F. A. (2007). Modeling in injury rehabilitation: Seeing helps believing. In D. Pargman (Ed.), *Psychological bases of sport injuries* (3rd ed., pp. 95–108). Morgantown, WV: Fitness Information Technology.

Glazer, D. D. (2009). Development and preliminary validation of the Injury-Psychological Readiness to Return to Sport (I-PRRS) scale. *Journal of Athletic Training*, 44(2), 185–189. doi:10.4085/1062-6050-44.2.185.

Hauret, K. G., Bostick, R. M., Matthews, C. E., Hussey, J. R., Fina, M. F., Geisinger, K. R., & Roufail, W. M. (2004). Physical activity and reduced risk of incident sporadic colorectal adenomas: Observational support for mechanisms involving energy balance and inflammation modulation. *American Journal of Epidemiology*, 159(10), 983–992. doi:10.1093/aje/kwh130.

Heil, J. (1993). *Psychology of sport injury*. Champaign, IL: Human Kinetics.

Johnson, U. (2000). Short-term psychological intervention: A study of long-term-injured competitive athletes. *Journal of Sport Rehabilitation*, 9(3), 207–218. doi:10.1123/jsr.9.3.207.

Knapik, J. J., Reynolds, K., & Hoedebecke, K. L. (2017). Stress Fractures: Etiology, Epidemiology, Diagnosis, Treatment, and Prevention. *Journal of Special Operations Medicine*, 17(2), 120–130.

Koren, D., Norman, D., Cohen, A., Berman, J., & Klein, E. M. (2005). Increased PTSD risk with combat-related injury: A matched comparison study of injured and uninjured soldiers experiencing the same combat events. *The American Journal of Psychiatry*, 162(2), 276–328. doi:10.1176/appi.ajp.162.2.276.

Larson, G. E., Booth-Kewley, S., & Ryan, M. A. K. (2002). Predictors of navy attrition: I. Analysis of 1-year attrition. *Military Medicine*, 167(9), 760–769.

Laubach, W. J., Brewer, B. W., Van Raalte, J. L., & Petitpas, A. J. (1996). Attributions for recovery and adherence to sport injury rehabilitation. *Australian Journal of Science and Medicine in Sport*, 28(1), 30–34.

Lee, D. (2011). Stress fractures, active component, US Armed Forces, 2004–2010. *Medical Surveillance Monthly Report*, 18(5), 8–11.

Mattila, V. M., Niva, M., Kiuru, M., & Pihlajamäki, H. (2007). Risk factors for bone stress injuries: a follow-up study of 102,515 person-years. *Medicine and Science in Sports and Exercise*, 39(7), 1061–1066.

Morgan, B. J., & Bibb, S. C. G. (2011). Assessment of military population-based psychological resilience programs. *Military Medicine*, 176(9), 976–985. doi:10.7205/MILMED-D-10-00433.

Murphy, G. C., Foreman, P. E., Simpson, C. A., Molloy, G. N., & Molloy, E. K. (1999). The development of a locus of control measure predictive of injured athletes' adherence to treatment. *Journal of Science and Medicine in Sport*, 2(2), 145–152. doi:10.1016/S1440-2440(99)80194-80197.

Neff, K. D., & McGehee, P. (2010). Self-compassion and psychological resilience among adolescents and young adults. *Self and Identity*, 9(3), 225–240. doi:10.1080/15298860902979307.

Podlog, L., Dimmock, J. A., & Miller, J. (2011). A review of return to sport concerns following injury rehabilitation: Practitioner strategies for enhancing recovery outcomes. *Physical Therapy in Sport*, 12(1), 36–42. doi:10.1016/j.ptsp.2010.07.005.

Podlog, L., & Eklund, R. C. (2006). A longitudinal investigation of competitive athletes' return to sport following serious injury. *Journal of Applied Sport Psychology*, 18(1), 44–68. doi:10.1080/10413200500471319.

Podlog, L., & Eklund, R. C. (2007a). Professional coaches' perspectives on the return to sport following serious injury. *Journal of Applied Sport Psychology*, 19(2), 207–225. doi:10.1080/10413200701188951.

Podlog, L., & Eklund, R. C. (2007b). The psychosocial aspects of a return to sport following serious injury: A review of the literature from a self-determination perspective. *Psychology of Sport & Exercise*, 8(4), 535–566. doi:10.1016/j.psychsport.2006.07.008.

Podlog, L., Heil, J., & Schulte, S. (2014). Psychosocial factors in sports injury rehabilitation and return to play. *Physical Medicine and Rehabilitation Clinics*, 25(4), 915–930. doi:10.1016/j.pmr.2014.06.011.

Podlog, L., Lochbaum, M., & Stevens, T. (2010). Need satisfaction, well-being, and perceived return-to-sport outcomes among injured athletes. *Journal of Applied Sport Psychology*, 22(2), 167–182. doi:10.1080/10413201003664665.

Reel, J. J., Podlog, L., Hamilton, L., Greviskes, L., Voelker, D. K., & Gray, C. (2018). Injury and disordered eating behaviors: What is the connection for female professional dancers? *Journal of Clinical Sport Psychology*, 12(3).

Russell, D. W. (1996). UCLA Loneliness Scale (version 3): Reliability, validity, and factor structure. *Journal of Personality Assessment*, 66(1), 20–40. doi:10.1207/s15327752jpa6601_2.

Ryan, R. M., & Deci, E. L. (2000). Self-determination theory and the facilitation of intrinsic motivation, social development, and well-being. *American Psychologist*, 55(1), 68–78. doi:10.1037/0003-066X.55.1.68.

Ryan, R. M., & Deci, E. L. (2002). An overview of self-determination theory: An organismic dialectical perspective. In E. L. Deci & R. M. Ryan (Eds.), *Handbook of self-determination research* (pp. 3–33). Rochester, NY: University of Rochester Press.

Waumsley, J., & Katz, J. (2013). Using a psychological model and counselling skills in sport injury rehabilitation. In M. Arvinen-Barrow & N. Walker (Eds.), *The psychology of sport injury and rehabilitation*. Abingdon: Routledge.

Williams, A., Hagerty, B. M., Yousha, S. M., Horrocks, J., Hoyle, K. S., & Liu, D. (2004). Psychosocial effects of the Boot Strap intervention in Navy recruits. *Military Medicine*, 169(10), 814–820. doi:10.7205/MILMED.169.10.814.

9

REACTIONS TO RETURN TO THE DECKS

Melissa Scruton, a professional disc jockey

Ross Wadey and Leanne Griffiths

Key Words: 37-year-old female, professional dancing disk jockey, return to work concerns, re-injury anxiety, over-adherence, performance narrative, Grade II hamstring strain

Case description

Melissa Scruton (this name is a pseudonym and used for descriptive purposes only) is 37 years old and she refers to herself as a professional disc jockey (DJ). She is white, heterosexual, middle-class, single, and lives in Manchester (England) by herself in an unfurnished studio apartment. When it comes to Melissa, music is life and life is music. She embodies music; it runs through her veins. When she is not performing in London, Paris, or New York, she is listening, thinking, and debating about music with other DJs. Music understands her and she understands music. It is a marriage. A marriage that has evolved over time. It all began when her dad gave her a 78 record on her thirteenth birthday. She played it repeatedly on his gramophone. She loved cranking up the gramophone, placing the record on the turntable, and, amongst the crackles, hearing the songs transcend the horn to engulf her living room. She would sit on her dad's lap using his arms as a blanket, grinning from ear-to-ear. These are fond memories; memories Melissa cherishes dearly.

Melissa's dad passed away when she was 19 years old. Unable to talk to anyone about her loss, she found comfort in music. Music knew how to help; how to relax her, how to energize her, and how to let her just be. It also went on to set the stage for her career. Melissa made the decision on her twentieth birthday that she was going to be a DJ. The gramophone was soon replaced with a set of decks. Although there were many setbacks and obstacles to overcome on her journey to becoming a DJ, she quickly moved up the ranks and soon found herself performing at some of the most iconic venues around the world. Melissa was amazed how this new world was opening in front of her very eyes. She loved every minute and wanted more. A newspaper article labelled her an *International Success*. She had "made it". She knew celebrities. She had money. Life was good. After all, music is life and life is music.

Aside from music, Melissa had little time for anything else. She was single-minded and determined to live up the hype surrounding her, continually striving for prestigious awards and accolades. If other aspects of her life are storied at all, they were of secondary importance and whether they would help or hinder her career. The costs of this way of life were that she rarely saw or spoke to her mum and regularly missed key family events (e.g., weddings, funerals, christenings). She recalls being in love once, but he demanded too much of her time. Unlike "normal" people, a typical day for Melissa involved sleeping during the day and performing throughout the night. Once home, she would draw the curtains and collapse on her bed. She would be physically exhausted. The thing is, what made Melissa's performances different from other DJs was that they not only involved mixing on the decks, but dancing with the music to engage the audience. Her sets would last two to eight hours. Some sets she described were like running two marathons.

Melissa prided herself on her fitness and described her body as a "machine." A relentless and powerful machine. Although her body goes against society's feminine ideas, she loved her body, especially her defined muscles. Yet, what Melissa did not realize was that her body was "running out of steam"; it was about to let her down. Indeed, one night after a gig, Melissa felt a tightening in her hamstring. She thought nothing of it. It was nothing some painkillers and vodka could not address. However, the pain came back with added vengeance in a subsequent gig to the extent that it made it impossible for her to walk or even stand. Melissa was forced to cancel her next gig. She was devastated. She felt dreadful. She let everyone down. She let herself down.

For the first time in five years, Melissa called her mum. Her mum came immediately and drove her to see the general practitioner (GP). Nothing was said in the car. At the clinic, the GP was extremely insensitive to Melissa's needs, saying that her injury was her fault and that she needed to rest, for at least eight weeks. Melissa burst into tears and was inconsolable. The GP looked at Melissa's mum and said that they needed to leave because his next patient was waiting; they never saw that GP again. Through word of mouth, Melissa met a sports physiotherapist who had worked with high-performing individuals, many of whom operated within a similar culture and shared a similar mindset to Melissa. The physiotherapist diagnosed Melissa's injury as a Grade II hamstring strain due to overuse and fatigue. Melissa's mum drove her to and from each physiotherapy appointment.

Melissa worked with her physiotherapist throughout her rehabilitation, which went from strength to strength. Her pain and inflammation reduced, while her range of motion and extensibility greatly improved. However, as the prospect of Melissa returning to her desks became closer, issues surfaced that could not be resolved solely within the physiotherapist-client relationship. Melissa, eager to return, had started to overdo her rehabilitation, which negatively impacted her physical recovery. One day, during a physical therapy (PT) session, Melissa explained:

> I am not sure why, but I feel less ready to go back to work than I did three weeks ago. I do all these exercises that I am supposed to do, and way more, but I feel unprepared, fatigued and scared. What if I book a gig and cannot sustain my energy and dancing for the duration? That's my professional reputation on the line. What if I get re-injured? And then, if I cannot return to the decks, what would I do? If I am not a DJ, who am I?

It was after this conversation that Melissa, with a little encouragement from her PT, decided it was time to meet with the sport psychologist (SP) her PT had recommended.

The injury

A Grade II hamstring strain is a common leg injury involving a tear in one or more of the hamstring muscles (Kaeding & Borchers, 2014). Melissa had strained her semimembranosus and semitendinosus. Common symptoms include sudden and severe pain (e.g., snapping or popping feeling), hamstring tenderness and bruising (Brukner, 2015). An ultrasound scan and MRI are able to identify the location and extend of the hamstring tear. Recovery times for a Grade II strain is typically between four and eight weeks (Brukner, 2015). Treatment aims to reduce hamstring pain and inflammation, normalize muscle range of motion and extensibility, and strengthen knee muscles and hamstrings. Hamstring re-injury rates are also high due a poor rehabilitation process (Kaeding & Borchers, 2014).

Key factor 1: Re-injury anxiety

The most commonly reported psychological factor that individuals experience when they return to performance following an injury is re-injury anxiety (Johnston & Carroll, 1998; Kvist, Ek, Sporrstedt, & Good, 2005; Podlog & Eklund, 2007; Walker, Thatcher, Lavallee, & Golby, 2004). It is defined as a negatively toned emotional response, with cognitive (e.g., negative thoughts and images) and somatic symptoms (e.g., feeling nauseous and tense) that arise due to the possibility of an injury reoccurring after an initial injury of the same type and location (Walker et al., 2004). Re-injury anxiety has been observed to manifest itself in several ways: during one's return, including holding back and not giving 100% effort, avoiding situations that could cause re-injury, trying too hard and overcompensating in other aspects of performance, and questioning physical and psychological readiness to return. All of the above can negatively impact performance and increase the risk of (re)injury (e.g., Andersen, 2001; Evans, Hardy, & Fleming, 2000; Johnston & Carroll, 2000). The demands and cognitions that precede re-injury anxiety typically include a lack of confidence in the injured body part, pain and soreness at the site of injury, performing the same skill in the same situation that the injury was incurred, concerns for potential setbacks, the physical demands of training and competition, and reminders of the injury incident (e.g., Bianco, Malo, & Orlick, 1999; Gould, Udry, Bridges, & Beck, 1997; Podlog & Eklund, 2006). In Melissa's case, her re-injury anxiety largely stemmed from her concerns with her identity. Similar to athletes who have an exclusive athletic identity (i.e., the degree to which an individual identifies with the athlete role; Brewer, Van Raalte, & Linder, 1993), Melissa's identity appeared to be wholly tied up with being a successful DJ. As evidenced in the case, her main concerns circled around worries about getting re-injured and the consequences of not being able to continue being a DJ. For as long as she can remember, Melissa has regulated other areas of her life to be a successful DJ.

Re-injury anxiety can be measured using the Re-Injury Anxiety Inventory (RIAI; Walker, Thatcher, & Lavallee, 2010). The RIAI is a 28-item measure designed to measure re-injury anxiety. The measure consists of two factors: rehabilitation re-injury anxiety and re-entry into competition re-injury anxiety. Items are scored on a 4-point Likert scale (0 = not at all; 3 = very much so). Initial research has shown the instrument to valid (i.e., face, content, and factorial), with good internal reliability with an alpha coefficient of .98 for RIA-R and .96 for RIA-RE (Walker et al., 2010).

Key factor 2: over-adherence

Adherence to injury rehabilitation has been examined extensively in the sports medicine and psychology of sport injury literature (for reviews, see Brewer, 1998; Levy, Polman, Clough, & McNaughton, 2006). Granquist, Gill, and Appaneal (2010) defined adherence as behaviors an individual demonstrates by pursuing courses of action that coincides with the recommendations of a physiotherapist or athletic trainer. Thus far, research has largely illustrated positive adherence-outcome associations for indices of adherence such as attendance at physiotherapy sessions (e.g., Derscheid & Feiring, 1987; Treacy, Barron, Brunet, & Barrack, 1997), clinical ratings of adherence (e.g., Brewer et al., 2004; Brewer et al., 2000), and self-ratings of adherence (e.g., Alzate Saez de Heredia, Ramirez, & Lazaro, 2004; Pizzari, Taylor, McBurney, & Feller, 2005). Recently, Podlog et al. (2013) suggested that more research attention is needed on over-adherence (i.e., doing too much too quickly), which resonates with Melissa's actions that stem from her relationship with her body. Melissa has punished her body for years, subjecting it to demanding and at times abusive practices and performances. She describes her body as a relentless and powerful "machine", aligning with research by Douglas and Carless (2015) that shows how the media and certain cultural narratives reinforce the "body-as-machine" metaphor. Rather than demonstrating self-compassion for her body and listening to and understanding the messages it sends her, Melissa is using this metaphor to depersonalize and detach herself from her body. This has enabled her to tolerate pain, push herself harder by doing more rehabilitation than required, subsequently hampering her recovery and readiness to return to the decks.

Over-adherence can be measured using the Rehabilitation Over-adherence Questionnaire (ROAQ; Podlog et al., 2013). The ROAQ is a 10-item measure, comprising two subscales assessing over-adherence behaviours and beliefs: ignore practitioner recommendations and attempt an expedited rehabilitation measured on a 5-point Likert scale (1 = strongly disagree; 5 = strongly agree). Initial research has shown the instrument to have face, content, and factorial validity as well as good internal reliability with an alpha coefficient of .86 and .75 for the two subscales, respectively (Podlog et al., 2013).

Key factor 3: Performance narrative

Another key factor to consider in Melissa's care is the broader cultural narrative she draws upon to construct how her life is storied. Recent research operating at the intersection between sociology and psychology have helped to provide a more detailed understanding of the influence of social-cultural phenomenon on injured athletes' psychological experiences and actions. This is perhaps best illustrated in the work of Smith and Sparkes (2002, 2004, 2005), who have explored the stories of athletes who suffered a spinal cord injury through sport. Their research illustrates how, "A person's own story and their experience is shaped, facilitate, and contained by narratives that circulate within the culture that he or she is immersed" (Smith & Sparkes, 2009, p. 5). One approach that has been effective in connecting the social and personal is narrative inquiry (McGannon & Smith, 2015). In the context of competitive sport, Douglas and Carless (2009) identified a dominant narrative: *performance narrative*; a story of single-minded dedication to sport performance that justifies, and even demands, the exclusion or relegation of all other areas of life and self. Performance narratives provide illustrations of how and why, for some athletes at least, "sport is life and life is sport", which clearly resonates with Melissa's story (i.e., "music is life and life is music").

Within the performance narrative, success is pre-eminent and linked closely to the storyteller's identity and self-worth (Douglas & Carless, 2009). For example, performance stories can often reveal the fragile nature of self-worth when it is dependent on sport performance and how it can be affected during performance fluctuations or other disruptive factors (e.g., injury). Within this performance narrative, Douglas and Carless (2015) outlined several of its characteristics, two of which resonated with Melissa's experiences and actions: fragile and contingent sense of self (i.e., identity) and the work of performance enhancement (e.g., detached body-self relationship). To address the above, researchers are now recommending that practitioners critically consider helping clients to consider alternative narratives to counter existing destructive master narratives such as the performance narrative (e.g., Cavallerio, Wadey, & Wagstaff, 2017; Papathomas & Lavallee, 2014).

Theoretical considerations

Melissa's case is best explained by the *multilevel model of sport injury* (MMSI; Wadey, Day, Cavallerio, & Martinelli, 2018). The MMSI contextualizes the wider social-organizational-cultural influences that impact sport injury process. Specifically, the MMSI recognizes and accounts for five distinct, yet relational units of analysis that are proposed to impact and be impacted by sport injury. The first level, *Intrapersonal*, reflects the characteristics of the individual (e.g., values, beliefs, attitudes) and their thoughts, feelings, and behaviours pre- and post-injury. The second level of analysis, *Interpersonal*, focuses on formal and informal social networks and support systems (e.g., social support, other social processes). The third level, *Institutional*, is concerned with the institutions and organizations (e.g., strategy, functioning, climate), the physical environment (e.g., material provisions), and the psychosocial architecture (e.g., key stakeholder relationships). The fourth level, *Cultural*, reflects the media, cultural narratives, and collective norms and values. The fifth and final level, *Policy*, represents the relevant local and national policies and practices.

One of the benefits of the MMSI is that it can accommodate additional models and theories within and across its levels. Considering Melissa's case largely operates at the intrapersonal (i.e., re-injury anxiety, over-adherence) and cultural levels (i.e., performance narrative), these can be further explained through the integrated model of psychological response to sport injury and rehabilitation process (Wiese-Bjornstal, Smith, Shaffer, & Morrey, 1998) and narrative theory (Frank, 1995). At an intrapersonal level, Wiese-Bjornstal et al.'s (1998) integrated model proposes that emotional and behavioural responses to injury affect recovery outcomes, which are moderated by both personal and situational factors and mediated by the process of cognitive appraisal. Indeed, Melissa's emotional (e.g., re-injury anxiety) and behavioural (e.g., over-adherence) responses are affecting her recovery and readiness to return to the decks. The interaction of Melissa's thoughts, feelings, and behaviours are further understood by drawing from narrative theory. Sparkes and Partington (2003) suggested that narrative theory can help provide a more sophisticated appreciation of people as active social beings. Although individuals tell personal stories, these stories are drawn from more general narratives that are embedded within social-cultural contexts. Frank (1995) uses the term "narrative types" to describe what he considered to be the most general storyline that can be recognized underlying the plot and tensions of particular stories. According to Frank, culturally available narrative types structure, locate, and underpin personal stories acting as a guide for the way life should be lived and providing a framework within which accounts of personal experiences are created. This helps to explain why the performance narrative that Melissa is operating within is influencing her experiences and actions at an intrapersonal level.

Interprofessional plan of care

The plan of care for Melissa's case was multidisciplinary, and more reactive than proactive. Rather than having an established team in place from the outset to support Melissa throughout her return to the decks, additional members of her rehabilitation team were referred in or out as and when required. Initially, the rehabilitation "team" consisted of only the PT, which was a successful working alliance throughout rehabilitation. As Melissa's return to the decks approached, additional issues emerged that went above and beyond the PT's professional boundaries and competence (i.e., emergence of re-injury anxiety, over-adherence). It was at this stage, the sport psychologist (SP) was included into the rehabilitation team with a goal of working with the PT and Melissa to support her successful return to the decks. The PT and SP held several collective meetings, mainly focused on strategies how to help regulate Melissa's over-adherence. It was agreed that issues related to re-injury anxiety were best discussed in a series of one-to-one sessions with the SP. It was during these sessions that the focus shifted from using psychological skills to a more rigorous examination of self. While the SPs efforts enhanced Melissa's readiness and ultimate return to the decks, the examination of self also brought with it more questions and several negative affective states (e.g., feelings of depression, sadness, and regret). This led to the inclusion of a clinical psychologist in Melissa's care team to ensure her successful return to the decks and beyond.

Perspective 1: The physiotherapist's perspective

From the injury onset and throughout the rehabilitation, the PT and Melissa had developed a strong working alliance (Keegan, 2015). Yet, upon Melissa's return to performance, trust within their relationship emerged as a concern. Melissa was saying one thing (i.e., I'm doing the rehabilitation program as advised) yet doing another (i.e., doing too much rehabilitation at home). The PT could not understand Melissa's lower than expected progress and continued pain. First, the PT questioned herself and the advice she had offered Melissa. Then, the PT reflected on previous experiences with other clients sharing Melissa's background and mindset and concluded that Melissa is likely to be over-adhering. The PT brought this up during their next consultation and challenged Melissa to disclose all activities she had been doing. Upon further questioning and probing, Melissa confessed that against her PT's instructions she had been doing additional runs and going to aerobic classes with the aim to maintain her level of fitness. Yet, despite emphasizing to Melissa how her over-adherence had the potential to do more harm than good, Melissa continued to ignore the PT's advice. Melissa's mindset was "no pain, no gain". It was at this stage, when the PT suggested Melissa should also see a SP, and upon Melissa's consent, the PT and the SP worked together to address Melissa's over-adherence. Together with Melissa, the PT and SP agreed upon two strategies to address Melissa's over-adherence: simulation training and setting process goals.

Simulation training has proven an effective technique during the return to participation phase of recovery (e.g., Cox, 2002; Evans et al., 2000; Podlog & Eklund, 2007). As Melissa was adamant that she wanted to continue to train to increase her fitness and physical readiness to return to the decks, other types of physical practice were discussed between Melissa, PT, and SP. It was decided that Melissa would continue her training if she did it in a swimming pool (i.e., performing actions that replicated her performing on stage). She could also continue aerobics, but again, only water aerobics. This was a compromise that the PT and Melissa made to allow Melissa to keep training while in rehabilitation, yet simultaneously ensuring that Melissa did not further harm her hamstring, which would have ultimately prolonged her return to the decks.

The second strategy implemented to address Melissa's over-adherence was goal-setting. Goal-setting has been found to decrease recovery time and that short-term goals appear to be more effective than long-term goals in expediting recovery (Ievleva & Orlick, 1991). Studies have also illustrated that injured athletes have a preference for the use of goal-setting over other psychological skills (Brewer, Jeffers, Petitpas, & Van Raalte, 1994) and physiotherapists consider goal-setting to be an integral part of rehabilitation (Arvinen-Barrow, Penny, Hemmings, & Corr, 2010). The PT was familiar with goal-setting literature and knew how to set long- and short-term SMART goals to facilitate goal-setting effectiveness (Arvinen-Barrow & Hemmings, 2013; Podlog, Dimmock, & Miller, 2011). However, issues arose when the PT found out that Melissa would religiously stick to her exercise goals, even if she was in pain. This was discussed between the PT and the SP, which led to further discussions about the importance of goal flexibility to account for the unpredictability nature of recovery (Evans & Hardy, 2002). The PT and SP spoke about importance of setting process goals (i.e., focusing on form and technique over outcome), that are self-referent in nature and under the control of the athlete (Kingston & Hardy, 1997).

The PT had not come across process goals before. The SP explained how focusing more on the processes involved in the movement rather than specific sets or repetitions, Melissa would be more attuned to the messages her body is sending her rather than meeting specific outcomes. As a result, the PT's knowledge of rehabilitation exercises and the SP's knowledge of goal-setting was integrated and shared with Melissa. She found the new process goals to be effective, as she felt she was more attuned with the messages her body was sending her, less focused on completing certain number of repetitions, and more likely to stop when she experienced pain. Ultimately, this greatly enhanced Melissa's adherence to her rehabilitation, increased her confidence in her hamstring subsequently decreasing her re-injury anxiety, and ultimately led to her psychological readiness to return (Podlog, Banham, Wadey, & Hannon, 2015).

Perspective 2: The sport psychologist's perspective

Considering Melissa's psychosocial concerns and associated research, the SP initially worked with Melissa to teach her psychological skills aimed to regulate her re-injury anxiety and adherence levels. Although research has shown that imagery, relaxation, and goal-setting are effective psychological skills in reducing re-injury anxieties and regulating levels of adherence (e.g., Cupal & Brewer, 2001; Evans &

Hardy, 2002; Evans et al., 2000; Podlog et al., 2011), these psychological skills proved ineffective in meeting Melissa's needs. She reported having low imagery ability and little interest in learning how to use imagery: "I think with words, not pictures." The SP also encouraged Melissa to try progressive muscular relaxation technique (Jacobson, 1938) and mediation with the aim to lower her anxiety and promote blood flow to the injured limb, thus promoting healing and reducing the likelihood of re-injury (Heil, 1993). However, Melissa reported that she could not stop ruminating about the possibility of getting re-injured and found the relaxation techniques more frustrating than relaxing. While goal-setting helped to regulate Melissa's adherence (see above, the physiotherapist's perspective), it had no effect on her re-injury anxiety. The SP also tried cognitive restructuring to normalize her anxiety-related symptoms and modelling with individuals who had successfully overcome their re-injury anxiety. Informational support from her PT aimed to reinforce Melissa that she was meeting physical levels of proficiency, none of which alleviated Melissa's re-injury anxiety.

At this stage, the SP was at a loss about what to do next. The SP engaged himself in conversations with his sport psychology peers, reflected on their previous consultations with Melissa and other clients, and immersed themselves in wider reading, after which the SP decided to adopt a more Socratic approach with Melissa. That is, rather than being technique-driven and concerned solely with specific skills (i.e., Sophist approach), the SP encouraged Melissa to engage in rigorous personal examination and seek to gain an improved knowledge of self (Corlett, 1996). The term "knowledge of self" is not used here in the same way that "self-awareness" is used in sport psychology literature (Ravizza, 1993). The term "self-awareness" refers to a highly developed and immediate attentional focus on one's physical and mental states, whereas "knowledge of self", is a more broader and general sense of self that reflects one's values, and in Melissa's case, her relationship with music and the meaning of her re-injury anxiety. Corlett (1996) argued that "during their busy and narrow sport careers, athletes have had ample experience developing mental skills, including the attentional focus that self-awareness demands, but they have not always had parallel experiences developing knowledge of self" (p. 87). The SP determined that the same could apply to Melissa. Rather than seeking to regulate or gain "control" over Melissa's re-injury anxiety, the SP decided to confront and understand what was causing her re-injury anxiety by understanding what it meant to her.

At the next consultation, the SP approached Melissa with cause-illuminating questions. What does your re-injury anxiety mean to you? What is your relationship with music? What do you value? Who are you? The consultations that followed were challenging (for both parties), painful, and filled with awkward silences; but they ultimately pushed Melissa to stop and think about what she values and who she is. To assist Melissa on her journey towards greater self-discovery, the SP drew from Acceptance and Commitment Therapy (ACT) and its associated techniques (e.g., Harris, 2008; Hayes & Smith, 2011; LeJeune, 2007). One technique that proved helpful was the imaginary "mind-reading machine" exercise aimed to uncover Melissa's values (Harris, 2008). First, the SP told Melissa that he had invented a fictitious mind-reading machine that can read the mind of anybody of the planet. Then the SP asked Melissa to think of someone very important to her; she chose her dad, who had passed away when she was younger. The SP then asked Melissa to imagine her dad's face, he pulled an "imaginary lever", and said to Melissa: "you can now read your Dad's mind, and it just so happens that he is thinking of you. He's thinking about your character, about the sort of person you are, the personal strengths and qualities you have, and what you stand for in life. He is also thinking about what you meant to him, and the role you played in his life." While Melissa is thinking, the SP asked: "What would you love to hear your Dad saying about you?" At this point, Melissa broke down in uncontrollable tears.

The aim of the exercise was not to predict what Melissa's dad would have said but rather to uncover what Melissa would love him to be thinking about her during this exercise. Melissa identified a significant gap between her values and her actions. Melissa said how much she valued love for others, particularly her mum, whom she had barely seen or spoke to in over half a decade, apart from her mum driving Melissa to the PT sessions during the initial stages of the rehabilitation. Over the next ten sessions, Melissa and the SP worked together to identify strategies how to reduce this gap between her values and actions. One effective strategy was a gratitude task (Seligman, Steen, Park, & Peterson, 2005). Emerging from the positive psychology literature, this task involves writing and delivering a letter of gratitude in person to someone who has been especially kind to them but had never properly been thanked. Melissa chose to write and deliver a letter to her mum, who had helped Melissa during the PT appointments, yet Melissa had never thanked her. Before the next consultation, Melissa had called her mum, they met for a coffee, where Melissa read the letter to her mum verbatim and then reported back to her SP:

SP: How was coffee with your Mum?

Melissa: Aw, it was lovely. It wasn't awkward at all. I know we haven't seen each other in ages, but it was so nice to see her again.

SP: I'm so pleased to hear this. And the letter …

Melissa: Yes, I did it. I took it out and told her that I'd like to read her something I had written about her. It was a little strange at first, but felt more natural as it went on. I could see tears welling up in my Mums eyes as I was reading it, but I made sure I finished it. Afterwards, we just hugged each other and we both burst into tears. It was a real ice-breaker. We talked for hours then. About old times. About Dad. About what we're both doing now. It was, just, I don't know, it was so nice.

SP: So, what now …

Melissa: Oh, we've planned to meet every Wednesday morning for breakfast from now on. She's also coming to one of my gigs! She'll hate it, but it'll be great for her to see me perform. She's never seen me perform. I'm also going to watch her. She recently joined the church choir, so I'm going to that. I'm really looking forward to it, and to getting to know my Mum more. I've realized from doing this task that I'm not just a DJ, I have other roles and responsibilities in life too. I want to be a good daughter to my Mum.

From the SP adopting a Socratic approach, Melissa started to make progress in her psychological recovery. She had started to develop a greater knowledge of self, something the psychological skills used at the start of the consultation would have perhaps not have allowed. She started to develop a more multidimensional sense of self; not only was she a DJ, she was also a daughter. She realized there is more to life than her career, subsequently reducing her Melissa's re-injury anxiety, and enhancing her psychological readiness to return to the decks, thus supporting research findings from Podlog et al. (2015). Melissa also believed that upon her return to the decks, she had returned beyond her pre-injury level of psychological functioning (cf. Roy-Davis, Wadey, & Evans, 2017). Specifically, she explained that she had returned with a greater understanding of what she values in life, and how those values were now more aligned with her actions. Melissa also felt that her relationship with her mum was going from strength to strength. The above resonates with a growing body of research that illustrates that injury can be trans-formed from a potentially debilitating experience into an opportunity for growth and development (Roy-Davis et al., 2017; Salim & Wadey, 2018).

On the downside, Melissa's journey towards self-discovery also led to her ask herself challenging questions, resulting in her experiencing unpleasant emotional states (e.g., feelings of depression, sadness, regret). Perhaps due to his professional inexperience at the time, the SP felt it was best to refer Melissa to a clinical psy-chologist. Whether this referral was necessary, is up for debate. Indeed, Corlett (1996) reported:

> Referral is certainly the correct response in some situations, but not all athletic experiences of sadness, anger or doubt are rooted in psychotherapy. Many are simply difficult counselling challenges whose demands transcend mental skills training but do not, and should not, fall within the realm of clinical psychology (p. 90).

Perspective 3: The clinical psychologist's perspective

Melissa was referred to the clinical psychologist during her process of returning to the decks after she reported to her SP that she was experiencing increased feelings of depression, sadness, and regret. The emergence of these affective states even-tually led to discussions about the loss of her father, and how she had not grieved at this loss. However, prior to these discussions, and more relevant to Melissa's return to the decks, the clinical psychologist used counselling and narrative therapy (Denborough, 2014). Specifically, the therapist collaborated with Melissa to con-struct a counter-narrative that eschewed the dominant performance narrative. This involved four main themes: (a) reconceptualizing what "success" meant to her; (b) making her self-worth less fragile and contingent; (c) encouraging her to consider what life might be like following retirement from being a DJ; and (d) helping Melissa to alleviate the guilt and self-blame experienced as a result of reflecting back on how she had prioritized her career above all else. This approach proved to be beneficial for Melissa, as it allowed her to explore alternative narrative types to her dominant performance narrative. Through her work with the clinical psychologist, Melissa was able to find a different way of storying her life by being able to create a discovery narrative, which is the antithesis of the performance narrative (Douglas & Carless, 2015). A discovery narrative is a story of exploration and discovery, in which the storyteller recounts achieving success without prioritizing their performance ahead of all other areas of life. In discovery stories, the teller presents a diverse and multifaceted self, describing a life full of people, places, and experiences, using sport as a vehicle to facilitate these experiences. Signs of an exclusive identity are absent. Self-worth is not dependent on performance achievement; rather it is related to negotiating, sustaining, and valuing multiple roles and activities (Douglas & Carless, 2015).

The plot of the discovery narrative resolves around exploration of the full and multidimensional possibilities of life (Douglas & Carless, 2015). There is no single destination; rather, a multiplicity of potential journals that become available through the storyteller's opening to new experiences. Through diverse experiences over time the storyteller tells or personal growth, development and change that he or she perceives as continuing indefinitely into the future. Should winning be referred to at all, it is most likely on the basis of opening up or facilitating new opportunities and experiences. For example, one elite golfer described how she enjoyed travelling abroad to tournaments, "You're going to see new people, discover new towns, new foods, the hotel, you know, a different bed. Everything is very exciting" (Douglas & Carless, 2015, p. 94). The above example could very much relate to Melissa in that she has performed at some of the most the most iconic venues around the world in London, Paris, and New York. Despite travelling to these locations, Melissa had never experienced these cities other than commuting between her hotel room and where she was performing. However, due to her narrative therapy, this appeared to have changed upon her successful return to the decks. Melissa spoke of this during a meeting she had arranged to reconnect with PT and SP when asked about how she was feeling:

> I'm doing so well, thank-you. Really starting to enjoy life again. Ever since that injury my life has changed so dramatically. I'm spending more time with my family. Still meeting my Mum every Wednesday morning, which I love. I also really enjoy travelling now too. Rather than spending all my time in hotel rooms, when I travel abroad now, I always buy a Lonely Planet guide to make sure I explore the surrounding area. I just love exploring. I've also taken up more hobbies. I'm learning to play the guitar and have started painting. It's been brilliant to meet new people, and to develop a set of friends that aren't DJs. I don't know, I guess, I've opened myself up to life more. I'm happier, much happier.

Ethical considerations and need(s) for referral

Melissa's case had two main ethical considerations. First, the practitioners working together needed to respect client confidentiality. Although many meetings were held together (i.e., Melissa, PT, and SP), the PT and SP also held one-to-one meetings with Melissa. Therefore, during the team meetings, the practitioners needed to be mindful of which conversations were appropriate to disclose and what were not. Aligned with professional standards, this ethical issue was addressed through the practitioners engaging in reflective practice, and by gaining consent from Melissa for the PT and SP to disclose details from one-on-one consultations to each other until Melissa would say otherwise. Additional consideration emerged during the referral process to the clinical psychologist. Although not ideal, due to logistical constraints, the clinical psychologist was not a part of the primary team (PT and SP). As such, any information between the clinical psychologist, PT, and SP would be relayed through Melissa, rather than considered as part of a wider team consultation.

Case update

Two years after returning to the decks, Melissa has now retired from being a DJ. She still lives in her apartment back in Manchester (which is now furnished) and she does the occasional local gig now and then. She is a lot closer to her mum and has also reconnected with some of her school friends. She feels lucky that she does not need to work, as her life as a DJ paid well; however, she dreams of owning a music shop that sells gramophones and vinyl players. She keeps fit by doing several classes in her local gym, but she does not push her body of the limits anymore. Melissa is more compassionate to her body, listening the message it sends her. All in all, Melissa looks forward to and is excited about what the future holds for her.

Conclusion

This chapter examined Melissa's return to performance following a Grade II hamstring strain. At the return-to-decks phase, two main concerns were raised: re-injury anxiety and over-adherence. Underpinning the above were "deeper" concerns surrounding Melissa's sense of self, identity and her body-self relationship. These, as demonstrated, were linked to the broader cultural influence acting on Melissa (i.e., performance narrative). Melissa's needs were met by her primary rehabilitation team (i.e., PT, SP), by adopting a sophist (i.e., skill driven) and Socratic (i.e., rigorous personal examination) approach respectively. Upon referral, the clinical psychologist used narrative therapy to construct a counter-narrative that eschewed the dominant performance narrative. Taken together, this co-constructed intervention led to a reduction in Melissa's re-injury anxiety and regulation of over-adherence, which led to her physical and psychological readiness to return to the decks and beyond.

KEY POINTS

- Melissa, a disc jockey, suffered a Grade II hamstring strain.
- Prior to returning to the decks, consultations with the practitioners identified two main concerns: re-injury anxiety and over-adherence. These concerns were the result of how Melissa's injury threatened her identify and from her having a destructive relationship with her body.
- Melissa's case can best be explained by drawing on the multilevel model of sport injury (Wadey et al., 2018), narrative theory (Frank, 1995), and the integrated model (Wiese-Bjornstal et al., 1998).
- A multidisciplinary approach was used to address Melissa's negative concerns and actions. Specifically, the physiotherapist used simulation training and process goals, the sport psychologist took a Socratic perspective to challenge the meaning of the re-injury anxiety, and the clinical psychologist used counselling and narrative therapy to challenge the dominant cultural narrative Melissa operated within.
- The interventions co-structured with Melissa led to a reduction in her re-injury anxiety, an increase in physical and psychological readiness to return to the decks, a more compassionate body-self relationship, and the experience of growth and personal development.

CRITICAL THINKING QUESTIONS

1. How did Melissa's thoughts impact her feelings (e.g., re-injury anxiety) and actions (e.g., over-adherence)?
2. Acknowledging cultural narratives, to what extent did the performance narrative do things *on, in,* and *for* Melissa during her return to the decks?
3. Moving beyond traditional psychological skills training, what other approaches and strategies might have been effective in addressing Melissa's re-injury anxiety and over-adherence?

RESEARCH QUESTIONS

1. Does over-adherence mediate the relationship between re-injury anxiety and recovery outcomes? (e.g., return vs. non-return, physical, and/or psychological readiness)?
2. Moving beyond an intrapersonal perspective, what interpersonal, institutional, and cultural factors are influencing return to performance following injury?
3. How can injury be transformed from a potentially debilitating experience into an opportunity for personal growth and development?

KEY PUBLICATIONS

1. Corlett, J. (1996). Sophistry, Socrates, and sport psychology. *The Sport Psychologist, 10*, 84–94. doi: 10.1123/tsp.10.1.84.

This paper contrasts two philosophical approaches in professional practice (i.e., sophist and Socratic). Sophists are technique-driven and concerned with specific skills that produce successful performance results. Socratics, in contrast, encourage rigorous personal examination and improved knowledge of self. The application of each philosophy is described with examples.

2. Podlog, L., Dimmock, J., & Miller, J. (2011). A review of return to sport concerns following injury rehabilitation: Practitioner strategies for enhancing recovery outcomes. *Physical Therapy in Sport, 12*, 36–42. doi: 10.1016/j.ptsp.2010.07.005.

Underpinned by self-determination theory, this paper provides a review of return to sport concerns (e.g., re-injury anxiety, inability to perform to pre-injury standards, feelings of isolation), together with practical suggestions that practitioners can use to enhance recovery outcomes.

References

Alzate Saez de Heredia, R., Ramirez, A., & Lazaro, I. (2004). The effects of psychological response on recovery of sport injury. *Research in Sports Medicine, 12*(1), 15–31. doi:10.1080/15438620490280567.

Andersen, M. B. (2001). Returning to action and the prevention of future injury. In J. Crossman (Ed.), *Coping with sports injuries: Psychological strategies for rehabilitation* (pp. 162–173). New York, NY: Oxford University Press.

Arvinen-Barrow, M., & Hemmings, B. (2013). Goal setting in sport injury rehabilitation. In M. Arvinen-Barrow & N. Walker (Eds.), *Psychology of sport injury and rehabilitation* (pp. 56–70). Abingdon: Routledge.

Arvinen-Barrow, M., Penny, G., Hemmings, B., & Corr, S. (2010). UK chartered psychotherapists' personal experiences in using psychological interventions with injured athletes: An interpretative phenomenological analysis. *Psychology of Sport and Exercise, 11*(1), 58–66. doi:10.1016/j.psychsport.2009.05.004.

Bianco, T. M., Malo, S., & Orlick, T. (1999). Sport injury and illness: Elite skiers describe their experiences. *Research Quarterly for Exercise & Sport, 70*(2), 157–169. doi:10.1080/02701367.1999.10608033.

Brewer, B. W. (1998). Adherence to sport injury rehabilitation programs. *Journal of Applied Sport Psychology, 10*(1), 70–82. doi:10.1080/10413209808406378.

Brewer, B. W., Cornelius, A. E., Van Raalte, J. L., Brickner, J. C., Sklar, J. H., Corsetti, J. R ..., Emery, K. (2004). Rehabilitation adherence and anterior cruciate ligament outcomes. *Psychology, Health, and Medicine, 9*(2), 163–175. doi:10.1080/13548500410001670690.

Brewer, B. W., Cornelius, A. E., Van Raalte, J. L., Petitpas, A. J., Sklar, J. H., Pohlman, M. H ...Ditmar, T. D. (2000). Attributions for recovery and adherence to rehabilitation following anterior cruciate ligament reconstruction: A prospective analysis. *Psychology and Health, 15*(2), 283–291. doi:10.1080/08870440008400307.

Brewer, B. W., Jeffers, K. E., Petitpas, A. J., & Van Raalte, J. L. (1994). Perceptions of psychological interventions in the context of sport injury rehabilitation. *The Sport Psychologist*, 8(2), 176–188. doi:10.1123/tsp.8.2.176.

Brewer, B. W., Van Raalte, J. L., & Linder, D. E. (1993). Athletic identity: Hercules' muscles or Achilles' heel? *International Journal of Sport Psychology*, 24(2), 237–254.

Brukner, P. (2015). Hamstring injuries: Prevention and treatment-an update. *British Journal of Sports Medicine*, 49, 1241–1244. doi:10.1136/bjsports-2014-094427.

Cavallerio, F., Wadey, R., & Wagstaff, C. (2017). Adjusting to retirement from sport: Narratives of former competitive rhythmic gymnasts. *Qualitative Research in Sport, Exercise, and Health*, 9(5), 533–545. doi:10.1080/2159676X.2017.1335651.

Corlett, J. (1996). Sophistry, Socrates, and sport psychology. *The Sport Psychologist*, 10(1), 84–94. doi:10.1123/tsp.10.1.84.

Cox, R. (2002). The psychological rehabilitation of a severely injured rugby player. In I. Cockerill (Ed.), *Solutions in sport psychology* (pp. 159–172). London: Thompson.

Cupal, D. D., & Brewer, B. W. (2001). Effects of relaxation and guided imagery on knee strength, re-injury anxiety, and pain following anterior cruciate ligament reconstruction. *Rehabilitation Psychology*, 46(1), 28–43. doi:10.1037/0090-5550.46.1.28.

Denborough, D. (2014). *Retelling the stories of our lives: Everyday narrative therapy to draw inspiration and transform experience*. New York, NY: W. W. Norton Company.

Derscheid, G. L., & Feiring, D. C. (1987). A statistical analysis to characterize treatment adherence for the 18 most common diagnoses seen at a sports medicine clinic. *Journal of Orthopedic and Sports Physical Therapy*, 9(1), 40–46. doi:10.2519/jospt.1987.9.1.40.

Douglas, K., & Carless, D. (2009). Abandoning the performance narrative: Two women's stories of transition from professional sport. *Journal of Applied Sport Psychology*, 21(2), 213–230. doi:10.1080/10413200902795109.

Douglas, K., & Carless, D. (2015). *Life story research in sport: Understanding the experiences of elite and professional athletes through narrative*New York, NY: Routledge.

Evans, L., & Hardy, L. (2002). Injury rehabilitation: A goal-setting intervention study. *Research Quarterly for Exercise and Sport*, 73, 310–319. doi:10.1080/02701367.2002.10609025.

Evans, L., Hardy, L., & Fleming, S. (2000). Intervention strategies with injured athletes: An action research study. *The Sport Psychologist*, 14(2), 188–206. doi:10.1123/tsp.14.2.188.

Frank, A. (1995). *The wounded storyteller: Body, illness, and ethics*. Chicago, IL: University of Chicago Press.

Gould, D., Udry, E., Bridges, D., & Beck, L. (1997). Stress sources encountered when rehabilitating from season-ending ski injuries. *The Sport Psychologist*, 11(4), 361–378. doi:10.1123/tsp.11.4.361.

Granquist, M. D., Gill, D. L., & Appaneal, R. N. (2010). Development of a measure of rehabilitation adherence for athletic training. *Journal of Sport Rehabilitation*, 19(3), 249–267. doi:10.1123/jsr.19.3.249.

Harris, R. (2008). *The happiness trap: Stop struggling, start living*. London: Little, Brown Book Group: Robinson Publishing.

Hayes, S. C., & Smith, S. (2011). *Get out of our mind and into your life: The new acceptance and commitment therapy*. Oakland, CA: New Harbinger Publications.

Heil, J. (1993). *Psychology of sport injury*. Champaign, IL: Human Kinetics.

Ievleva, L., & Orlick, T. (1991). Mental links to enhanced healing: An exploratory study. *The Sport Psychologist*, 5(1), 25–40. doi:10.1123/tsp.5.1.25.

Jacobson, E. (1938). *Progressive relaxation*. Chicago, IL: University of Chicago Press.

Johnston, L. H., & Carroll, D. (1998). The context of emotional responses to athletic injury: A qualitative analysis. *Journal of Sport Rehabilitation*, 7(3), 206–220. doi:10.1123/jsr.7.3.206.

Johnston, L. H., & Carroll, D. (2000). The psychological impact of injury: Effects of prior sport and exercise involvement. *British Journal of Sports Medicine*, 34, 436–439. doi:10.1136/bjsm.34.6.436.

Kaeding, C. C., & Borchers, J. R. (2014). *Hamstring and quadriceps injuries in athletes: A clinicals guide*. New York, NY: Springer Science.

Keegan, R. (2015). *Being a sport psychologist*. London: Palgrave.

Kingston, K. M., & Hardy, L. (1997). Effects of different types of goals on processes that support performance. *The Sport Psychologist*, 11, 277–293.

Kvist, J., Ek, A., Sporrstedt, K., & Good, L. (2005). Fear of re-injury: A hindrance for returning to sports after anterior cruciate ligament reconstruction. *Knee Surgery, Sports Traumatology, Arthroscopy*, 13(5), 393–397.

LeJeune, C. (2007). *The worry trap: How to free yourself from worry and anxiety using acceptance and commitment therapy*. Oakland, CA: New Harbinger Publications.

Levy, A. R., Polman, R. C. J., Clough, P. J., & McNaughton, L. R. (2006). Adherence to sport injury rehabilitation programmes: A conceptual review. *Research in Sports Medicine*, 14(2), 149–162.

McGannon, K. R., & Smith, B. (2015). Centralizing culture in cultural sport psychology research: The potential of narrative inquiry and discursive psychology. *Psychology of Sport & Exercise*, 17(1), 79–87. doi:10.1016/j.psychsport.2014.07.010.

Papathomas, A., & Lavallee, D. (2014). Self-starvation and the performance narrative in competitive sport. *Psychology of Sport & Exercise*, 15(6), 688–695. doi:10.1016/j.psychsport.2013.10.014.

Pizzari, T., Taylor, N. F., McBurney, H., & Feller, J. A. (2005). Adherence to rehabilitation after anterior cruciate ligament reconstructive surgery: Implications for outcome. *Journal of Sport Rehabilitation*, 14(3), 201–214. doi:10.1123/jsr.14.3.202.

Podlog, L., Banham, S. M., Wadey, R., & Hannon, J. C. (2015). Psychological readiness to return to competitive sport following injury: A qualitative study. *The Sport Psychologist*, 29(1), 1–14. doi:10.1123/tsp.2014-0063.

Podlog, L., Dimmock, J. A., & Miller, J. (2011). A review of return to sport concerns following injury rehabilitation: Practitioner strategies for enhancing recovery outcomes. *Physical Therapy in Sport*, 12(1), 36–42. doi:10.1016/j.ptsp.2010.07.005.

Podlog, L., & Eklund, R. C. (2006). A longitudinal investigation of competitive athletes' return to sport following serious injury. *Journal of Applied Sport Psychology*, 18(1), 44–68. doi:10.1080/10413200500471319.

Podlog, L., & Eklund, R. C. (2007). The psychosocial aspects of a return to sport following serious injury: A review of the literature from a self-determination perspective. *Psychology of Sport & Exercise*, 8(4), 535–566. doi:10.1016/j.psychsport.2006.07.008.

Podlog, L., Gao, Z., Kenow, L., Kleinert, J., Granquist, M. D., Newton, M., & Hannon, J. (2013). Injury rehabilitation overadherence: Preliminary scale validation and relationships with athletic identity and self-presentation concerns. *Journal of Athletic Training*, 48(3), 372–381. doi:10.4085/1062-6050-48.2.20.

Ravizza, K. (1993). Increasing awareness for sport performance. In J. M. Williams (Ed.), *Applied sport psychology: Personal growth to peak performance* (2nd ed., pp. 148–155). Mountain View, CA: Mayfield Publishing.

Roy-Davis, K., Wadey, R., & Evans, L. (2017). A grounded theory of sport injury-related growth. *Sport, Exercise and Performance Psychology*, 9(4), 35–52. doi:10.1080/2159676X.2017.1328460.

Salim, J., & Wadey, R. (2018). Can emotional disclosure promote sport injury-related growth? *Journal of Applied Sport Psychology*, 30(4), 367–387. doi:10.1080/10413200.2017.1417338.

Seligman, M. E. P., Steen, T. A., Park, N., & Peterson, C. (2005). Positive psychology progress: Empirical validation of interventions. *American Psychologist*, 60(5), 410–421. doi:10.1037/0003–066X.60.5.410.

Smith, B., & Sparkes, A. C. (2002). Men, sport, spinal cord injury, and the construction of coherence: Narrative practice in action. *Qualitative Research*, 2(2), 143–171. doi:10.1177/146879410200200202.

Smith, B., & Sparkes, A. C. (2004). Men, sport, and spinal cord injury: An analysis of metaphors and narrative types. *Disability and Society*, 19(6), 613–626. doi:10.1080/0968759042000252533.

Smith, B., & Sparkes, A. C. (2005). Men, sport, spinal cord injury, and narratives of hope. *Social Science and Medicine*, 61(5), 1095–1105. doi:10.1016/j.socscimed.2005.01.011.

Smith, B., & Sparkes, A. C. (2009). Narrative inquiry in sport and exercise psychology: What can it mean, and why might we do it? *Psychology of Sport & Exercise*, 10(1), 1–11. doi:10.1016/j.psychsport.2008.01.004.

Sparkes, A., & Partington, S. (2003). Narrative practice and its potential contribution to sport psychology: The example of flow. *The Sport Psychologist*, 17(3), 292–317. doi:10.1123/tsp.17.3.292.

Treacy, S. H., Barron, O. A., Brunet, M. E., & Barrack, R. L. (1997). Assessing the need for extensive supervised rehabilitation following arthroscopic surgery. *American Journal of Orthopedics*, 26(1), 25–29.

Wadey, R., Day, M., Cavallerio, F., & Martinelli, L. (2018). The multi-level model of sport injury: Can coaches impact and be impacted by injury? In R. Thelwell & M. Dicks (Eds.), *Professional advances in sports coaching: Research and practice*. Abingdon: Routledge.

Walker, N., Thatcher, J., & Lavallee, D. (2010). A preliminary development of the re-injury anxiety inventory (RIAI). *Physical Therapy in Sport*, 11(1), 23–29.

Walker, N., Thatcher, J., Lavallee, D., & Golby, J. (2004). The emotional response to athletic injury: Re-injury anxiety. In D. Lavallee, J. Thatcher & M. V. Jones (Eds.), *Coping and emotion in sport* (pp. 91–103). Hauppauge, NY: Nova Science.

Wiese-Bjornstal, D. M., Smith, A. M., Shaffer, S. M., & Morrey, M. A. (1998). An integrated model of response to sport injury: Psychological and sociological dynamics. *Journal of Applied Sport Psychology*, 10(1), 46–69. doi:10.1080/10413209808406377.

10

REACTIONS TO A CAREER-ENDING SPORT INJURY

Pekka Hirvonen, a professional ice hockey player

Montse C. Ruiz, Satu Kaski, Päivi Frantsi, and Claudio Robazza

Keywords: 33-year-old male, professional ice hockey, forced retirement, athletic identity, coping, pre-retirement planning, multi-ligament knee injury

Case description

Pekka Hirvonen (this name is a pseudonym and used for descriptive purposes only), is a 33-year-old professional ice hockey player, who suffered a multi-ligament knee injury during a regular practice session. A detailed evaluation of the injury revealed that his medial collateral (MCL), anterior cruciate (ACL), and posterior (PCL) cruciate ligaments were torn with medial meniscus damage and needed reconstructive surgery. His initial response to his injury was: "this is no big deal. I am a strong, healthy ice hockey player. I have been through worse. Let's get this fixed." Pekka remained very positive throughout his medical care and post-surgery rehabilitation, and according to his physiotherapist, the rehabilitation process went well. Pekka did notice some periodical swelling and pain in his knee during rehabilitation, but said that it was "something a little ice and sisu[1] would take care of". However, at his three-month post-surgery evaluation, his orthopaedic surgeon revealed that the ligament repair went well, but the meniscus repair was unsuccessful, and that Pekka needed a meniscectomy. The surgeon also indicated that because of the extent of this second surgery, it was very likely that Pekka would not be able to return back to professional sport. This medical judgement was a huge shock to Pekka. He had been playing hockey from the age of 5. Even during primary school, he knew he wanted to be a professional hockey player. In all his life choices, hockey had always come first.

Prior to his multi-ligament injury, Pekka had played his best season and the expectations from the coaches and the club were high. Pekka's plans were to return back to the ice for a few more years "I cannot believe this is happening. If

I don't have this meniscectomy, my career is over. If I do have this surgery … my career is still over. I mean, I am a 33-year old guy who has played ice hockey all his life. I am a hockey player. What else could I even do?" On that evening, Pekka went home and could not sleep. Pekka kept tossing and turning in his bed and thinking: "What am I going to do? I cannot support my family if I don't play hockey. I wish I had listened to my parents when they insisted that I should get an education." As a hockey player, Pekka had always been able to deal with any worrying thoughts and stressors that came his way, and many considered him mentally and physically strong. However, this time it was different. Pekka felt overwhelmed, he did not know how to deal with all of this. The unforeseen end to his career as a professional ice hockey player meant his wife Nina and two children, Onni (8 years old) and Ilona (6 years old) would face a great financial loss. Being high school sweethearts, Pekka and Nina had been married for over ten years, and hockey had always been at the core of things, determining how and where they lived. Nina was a hockey wife. She had sacrificed her professional career to support Pekka, and when their children were born, she focused on the family. As Nina put it: "family comes first … I want to support Pekka in pursuit of his dreams, and you know, if you want to get things in life, you have to make sacrifices. The future will pay off."

After the second surgery, Pekka stayed home and refused to answer the phone, or to participate in any conversations with the club officials, coaches, or even his loved ones. Pekka felt overwhelmed by all of this, and thought that he was just a big disappointment to everyone. "I have let my family, coaches, and teammates down. So shameful that a grown man can't take care of his business. How weak is that?" Over the next few weeks, Nina became increasingly worried about Pekka and his behaviour. Nina has noticed that Pekka had become increasingly withdrawn from his family and friends. For example, Pekka and his closest teammates would typically spend one night a week together playing videogames, and have a sauna, but since his injury, Pekka has not seen his teammates at all. When asked about it, Pekka stated: "I cannot go there and be reminded about how my body has betrayed me."

One month on, nothing had really changed. Pekka was still very withdrawn, and took strong painkillers to ease the physical pain and discomfort. At times, the pain was so intense that Pekka got angry and relieved his anger by punching a wall or breaking objects. Pekka appeared to struggle with normal daily activities, he was eating and sleeping too much, and was annoyed by his children. "They are so annoying. All they want to do is play with me. Can't they see that I just want to rest?" At times, Pekka found himself recalling the good times and his past achievements, which quickly turned into despair. "I could have been so much better, and achieved so much more. Now I have nothing." Overwhelmed by the whole situation, it was at this point when his wife Nina decided to call Pekka's coach for help. After all, the coach had been Pekka's confidant for several years, and knew him better than anyone else.

The injury

The anterior cruciate (ACL) and posterior cruciate (PCL) ligaments enable the knee to support the body's weight and provide front-to-back and rotational stability, while the medial collateral ligament (MCL) helps support the inside of the knee providing side-to-side stability (Parkar, 2016; Phisitkul, James, Wolf, & Amendola, 2006). In the case of Pekka, the ACL, PCL, MCL, and meniscus were torn after receiving a strong impact to the knee while his foot was fixed on the ground. Typically, individuals with this type of injury experience pain, loss of knee motion, swelling and instability (Millett, Wickiewicz, & Warren, 2001). Early surgical intervention before scar tissue forms is usually required. Treatment usually involves surgical repair/reconstruction to regain stability and the function of the torn ligaments (Laprade & Wijdicks, 2012). The rehabilitation process is painful and lengthy. Recovery can start after swelling subsides. Early rehabilitation may start with exercise on a stationary bike. Later exercises involve more intense training aimed at improving the range of motion and strength.

Key factor 1: Athletic identity

One of the factors affecting Pekka's responses to his career-ending injury was his identity. An individual's identity, which refers to the traits, social relations, roles, and social group memberships that define who one is (Oyserman, Elmore, & Smith, 2012), is considered one of the most critical psychological constructs that influence their transition out of sport (Arvinen-Barrow, Hurley, & Ruiz, 2017; Brewer, Cornelius, Stephan, & Van Raalte, 2010).

Athletic identity has been defined as "the degree to which an individual identifies with the athlete role" (Brewer, Van Raalte, & Linder, 1993, p. 237). A strong athletic identity is present when athletes identify their self-worth in terms of their participation and achievement in sports to the exclusion of other activities. An individual with a strong athletic identity may perceive transitioning out of sport as threatening as they may have little input to support their sense of self-worth once they retire from their sport (Taylor & Ogilvie, 1994). Research has shown that athletes with a high athletic identity, when forced to retire due to injury, may be prone to experience unpleasant emotions, dissatisfaction with time of retirement, and adjustment difficulties (Alfermann, Stambulova, & Zemaityte, 2004; Arvinen-Barrow et al., 2017; Mankad, Gordon, & Wallman, 2009; Webb, Nasco, Riley, & Headrick, 1998), viewing retirement as something that is lost and cannot be recovered (Werthner & Orlick, 1982).

A widely used tool to assess athletic identity is the Athletic Identity Measurement Scale (AIMS; Brewer & Cornelius, 2001). The AIMS is a 7-item self-report tool that measures athletic identity and the strength and exclusivity of the athletic role. The scale includes three subscales assessing social identity, exclusivity, and negative affectivity, rated on a 6-point Likert scale (0 = strongly disagree; 5 = strongly agree). The AIMS is characterized by sound psychometric properties, with reported adequate internal consistency on samples of American athletes representing diverse sports. The AIMS is available in several languages other than English (e.g., Chinese, Dutch, German, Portuguese, Russian). In Pekka's case, since there is no Finnish version available, the practitioner could use the English version, given that Pekka had good English skills.

Key factor 2: Pre-retirement planning

Pekka faced a serious adjustment crisis due to the non-existence of a pre-retirement plan. Retirement planning refers to the individuals' long-term effort in preparation for the end of their career and is typically associated with realistic expectations of retirement and clear long-term goals. Pekka, who suffered a non-normative injury after which he expected to recover and return to sport, had not considered a future without sports until he was faced with it. Pre-retirement planning is a valuable resource that can significantly impact the quality of the adaptation to career transition and effective coping (Arvinen-Barrow, DeGrave, Pack, & Hemmings, in press; Arvinen-Barrow et al., 2017; Arvinen-Barrow, Nässi, & Ruiz, 2015; Stambulova, 2000). Research has shown that pre-retirement planning is predictive of changes in athletes' psychological health, with the existence of planning being associated with a more successful transition out of sport compared to those who do not have an alternative plan (Lavallee, 2005; Roberts, Mullen, Evans, & Hall, 2015; Stoltenburg, Kamphoff, & Lindstrom Bremer, 2011). Equally, athletes involved in sports that require a large amount of their time and energy appear to have no time for pre-retirement planning during their careers (Lavallee, 2005).

There are different career and education programs offered by Olympic Centres (e.g., Australia, Canada, USA) to help athletes in preparing for the life after sport. In the USA, professional sports teams such as the National Hockey League (NHL), National Football League (NFL), and National Basketball Association (NBA) also offer career-counselling services or pension plans to their members. Unfortunately, such services are not as common in Finland, and of the services available, Pekka had not considered them as important, since his intentions were to play professional ice hockey for the following five years. "I was planning to get around to it … I mean all these income protection insurances are out there, I just did not think I needed them yet."

Key factor 3: Coping skills

In Pekka's case, it appears he does not possess adequate skills to cope with his abrupt career transition. For him, transitioning out of sport had become a stressful situation, involving several financial, occupational, emotional, and social adjustments. Coping skills are important factors influencing the quality of the adjustment to athletic retirement (Grove, Lavallee, & Gordon, 1997; Stambulova, Stephan, & Jäphag, 2007). Coping has been defined as "constantly changing cognitive and behavioural efforts to manage specific external and/or internal demands that are appraised as taxing or exceeding the resources of the person" (Lazarus & Folkman, 1984, p. 141). Lazarus and Folkman distinguished between problem-focused coping, which targets the stressor involving plans or actions to change a situation causing distress, and emotion-focused coping, aimed at managing emotional distress, typically used when the individuals perceived that the situation could not be modified. Research indicates that athletes with strong athletic identities may fail to develop appropriate coping skills, and thus be more vulnerable to career transition difficulties (Crook & Robertson, 1991). The way in which individuals appraise their injury may trigger different emotional responses and could lead to using diverse strategies for coping (Grove et al., 1997; Lazarus, 2006).

To assess coping strategies, practitioners can use either the COPE inventory (Carver, Scheier, & Weintraub, 1989) or the sport version of the tool, the Modified-COPE (MCOPE; Crocker & Graham, 1995). The COPE (Carver et al., 1989) is a widely used 60-item self-report that assesses 15 different ways in which people cope with stress including problem- and emotion-focused coping strategies. The MCOPE (Crocker & Graham, 1995) comprises 12 scales assessing active coping, planning, suppression of competing activities, seeking instrumental social support, seeking emotional social support, denial, humour, venting of emotion, behavioural disengagement, wishful thinking, self-blame, and increased effort.

Theoretical considerations

Taylor and Ogilvie's (1994) conceptual model of adaptation to career transition provides a useful framework to conceptualize the career transition process. The model integrates theoretical and empirical findings addressing relevant aspects in the career transition process from sport to the post-career, focusing on the reasons for their sport career retirement. According to Taylor and Ogilvie's model, there are five basic stages to consider when assisting athletes in their transition: (1) the cause for career termination; (2) the adaptation to the transition; (3) available resources; (4) the quality of transition; and (5) interventions. The main causes for termination of sports career may depend on age, de-selection, the consequences of an injury, and free choice. A career-ending injury, considered as the most negative transition in sport, may trigger a wide range of unpleasant emotions, and cause various degrees of physical disabilities, which may limit the choices of new careers (Arvinen-Barrow et al., 2017). Important factors related to athletes' adaptation involve the extent of the psychological, social, financial, and occupational changes, as well as athletes' self- and social identity, and perceived control. Athletes' adaptation to career transition depends on the availability of resources, such as coping strategies, social support, and pre-retirement planning (Stambulova et al., 2007). These factors need to be considered in interventions aimed at addressing the potentially negative psychosocial consequences of career transition crises.

When applying Taylor and Ogilvie's (1994) model to Pekka's case, it is clear that the involuntary nature of his career termination, mainly caused by a severe and unexpected injury, was indicative of a post-retirement adjustment crisis. Pekka's strong athletic identity was helpful after the first surgery, because it has been associated with a positive attitude towards the rehabilitation process. However, his initial reaction after the second surgery and being informed that he would not be able to return to sport was perceived as a shock, and appraised as a loss. The lack of available resources, pre-retirement planning in particular, was threatening Pekka's quality of adaptation and having negative consequences for his family. As evidenced in the case, Pekka had poor coping skills to deal with the situation, in that he used avoidance-based coping strategies (e.g., denial, mental, and behavioural disengagement) instead of problem-focused techniques. Altogether, his strong athletic identity, negative appraisal of the situation and lack of available resources had adverse psychosocial consequences for his transition out of sport and well-being.

Interprofessional plan of care

Following his initial injury, different health professionals were involved in Pekka's plan of care. His primary rehabilitation team consisted of the team orthopaedic surgeon, the physician, and the physiotherapist. The physiotherapist was in charge of Pekka's post-surgery rehabilitation. Following standard procedures within the ice hockey team Pekka played for, the team physician referred Pekka to a certified sport psychologist (SP) immediately after Pekka's first surgery. There was no previous relationship between Pekka and the SP. Following the first surgery, the physiotherapist and the SP worked with Pekka with the goal of full recovery and return to sport. After the second surgery, however, it was clear that Pekka would not be able to return to professional sport. As a result, the focus of the plan of care shifted, and the goal of Pekka's physiotherapist was to decrease his pain and work with him on functional recovery exercises.

The role of the SP also changed following the second surgery. The SP focused on psychological adjustment, with a goal of facilitating successful transition out of sport. The intervention plan of care sought to address the psychological, behavioural, and social impact of retirement. Since Pekka exhibited behavioural signs of poor coping, and emotional and behavioural disengagement (refusing to answer the phone or to talk), especially with his loved ones, it was decided that including Pekka's wife and coach to his care team would be beneficial. Thus, the three met with Pekka's permission. It was decided that the objective would be to increase Pekka's awareness of the transition process and demands to help him cope with traumatic experiences and stress-related emotions, and restore his self-esteem. The process also focused on a realistic evaluation of available resources, possible barriers, and coping strategies for a successful transition to life out of competitive sport. Part of this process would be that Nina too attends Pekka's sessions with the SP when relevant.

Perspective 1: The certified sport psychologist's perspective

Pekka met the SP immediately following the initial injury, after the first surgery. Much of the early sessions were focused on the rehabilitation process, goal setting, subsequent rehabilitation, and successful return to sport. However, this changed after Pekka was told he would not be able to return to professional ice hockey. During his first meeting with the SP after the devastating news, Pekka verbalized that he was "scared, afraid about what the future will bring, and not sure now what is there for me." When prompted further, Pekka explained: "I think that I'm in a vicious circle and can't find the way out. I feel that everything is falling apart. I think that my life has no meaning. Why do I get this kind of punishment?" The initial discussion with Pekka made clear that he perceived the end of his athletic career as a traumatic experience. Pekka demonstrated appraisals of athletic identity loss, and it was evident that he had not yet processed his transition out of sport. This had triggered a range of stress-related emotions, which in turn had negative psychological, behavioural, and social impact on Pekka.

It was at this point that the SP decided to switch his approach to working with Pekka. Instead of using a practical cognitive-behavioural therapy founded on goal setting, the SP decided to utilize a more person-cantered trauma-informed therapy. The sessions focused on creating a supportive environment where Pekka could express his emotions, providing a realistic perspective to consider life after sport, mobilizing his resources, and developing skills to cope with this transition.

The purpose of the first session after the devastating news was on conducting an initial assessment of the situation and creating a supportive environment. It was also important to give Pekka the opportunity to share his thoughts and express his feelings. Pekka was asked to provide a detailed account of what happened. The role of the SP was to actively listen to Pekka and give him the opportunity to fully recall and recount the event as he had experienced it. The recall and reconstruction of the incident was painful, but a step-wise approach to his crisis intervention made it easier to structure the whole story of what happened in his mind. The goal of this type of intervention was to help Pekka become aware of what had happened and the significance of it all for himself and for his own life (Hillman, 2002).

During the sessions, Pekka experienced a wide range of intense emotions. These included sadness, anger, relief, and anxiety, to name a few. In most sessions, Pekka cried intensively, which was something he would not typically do at home or with his peers. He repeatedly wondered what he could have done differently. Sometimes it was very difficult for Pekka to talk about his injury and its consequences, and he felt that coping with it all with a brave face was important:

> The feeling of shame is really strong and I do refuse to go to all social happenings, celebrations, etc. People are asking, how is it going and how is your knee? I give unclear answers, because I think that accepting it would be a sign of weakness, and the truth is very painful. It is better to stay away than answer people's questions. Giving explanations is really frustrating and it hurts. When

you are in trouble and feeling physical and psychological pain, you easily think that it is not anyone else's business.

At times, Pekka's grief was palpable. The SP remained present in Pekka's grief, being patient and giving him time to deal with it. Every time grief was experienced and dealt with, the healing process moved forward, and the next time the experience was less intense. Addressing this requires an effective use of time, silences, and professional skills (Mischke-Reeds, 2018):

> PEKKA: This is terrible … I don't know how I am going to survive this …
> SP: [Nodding, silence] … Would you tell me how you are feeling now when you are sitting there?
> PEKKA: Awful …
> SP: Hmmm … where does the awfulness feel in your body?
> PEKKA: [Silence … touching his chest] … In the chest [Pause] … It is terrible, why just me?
> SP: [nods, sits in silence … [Pause] How do you feel now, when talking about it?
> PEKKA: Angry.

Silence in itself, in particular when dealing with traumatic experiences, can be perceived as the inability to address the individual's needs. However, silence is part of non-verbal communication and should reflect active listening associated with the effective reception of information. When accompanied with other appropriate forms of non-verbal communication, such as making direct eye contact and nodding to confirm understanding, silence can transmit the idea of being actively involved in listening and able to fully understand the individual's needs (Weinberg & Gould, 2015). The role of the SP was to give Pekka time to deal with his emotions (anger, anxiety, grief), at the same time ensuring that he took care of himself and was involved in the family's daily routines. Family support can have a beneficial influence on the process of adjustment and protect from the negative impact of stressors (Venter & Grobbelaar, 2018). Specific questions such as "What have you eaten today with your family?", or "What are you going to do with your family when you leave from here?" were used to help Pekka cope with the situation one session at the time. When Pekka displayed signs of acceptance, such as being able to think about other things outside his shock of forced retirement from ice hockey, then the focus of the sessions shifted towards increasing his coping strategies and well-being.

To foster emotion self-regulation, namely, down-regulation of unpleasant emotions and up-regulation of pleasant emotions (see Robazza & Ruiz, 2018), the SP taught Pekka meditation and relaxation strategies (Walker & Heaney, 2013). Pekka was given audio exercises to practice at home and incorporate into his daily routine. In a similar manner, imagery was used to help Pekka down-regulate his anxiety and create a pleasant experience (Arvinen-Barrow, Clement, & Hemmings,

2013). For example, Pekka was asked to find a comfortable sitting position, take a few deep breaths, notice his bodily sensations, and imagine a warm wave of healing relaxation flowing throughout his whole body.

After some practice, Pekka used imagery to be prepared and cope with possible unpleasant emotions arising when confronting (Gross, 2014) situations that reminded him of his injury and triggered anxiety. As Pekka indicated "using imagery was useful before going to places that were threatening, such as going to the ice rink for a teammate's farewell party". In these situations, Pekka was also taught to focus on his breathing with a goal to calm down. This is consistent with Gross' process model of emotion regulation in which distracting attention away from the disturbing emotional cues of a situation and redirecting the focus on non-emotional aspects (e.g., relaxation and breathing) are viewed as part of the emotion regulation process.

The SP also used eye movement desensitization and reprocessing (EMDR; Shapiro, 2017) to help Pekka deal with stress. Eye movement desensitization and reprocessing is a therapeutic technique used to block the deleterious consequences of traumatic memories and related negative imagery. It was found effective in the treatment of post-traumatic disorders and a range of clinical issues (Luber, 2016), and has also been applied in sport (e.g., Falls, Barker, & Turner, 2018). It involves identifying specific situations, triggers, emotional and physical symptoms, and negative self-referencing statements linked to past, present, and future issues. Then, the person is asked to visually follow the predetermined sequence of rapid and rhythmic movement of the psychologist's fingers shifting from side to side across the range of eye movement. During this bilateral stimulation the person is required to pay attention to their own experience with a sense of mastery and more adaptive interpretations with respect to the traumatic event. Hand taps and auditory tones are used in case of visual impairments of eye movement intolerance. Prior to the teaching and implementation of this strategy, it was deemed necessary for Pekka to process previous experiences connected with personal traumatic experiences. This process in Pekka's words was "scary in the beginning, like watching a movie". However, after a couple of sessions he felt more distant to the traumatic incidence and felt that it was easier to cope with the anxiety. Gradually, he was able to include daily activities like watching an ice hockey match. He began to perceive that his mental well-being had improved and felt more energetic.

Counselling Pekka through retirement involved addressing his thoughts and emotions related to his adaptation to the current situation and his future. Once Pekka had processed his initial shock and grief, the sessions focused on helping him adjust his perceptions about himself to his new roles out of sport (e.g., starting a new business), to experience feelings of value and self-worth outside of ice hockey, and being more present in his relationships with his family.

Overall, Pekka's recovery process was slow and intensive. From the onset of the injury, Pekka met the SP once every second week. Following his devastating news, Pekka met the SP twice a week. After the initial shock phase, the frequency of the meetings was reduced to once a week, then to every second week, and in the final stages to once a month. Overall, Pekka's SP consultancy sessions lasted two years.

Perspective 2: The wife's perspective

When Nina approached Pekka's coach, she felt that watching her husband suffer in silence was affecting their family life. Pekka's injury was a shock to his family, and with Nina being a hockey wife, she too was tangibly affected by Pekka's transition out of sport. Although Nina was practically responsible for all everyday chores, Pekka was the emotional pillar for their family. Their two children, Onni and Ilona, were initially enjoying the idea that they could spend more time at home with their father, but they quickly realized that this would not be the case as Pekka was often angry and withdrawn from social interactions. As a consequence, the children reduced the interaction with their father to avoid irritating him. "It is like living on eggshells", Nina explained to her friends. "I know things are hard for him, but so it is for us too. I mean, I am worried about future, and how we can financially survive, and I am worried about Pekka and our family life. When I bring things up with Pekka, it is constant arguing. So I am starting to avoid interactions with him. And that's not healthy for any of us."

In the struggle to help her husband, Nina joined him in one of the sessions with the SP. Nina wanted to be able to share her feelings and to find a way to help her husband. For Pekka and Nina, being able to share feelings and listen to each other was very productive and brought with it a sense of relief. Nina discussed how she had been trying to support Pekka, by listening and providing an environment facilitative of conversation and how this had backfired. Pekka was dispirited while listening to his wife, as he found himself in a situation he had done nothing to create, but he and his family were suffering the consequences. When it was Pekka's turn to share his feelings, he opened up for the first time since the injury occurrence, and it made Nina deeply emotional.

Nina's experiences are not unique, in that the impact of career-ending injuries often extends beyond the injured athlete. According to a systemic approach to family therapy (Rivett & Buchmüller, 2018), communication provides the essence of a relationship. In addition, it is not possible not to communicate within a system, and any behaviour including silence is a form of communication. Pekka's avoidance to talk, triggered Nina's interaction withdrawal, and feeling depressed, which resulted in a circular and negative spiral, as Pekka blamed himself for this. Thus, the SP encouraged them to share their feelings for at least 15 minutes every day.

With the assistance of the SP, Nina was able to provide emotional support through physical presence, love and acceptance, empathy, and encouragement facilitating a sense of comfort and security. She also helped Pekka recover self-esteem through enacting behaviours such as involving him in daily activities and routines, and demonstrating belief in Pekka's ability to cope. Nina attempted to engage in active listening while refraining from making judgements, sharing positive and negative thoughts and feelings associated with the transition process. By planning and organizing activities with family friends, Nina offered a shared social reality, where she tried to restore social interactions and to provide a sense of normalcy. The SP, Nina, and Pekka agreed that Nina would come back to a session in a month time.

Perspective 3: The coach's perspective

Pekka was a highly regarded player by his coach, who had high expectations for him. Their relationship was one in which Pekka (as well as all players in the team) could express his thoughts and feelings in a genuine manner. The injury was also shocking news for the coach, who felt sad for Pekka not only for the consequences to his athletic career but also personally. The coach had been Pekka's confidant throughout his career and Pekka trusted him and had previously discussed even personal issues. From the onset of Pekka's injury, the coach as well as his team members were supportive at the early stages of the rehabilitation process and remained in contact by phone. After Pekka's second surgery, and once they knew he would not be able to play hockey again, the coach tried to remain in contact with him. Pekka, however, was not responding to phone calls. Pekka felt that his coach would stop calling and at some point lose interest on him. Typically, in situations where athletes face a career-ending injury, coaches have responsibilities to the rest of the team, and may not have as much time to devote to the injured athlete (Udry, 2001).

After a time without any news, the coach received Nina's phone call, who was overwhelmed by the whole situation. His attempts to talk to Pekka some room were unsuccessful, thus, he decided to take a step back and give Pekka some room to assimilate the situation. When Pekka started showing signs of acceptance and thinking what life could look like apart from being a professional player, the SP also contacted the coach and they shared ideas about how to facilitate a successful transition out of sport.

During an initial meeting with Pekka, the coach provided examples of athletes who had suffered career-ending injuries and were able to make a successful transition out of sport, and are currently integrated in society. Then the coach connected Pekka with another athlete who had suffered a career-ending injury a few years back. This helped Pekka realize that there were other people who have also suffered traumatic incidents, and allowed him to share his experiences with someone who could empathetically understand his struggles.

According to Podlog and Dionigi (2010), self-determination theory (SDT; Deci & Ryan, 1985; Ryan & Deci, 2017) provides a framework to examine coaches' strategies for addressing athletes' psychosocial challenges in returning to sport following injury rehabilitation. The theory emphasizes the importance of satisfying individual psychological needs for competence, autonomy, and relatedness. Needs satisfaction results in enhanced well-being, self-development, and self-determined behaviour, social functioning, and task involvement in a variety of settings. Competence reflects the perceptions of effectiveness in one's interactions with the environment, autonomy is typified by the belief that one's actions are volitional, and relatedness denotes a sense of connectedness with others. Self-determination theory can be used as a framework to develop a strategy where individuals transfer their athletic skills to other tasks within the sporting context or in other contexts. The coach was very instrumental in keeping Pekka involved in the team. For example, he was assisting Pekka in transferring his skills (competence) as a former athlete, and capitalizing on such skills, providing opportunities for Pekka to assist him in tasks such as organizing team activities, planning sessions and drills, or sharing his own experiences with novice athletes (autonomy). The coach explained to the other members of the team the new role that Pekka had on the team by acknowledging his unique competences and skills, in an effort to have him accepted and maintain his social involvement (relatedness) and social identity as a person. He also introduced Pekka to relevant people within the hockey player development network, which allowed him to develop new skills and a professional identity. Overall, the coach's intervention was very useful in helping Pekka make a successful transition out of competitive sport to establish a professional career.

During this intervention the coach was able to respond appropriately to Pekka's needs displaying positive interaction skills. The intervention, indeed, was characterized by closeness, commitment, complementarity, and co-orientation, in accordance with Shanmugam and Jowett (2017) conceptualization. Closeness was characterized by the coach and Pekka valuing and supporting each other. Commitment was reflected in the intent to maintain the relationship and continuing working with each other. Complementarity was manifested in reciprocal care in the relationship between the two of them. Finally, co-orientation represented the common ground that allowed both to share thoughts and plans for the future.

Ethical consideration(s)

In accordance with the American Psychological Association's standards for practice, as specified in the Ethical Principles of Psychologists and Code of Conduct (American Psychological Association, 2010) psychologists working with clients should possess appropriate education training and supervised experience prior to providing services to make sure that such services are within the boundaries of their competence. A key principle is the obligation that psychologists have to protect confidential information gathered during consultations. Only with the appropriate consent from the individual may psychologists disclose confidential information to others, unless law mandates it for valid specific purposes such as to protect the client, psychologist or others from harm. In the case of Pekka, the SP asked for his permission to meet with his wife Nina and the coach, and disclosed information they had agreed beforehand, appropriate for his adaptation and successful transition out of sport.

Case update

As indicated earlier, Pekka held regular meetings with the SP for two years post-injury occurrence. During this time, he had an opportunity to retrain himself to a new profession, which he successfully completed. We are pleased to note that despite his difficult career transition, Pekka and Nina are happily married and he has remained involved in ice hockey. Collaborating with the hockey player development network, and later working for the network has helped Pekka develop a professional identity. He now feels a sense of satisfaction "giving back" to the sport that gave him so much. He has also started a new business.

Conclusion

Pekka, a professional ice hockey player described in this case study, suffered a multi-ligament knee injury during a practice session. He received early medical care and a surgical intervention, with a positive prognosis and post-rehabilitation process. A three-month post-surgery evaluation revealed that a second surgery was needed to repair Pekka's meniscus, which resulted in the end of his career. A plan of care was implemented involving several medical health professionals. A SP, Pekka's wife and his coach interacted closely with Pekka during the process of transition out of sport. The intervention focused on Pekka's psychological adjustment and provision of help to make a successful transition out of sport. Once it was clear that Pekka would not be able to return to sport, the SP worked with Pekka to help him deal with his emotions, have a realistic view of available resources, and develop skills to cope with his transition. The role of his wife was directly related to the provision of several types of support, while the intervention from the coach was facilitative in establishing a professional career. The overall intervention resulted in a successful transition to professional life.

KEY POINTS

- Pekka, a professional ice hockey player, suffered a multi-ligament knee injury that needed reconstructive surgery.
- After two surgeries, Pekka was informed that he would not be able to return to sport.
- Pekka's strong athletic identity, lack of pre-retirement planning, negative appraisals of the situation and lack of appropriate coping skills to deal with his emotions influenced his adjustment to athletic retirement.
- To address Pekka's emotional reactions and facilitate a successful transition out of sport, a SP, his wife, and his coach were involved in the process. In particular the SP utilized a trauma-informed therapy approach (e.g. EMDR) to help Pekka deal with his stress-related experiences, while his wife and the

coach were sources of support, and instrumental in facilitating a successful transition.

- Pekka was able to accept his situation and to develop a professional identity (e.g., working in ice hockey development network and developing a business).

CRITICAL THINKING QUESTIONS

1. How did Pekka's strong athletic identity affect his transition out of sport?
2. What other aspects of Pekka's psychosocial environment may have played an important role in his transition?
3. Each person involved in Pekka's transition out of sport used different strategies to address his needs. What are other possible alternative strategies that could have been used? Why do you think they would be effective?

RESEARCH QUESTIONS

1. What is the role of the coach, family members, and teammates in the transition out of sport after a career-ending injury?
2. What psychological strategies can be used to help individuals retire from sport after an injury?
3. How can a coach, a family, teammates, and other professionals interact to assist in an individual's transition out of sport?

KEY PUBLICATIONS

1. Park, S., Lavallee, D., & Tod, D. (2013). Athletes' career transition out of sport: A systematic review. *International Review of Sport and Exercise Psychology, 6*(1), 22–53. doi: 10.1080/1750984X.2012.687053.

This paper presents a systematic review of 126 studies related to athletes' career transition out of sport. The review focuses on sample characteristics, with studies including from 1 to 1617 participants of both genders involved in all competition levels, and psychological correlates associated with athletes' career transition quality. The review presents several factors related to the quality of the career transition (e.g., athletic identity, demographic issues, voluntariness of the decision, injuries/ health problems, financial status), and available resources during the transition (e.g., coping strategies, pre-retirement planning, psychosocial support). Practical implications such as the provision of proactive (e.g. education in transferable skills) and reactive support (e.g., supporting their identity reformation process) are provided.

2.   Stambulova, N. (2010). Counseling athletes in career transitions: The five-step career planning strategy. *Journal of Sport Psychology in Action, 1,* 95–105. doi: 10.1080/21520704.2010.528829

This paper presents a counselling framework to help athletes in their career transition, termed the Five-Step Career Planning Strategy (5-SCP). The 5-SCP is a framework to facilitate consultant-athlete communication aimed to increase awareness of past experiences, present situation, and future perspectives in sport and out of sport. The first two stages deal with how the athlete structures the past. The third stage focuses on the identification of most important spheres of current life and the evaluation of the balance among them. The fourth stage deals with the anticipation of the future, while the last stage focuses on lessons learned and coping resources developed. The paper also provides a review of reflections on the application of the model.

Note

1   Sisu is a uniquely Finnish personality trait and a state of mind that is said to typify Finnish spirit of inner strength, endurance, resilience, tenacity, determination, and perseverance. It is also a cultural norm and a value that all Finns are proud to have.

References

Alfermann, D., Stambulova, N., & Zemaityte, A. (2004). Reactions to sport career termination: A cross-national comparison of German, Lithuanian, and Russian athletes. *Psychology of Sport & Exercise,* 5(1), 61–75. doi:10.1016/S1469-0292(02)00050-X.

American Psychological Association. (2010). 2010 Amendments to the 2002 "Ethical principles of psychologists and code of conduct". *American Psychologist,* 65(5), 493. www.apa.org/ethics/code/.

Arvinen-Barrow, M., Clement, D., & Hemmings, B. (2013). Imagery in sport injury rehabilitation. In M. Arvinen-Barrow & N. Walker (Eds.), *Psychology of sport injury and rehabilitation* (pp. 71–85). Abingdon: Routledge.

Arvinen-Barrow, M., DeGrave, K., Pack, S. M., & Hemmings, B. (forthcoming). Transitioning out of professional sport: The psychosocial impact of career-ending non-musculoskeletal injuries among male cricketers from England and Wales. *Journal of Clinical Sport Psychology.* doi:10.1123/jcsp.2017-0040.

Arvinen-Barrow, M., Hurley, D., & Ruiz, M. C. (2017). Transitioning out of professional sport: The psychosocial impact of career-ending injuries among elite Irish rugby football union players. *Journal of Clinical Sport Psychology,* 10(1). doi:10.1123/jcsp.2016-0012.

Arvinen-Barrow, M., Nässi, A., & Ruiz, M. C. (2015). Kun vamma päättää, milloin ura loppuu. [When injury determines when the career ends]. *Liikunta ja Tiede,* 52(6), 45–49.

Brewer, B. W., & Cornelius, A. E. (2001). Norms and factorial invariance of the Athletic Identity Measurement Scale. *Academic Athletic Journal,* 15, 103–113.

Brewer, B. W., Cornelius, A. E., Stephan, Y., & Van Raalte, J. L. (2010). Self-protective changes in athletic identity following anterior cruciate ligament reconstruction. *Psychology of Sport & Exercise,* 11(1), 1–5. doi:10.1016/j.psychsport.2009.09.005.

Brewer, B. W., Van Raalte, J. L., & Linder, D. E. (1993). Athletic identity: Hercules' muscles or Achilles' heel? *International Journal of Sport Psychology,* 24(2), 237–254.

Carver, C., Scheier, M., & Weintraub, J. (1989). Assessing coping strategies: A theoretically based approach. *Journal of Personality and Social Psychology*, 56(2), 267–283.

Crocker, P. R. E., & Graham, T. R. (1995). Coping by competitive athletes with performance stress: Gender differences and relationships with affect. *The Sport Psychologist*, 9(3), 325–338. doi:10.1123/tsp.9.3.325.

Crook, J. M., & Robertson, S. E. (1991). Transition out of elite sport. *International Journal of Sport Psychology*, 22, 115–127.

Deci, E. L., & Ryan, R. M. (1985). *Intrinsic motivation and self-determinaton in human behaviour*. New York, NY: Plenum.

Falls, N., Barker, J. B., & Turner, M. J. (2018). The effects of eye movement desensitization and reprocessing on prospective imagery and anxiety in golfers. *Journal of Applied Sport Psychology*, 30(2), 171–184. doi:10.1080/10413200.2017.1345999.

Gross, J. J. (2014). Emotion regulation: Conceptual and empirical foundations. In J. J. Gross (Ed.), *Handbook of emotion regulation* (2nd ed., pp. 3–20). New York, NY: The Guilford Press.

Grove, R. J., Lavallee, D., & Gordon, S. (1997). Coping with retirement from sport: The influence of athletic identity. *Journal of Applied Sport Psychology*, 9(2), 191–203. doi:10.1080/10413209708406481.

Hillman, J. L. (2002). *Crisis Intervention and trauma: New approaches to evidence-based practice*. New York, NY: Plenum Publishers.

Laprade, R. F., & Wijdicks, C. A. (2012). The management of injuries to the medial side of the knee. *Journal of Orthopaedic & Sports Physical Therapy*, 42(3), 221–233. doi:10.2519/jospt.2012.3624.

Lavallee, D. (2005). The effect of a life development intervention on sports career transition adjustment. *The Sport Psychologist*, 19(2), 193–202. doi:10.1123/tsp.19.2.193.

Lazarus, R. S. (2006). Emotions and interpersonal relationships: Toward a person-centered conceptualization of emotions and coping. *Journal of Personality*, 74(1), 9–46. doi:10.1111/j.1467-6494.2005.00368.x.

Lazarus, R. S., & Folkman, S. (1984). *Stress, appraisal, and coping*. New York, NY: Springer Publishing Company.

Luber, M. (Ed.). (2016). *Eye movement desensitization and reprocessing (EMDR): Therapy scripted protocols and summary sheets*. New York, NY: Springer Publishing Company.

Mankad, A., Gordon, S., & Wallman, K. (2009). Perceptions of emotional climate among injured athletes. *Journal of Clinical Sport Psychology*, 3(1), 1–14. doi:10.1123/jcsp.3.1.1.

Millett, P. J., Wickiewicz, T. L., & Warren, R. F. (2001). Motion loss after ligament injuries to the knee: Part II: Prevention and treatment. *American Journal of Sports Medicine*, 29(6), 822–828. doi:10.1177/03635465010290062701.

Mischke-Reeds, M. (2018). *Somatic psychotherapy toolbox*. Eau Claire, WI: PESI Publishing & Media.

Oyserman, D., Elmore, K., & Smith, G. (2012). Self, self-concept, and identity. In M. R. Leary & J. P. Tangney (Eds.), *Handbook of self and identity* (2nd ed., pp. 69–104). New York, NY: The Guilford Press.

Parkar, A. P. (2016). Imaging the anterior and posterior cruciate ligaments. *Journal of the Belgian Society of Radiology*, 100(1), 1–12. doi:10.5334/jbr-btr.1197.

Phisitkul, P., James, S. L., Wolf, B. R., & Amendola, A. (2006). MCL injuries of the knee: Current concepts review. *The Iowa Orthopaedic Journal*, 26, 77–90.

Podlog, L., & Dionigi, R. (2010). Coach strategies for addressing psychosocial challenges during the return to sport from injury. *Journal of Sports Sciences*, 28(11), 1197–1208. doi:10.1080/02640414.2010.487873.

Rivett, M., & Buchmüller, J. (2018). *Family therapy skills and techniques in action*. New York, NY: Routledge.

Robazza, C., & Ruiz, M. C. (2018). Emotional self-regulation in sport and performance. In O. Braddick (Ed.), *Oxford Research Encyclopedia of Psychology*. Oxford: Oxford University Press. Retrieved from http://psychology.oxfordre.com/view/10.1093/acrefore/9780190236557.001.0001/acrefore-9780190236557-e-154. doi:10.1093/acrefore/9780190236557.013.154.

Roberts, C.-M., Mullen, R., Evans, L., & Hall, R. (2015). An in-depth appraisal of career termination experiences in professional cricket. *Journal of Sports Sciences*, 33(9), 935–944. doi:10.1080/02640414.2014.977936.

Ryan, R. M., & Deci, E. L. (2017). *Self-determination theory: Basic psychological needs in motivation, development, and wellness*. New York, NY: The Guilford Press.

Shanmugam, V., & Jowett, S. (2017). Creating a successful and effective coaching environment through interpersonal sports coaching. In S. Cotterill, N. J. V. Weston & G. Breslin (Eds.), *Sport and exercise psychology: Practitioner case studies* (pp. 215–239). London: Wiley-Blackwell.

Shapiro, F. (2017). *Eye movement desensitization and reprocessing: Basic principles, protocols, and procedures* (3rd ed.). New York, NY: Guilford Press.

Stambulova, N. (2000). Athlete's crises: A developmental perspective. *International Journal of Sport Psychology, 31*(4), 584–601.

Stambulova, N., Stephan, Y., & Jäphag, U. (2007). Athletic retirement: A cross-national comparison of elite French and Swedish athletes. *Psychology of Sport & Exercise, 8*(1), 101–118. doi:10.1016/j.psychsport.2006.05.002.

Stoltenburg, A. L., Kamphoff, C. S., & Lindstrom Bremer, K. (2011). Transitioning out of sport: The psychosocial effects of collegiate athletes' career-ending injuries. *Athletic Insight*, 11(2), 1–11.

Taylor, J., & Ogilvie, B. (1994). A conceptual model of adaptation to retirement among athletes. *Journal of Applied Sport Psychology*, 6(1), 1–20. doi:10.1080/10413209408406462.

Udry, E. (2001). The role of significant others: Social support during injuries. In J. Crossman (Ed.), *Coping with sports injuries: Psychological strategies for rehabilitation* (pp. 148–161). Oxford: University Press.

Venter, R., & Grobbelaar, R. (2018). Perceptions and practices of recovery modalities in elite team athletes. In M. Kellerman & J. Beckmann (Eds.), *Sport, recovery, and performance: Interdisciplinary insights* (pp. 33–48). New York, NY: Routledge.

Walker, N., & Heaney, C. (2013). Relaxation techniques in sport injury rehabilitation. In M. Arvinen-Barrow & N. Walker (Eds.), *Psychology of sport injury and rehabilitation* (pp. 86–102). Abingdon: Routledge.

Webb, W. M., Nasco, S. A., Riley, S., & Headrick, B. (1998). Athlete identity and reactions to retirement from sport. *Journal of Sport Behavior*, 21(3), 338–362.

Weinberg, R. S., & Gould, D. (2015). *Foundations of sport and exercise psychology* (6th ed.). Champaign, IL: Human Kinetics.

Werthner, P., & Orlick, T. (1982). Retirement experiences of successful Olympic athletes. *International Journal of Sport Psychology*, 17, 331–363.

11

CASE MADE! WHAT'S NEXT?

Damien Clement and Monna Arvinen-Barrow

It was the aim of the book to demonstrate how *interprofessional* teams can work in an *interdisciplinary*, or, in some cases, *transdisciplinary* or *multidisciplinary* manner to use appropriate *psychological interventions* to address identified *key factors* within their own professional competencies to achieve mutually agreed goals for each injured performer. Within the book, nine unique "real-life inspired" fictional cases were presented, each focused on a specific phase of the injury rehabilitation process (Kamphoff, Thomae, & Hamson-Utley, 2013). Relevant factors associated with each case were discussed and conceptualized using relevant theoretical frameworks. Interprofessional care plans were formulated and discussed from three different, interprofessional perspectives relevant to the case.

In conceptualizing the book, the editors purposefully chose representation of injured performers from a variety of sport and performance domains. These "real-life inspired" fictional sport and performance injury cases have been carefully selected to focus on the three phases of rehabilitation: the reactions to injury, reactions to rehabilitation, and reactions to return to participation (Kamphoff et al., 2013), and in the case of Pekka Hirvonen, reactions to a career ending injury. Each case is also evaluated from three perspectives highlighting the importance of an interprofessional approach to sport and performance injury rehabilitation.

Despite the book containing a range of sport and performance settings, myriad of different injuries, and key factors influencing the post-injury responses, one common theme appeared to be constant across all cases. In each case, when examining it from the injured performer's perspective, there appeared to be cyclical interactions between the performer's thoughts, emotions, and behaviors, which in turn influenced their overall recovery and rehabilitation outcomes. This is not surprising, as both theoretical (e.g., Brewer, Andersen, & Van Raalte, 2002; Wiese-Bjornstal, Smith, Shaffer, & Morrey, 1998; Wiese-Bjornstal, White, Russell, & Smith, 2015) and empirical (e.g., Clement, Arvinen-Barrow, & Fetty, 2015;

Ruddock-Hudson, O'Halloran, & Murphy, 2014; Wiese-Bjornstal, 2010) evidence in support of the cyclical interaction has been well established in the literature.

When examining the cases presented from a practitioner's perspective, it is also clear that typically the primary treatment provider coordinates care for the injured performer. In most cases this is the athletic trainer or the physiotherapists. Such is in line with previous research (Arvinen-Barrow & Clement, 2015, 2017a, 2017b), and makes sense from competency, proximity, and trust/rapport/professional relationship perspective. Sport medicine professionals are, due to their unique position with the injured performer, in an ideal position to facilitate holistic, biopsychosocial care (Kolt & Andersen, 2004). However, they should do so within their professional competencies, and most importantly, recognize the need for referral when the performer shows signs and symptoms of psychological distress beyond normal responses while injured.

When it comes to using psychological interventions with injured performers, the cases presented also revealed a prominent theme. In all cases, sports medicine professionals (i.e., athletic trainers, physiotherapist) all appeared to focus on interventions that promote injury education, and facilitate adherence. These interventions, i.e., patient-education and goal-setting, are both strategies that sports medicine professionals are typically well-versed and trained in (Arvinen-Barrow, Hemmings, Weigand, Becker, & Booth, 2007; Arvinen-Barrow, Penny, Hemmings, & Corr, 2010; Clement, Granquist, & Arvinen-Barrow, 2013; Hamson-Utley & Stiller-Ostrowski, 2014; Zakrajsek, Fisher, & Martin, 2016), and can be very effective ways to facilitate positive changes in injured performers' cognitive appraisals of injury, as well as the resultant emotional and behavioral responses to injury (for more details, see Arvinen-Barrow & Walker, 2013; Ayers & de Visser, 2018; Brewer & Redmond, 2017).

Similarly, the cases also highlight the need to ensure that appropriately trained mental health/psychology professionals are within their competencies in using a range of psychological strategies with injured performers. What is evident from our cases is that professional competencies, as well as professional titles, can vary greatly depending on the country in which an individual is operating. As a rule of thumb however, it can be concluded that any psychological concern that is clinical in nature and classifiable by the Diagnostic and Statistical Manual of Mental Disorders (DSM-5) classification (American Psychiatric Association, 2013), should be treated by a licensed, clinically trained mental health professional.

Lastly, the cases also highlight the significant role of professionals and individuals outside of psychology of injury and sports medicine as being integral to successful injury rehabilitation. Depending on the specific personal and/or situational factors influencing the injured performers' responses, these can include members of their immediate families, and/or educational and spiritual communities. For instance, in one of the chapters, the performer presented with body image concerns, thus a dietician was included in the interprofessional team. In cases involving students, relevant members of the educational institution were included to ensure holistic care. In the case of Pekka Hirvonen who sustained a career ending injury, his wife was included in the interprofessional team. As demonstrated in the book, the composition of the interprofessional team can vary greatly. What is common among these individuals is that typically their role is to provide support to the injured performer, and this support can be emotional, motivational, tangible, technical, material, or spiritual, to name a few (Arvinen-Barrow & Pack, 2013; Clement, Arvinen-Barrow, & LaGuerre, 2019; Cohen & Wills, 1985; Crossman, 1997; Hardy, Burke, & Crace, 2007; Rosenfeld, Richman, & Hardy, 1989; Udry, 2001).

The cases presented in this book also provide the reader with tangible proof that the psychology of injury and sports medicine research and applied practice are in the midst of a transition. Traditionally, injured performers have been primarily cared for by a lone physician, whose focus was exclusively on the physiological aspects related to recovery (Hess, Gnacinski, & Meyer, forthcoming). This book demonstrates that such is no longer the case, while also highlighting that in many professional settings, adopting a transdisciplinary approach (Karol, 2014) is also not common practice (yet). Instead, the cases in this book represent the "middle ground" in professional practice approaches to sport and performance injury care, where depending on the individual case in question and the environment where the rehabilitation takes place, the practitioners have adopted an approach more in line with multidisciplinary and interdisciplinary approaches.

While not a comprehensive list, the cases in this book also highlight several key components for successful interprofessional collaboration. First, the interprofessional team members need to have "good lines of communication, mutual respect and rapport" (MacClean, 2010, p. 19). Second, the roles within the team need to be clearly defined so that objectives, responsibilities, and expected outcomes are established (Jones, 2005). Third, the team members need to be cognizant of their respective professional competencies, possible overlap in such competencies, and to ensure they "provide only those services and use only those techniques for which they are qualified by education, training, or experience"(Whelan, 2011). Lastly, in order to utilize their relevant expertise appropriately, team members need to be "culturally knowledgeable and sensitive" (Matthews, Mehta Barden, & Sherrell, 2018, p. 130). In other words, they must possess an acute awareness of their own cultural biases and assumptions and know how such might influence their work (American Counseling Association, 2014).

The interprofessional literature to date propose that teamwork among professionals produces better results (Kniffin & Hanks, 2018). However to fully understand how this happens in sport and performance injury rehabilitation setting, more research is needed. In particular, the editors are calling for research where the team approach used is grounded in appropriate theoretical approaches (e.g., Clement & Arvinen-Barrow, 2013; Dijkstra, Pollock, Chakraverty, & Alonso, 2014; Meyer, Merkur, Ebersole, & Massey, 2014) and consistent with existing practical guidelines for effective teamwork. Equally any psychological interventions implemented should be theoretically conceptualized (e.g., Brewer et al., 2002; Wiese-Bjornstal et al., 1998) in relation to desired biopsychosocial outcomes and evaluated using valid and reliable outcome measures for the population in question. Lastly, the editors also call for all psychological interventions to be designed and implemented following existing theoretical and empirical evidence to date (for more details on psychological interventions in injury rehabilitation see Arvinen-Barrow & Walker, 2013; Brewer & Redmond, 2017), and to be delivered by professionals adequately trained to do so.

As demonstrated in the earlier chapters, this book has been founded on a premise that sport and performance injury should be interprofessional, person-centered, and case-based. By adopting such an approach, any and all individuals involved in the process should work together in a team-based manner to identify key factors of concern, as well as design and deliver multidimensional treatment plans and interventions. It is the intent of this book to be a useful additional resource for students, researchers, and applied practitioners when considering the implementation of an interprofessional team approach to sport and performance injury rehabilitation. The editors hope that the cases presented will inspire additional interprofessional collaborations amongst professionals working within the sport and performance injury rehabilitation context.

> Unity is strength. When there is teamwork and collaboration wonderful things can be achieved
>
> *(unknown)*

References

American Counseling Association. (2014). *ACA code of ethics*. Alexandria, VA: American Counseling Association.

American Psychiatric Association. (2013). *Diagnostic and statistical manual of mental disorders (DSM–5)* (5th ed.). Washington, DC: American Psychiatric Publishing.

Arvinen-Barrow, M., & Clement, D. (2015). A preliminary investigation into athletic trainers' views and experiences of a multidisciplinary team approach to sports injury rehabilitation. *Athletic Training and Sports Health Care, 7*(3), 97–107. doi:10.3928/19425864-20150422-05.

Arvinen-Barrow, M., & Clement, D. (2017a). A Preliminary investigation into sport and exercise psychology consultants' views and experiences of an interprofessional care team approach to sport injury rehabilitation. *Journal of Interprofessional Care, 31*(1), 66–74. doi:10.1080/13561820.2016.1235019.

Arvinen-Barrow, M., & Clement, D. (2017b). A preliminary investigation into previously injured athletes' views and experiences of a rehabilitation team approach to sport injury rehabilitation. Unpublished manuscript.

Arvinen-Barrow, M., Hemmings, B., Weigand, D. A., Becker, C. A., & Booth, L. (2007). Views of chartered physiotherapists on the psychological content of their practice: A national follow-up survey in the United Kingdom. *Journal of Sport Rehabilitation, 16*(2), 111–121. doi:10.1123/jsr.16.2.111.

Arvinen-Barrow, M., & Pack, S. M. (2013). Social support in sport injury rehabilitation. In M. Arvinen-Barrow & N. Walker (Eds.), *Psychology of sport injury and rehabilitation* (pp. 117–131). Abingdon: Routledge.

Arvinen-Barrow, M., Penny, G., Hemmings, B., & Corr, S. (2010). UK chartered physiotherapists' personal experiences in using psychological interventions with injured athletes:

An interpretative phenomenological analysis. *Psychology of Sport & Exercise*, 11(1), 58–66. doi:10.1016/j.psychsport.2009.05.004.

Arvinen-Barrow, M., & Walker, N. (Eds.). (2013). *Psychology of sport injury and rehabilitation*. Abingdon: Routledge.

Ayers, S., & de Visser, R. (2018). *Psychology for medicine and healthcare* (2nd ed.). Thousand Oaks, CA: Sage Publications.

Brewer, B. W., Andersen, M. B., & Van Raalte, J. L. (2002). Psychological aspects of sport injury rehabilitation: Toward a biopsychological approach. In D. L. Mostofsky & L. D. Zaichkowsky (Eds.), *Medical aspects of sport and exercise* (pp. 41–54). Morgantown, WV: Fitness Information Technology.

Brewer, B. W., & Redmond, C. J. (2017). *Psychology of sport Injury*. Champaign, IL: Human Kinetics.

Clement, D., & Arvinen-Barrow, M. (2013). Sport medicine team influences in psychological rehabilitation: A multidisciplinary approach. In M. Arvinen-Barrow & N. Walker (Eds.), *The psychology of sport injury and rehabilitation* (pp. 156–170). Abingdon: Routledge.

Clement, D., Arvinen-Barrow, M., & Fetty, T. (2015). Psychosocial responses during different phases of sport injury rehabilitation: A qualitative study. *Journal of Athletic Training*, 50(1), 95–104. doi:10.4085/1062-6050-49.3.52.

Clement, D., Arvinen-Barrow, M., & LaGuerre, D. (2019). Role of religion and spirituality in sport injury rehabilitation. In B. Hemmings, N. J. Watson & A. Parker (Eds.), *Sport, psychology and Christianity: Welfare, performance and consultancy*. Abingdon: Routledge.

Clement, D., Granquist, M. D., & Arvinen-Barrow, M. (2013). Psychosocial aspects of athletic injuries as perceived by athletic trainers. *Journal of Athletic Training*, 48(4), 512–521. doi:10.4085/1062-6050-49.3.52.

Cohen, S., & Wills, T. A. (1985). Stress, social support, and the buffering hypothesis. *Psychological Bulletin*, 98, 310–357.

Crossman, J. (1997). Psychological rehabilitation from sports injuries. *Sports Medicine*, 23(5), 333–339.

Dijkstra, P. H., Pollock, N., Chakraverty, R., & Alonso, J. M. (2014). Managing the health of the elite athlete: A new integrated performance health management and coaching model. *British Journal of Sports Medicine*, 48(7), 523–531. doi:10.1136/bjsports-2013-093222.

Hamson-Utley, J. J., & Stiller-Ostrowski, J. L. (2014). Introduction to psychosocial aspects of athletic training. In M. D. Granquist, J. J. Hamson-Utley, L. Kenow & J. Stiller-Ostrowski (Eds.), *Psychosocial strategies for athletic training* (pp. 1–25). Philadelphia, PA: F.A. Davis Company.

Hardy, C. J., Burke, K. L., & Crace, R. K. (2007). Social support and injury: A framework for social support-based interventions with injured athletes. In D. Pargman (Ed.), *Psychological bases of sport injuries* (pp. 175–198). Morgantown, WV: Fitness Information Technology.

Hess, C. W., Gnacinski, S. L., & Meyer, B. B. (forthcoming). A review of the sport injury and rehabilitation literature: From abstraction to application. *The Sport Psychologist*.

Jones, M. L. (2005). Role development and effective practice in specialist and advanced practice roles in acute hospital settings: Systematic review and meta-synthesis. *Journal of Advanced Nursing*, 49(2), 191–209. doi:10.1111/j.1365-2648.2004.03279.x.

Kamphoff, C., Thomae, J., & Hamson-Utley, J. J. (2013). Integrating the psychological and physiological aspects of sport injury rehabilitation: Rehabilitation profiling and phases of rehabilitation. In M. Arvinen-Barrow & N. Walker (Eds.), *Psychology of sport injury and rehabilitation* (pp. 134–155). Abingdon, UK: Routledge.

Karol, R. L. (2014). Team models in neurorehabilitation: Structure, function, and culture change. *NeuroRehabilitation*, 34, 655–669.

Kniffin, K. M., & Hanks, A. S. (2018). The trade-offs of teamwork among STEM doctoral graduates. *American Psychologist*, 73(4), 420–432. doi:10.1037/amp0000288.

Kolt, G. S., & Andersen, M. B. (Eds.). (2004). *Psychology in the physical and manual therapies*. Philadelphia: Churchill Livingstone.

MacLean, C. (2010). Patient education: sharing a passion, sharing resources. *Canadian Family Physician* • *Le Médecin de famille canadien*, 56(7), 721.

Matthews, J. J., Mehta Barden, S., & Sherrell, R. S. (2018). Examining the relationships between multicultural counseling competence, multicultural self-efficacy, and ethnic identity development of practicing counselors. *Journal of Mental Health Counseling*, 40, 129–141. doi:10.17744/mehc.40.2.03.

Meyer, B. B., Merkur, A., Ebersole, K. T., & Massey, W. V. (2014). The realities of working in elite sport. What they didn't teach you in graduate school. In A. M. Lane, R. J. Godfrey, M. Loosemore & G. P. Whyte (Eds.), *Applied sport science and medicine: Case studies from practice* (pp. 137–142). CreateSpace: Self-published.

Rosenfeld, L. B., Richman, J. M., & Hardy, C. J. (1989). Examining social support networks among athletes: Description and relationship to stress. *The Sport Psychologist*, 3, 23–33.

Ruddock-Hudson, M., O'Halloran, P., & Murphy, G. (2014). The psychological impact of long-term injury on Australian football league players. *Journal of Applied Sport Psychology*, 26(4), 377–394. doi:10.1080/10413200.2014.897269.

Udry, E. (2001). The role of significant others: Social support during injuries. In J. Crossman (Ed.), *Coping with sports injuries: Psychological strategies for rehabilitation* (pp. 148–161). Oxford: University Press.

Whelan, J. (2011). Ethics code: AASP ethical principles and standards. Retrieved September 26, 2018, from https://appliedsportpsych.org/about/ethics/ethics-code/.

Wiese-Bjornstal, D. M. (2010). Psychology and socioculture affect injury risk, response, and recovery in high-intensity athletes: a consensus statement. *Scandinavian Journal of Medicine & Science in sports*, 20, 103–111.

Wiese-Bjornstal, D. M., Smith, A. M., Shaffer, S. M., & Morrey, M. A. (1998). An integrated model of response to sport injury: Psychological and sociological dynamics. *Journal of Applied Sport Psychology*, 10(1), 46–69. doi:10.1080/10413209808406377.

Wiese-Bjornstal, D. M., White, A. C., Russell, H. C., & Smith, A. M. (2015). Psychology of sport concussions. *Kinesiology Review*, 5, 169–189. doi:10.1123/kr.2015-0012.

Zakrajsek, R. A., Fisher, L. A., & Martin, S. B. (2016). Certified athletic trainers' understanding and use of sport psychology in their practice. *Journal of Applied Sport Psychology*. doi:10.1080/10413200.2016.1231722.

INDEX

RED-S *see* Relative Energy Deficiency in Sports (RED-S)
Reel, J. J. 117
Reese, Schwab 65
referral network 89, 92
referral process 142
reflective listening 30
reframing 17, 74–5, 87–8, 105
Rehabilitation Adherence Measure for Athletic Training (RAdMAT) 64
rehabilitation non-adherence 64
Rehabilitation Over-Adherence Questionnaire (ROAQ) 134
re-injury anxiety 101–2, 132–3, 138
Re-Injury Anxiety Inventory (RIAI) 102, 133
Relative Energy Deficiency in Sports (RED-S) 90
relaxation: with imagery 74,137–8, 155–6; strategy 16–17, 155; training 106
relief 48, 71, 154, 157
retirement planning 151
return-to-duty (RTD) 114–25; controllable and uncontrollable factors influencing **124**; ethical considerations 124; external locus of control 117; interprofessional plan of care 119–24; isolation and loss of a soldier identity 117–18; lack of confidence in 116; nurse practitioners' perspective 123–4; overview 114–15; physical therapist's perspective 121–2; SPC on 119–21; theoretical considerations 118–19
return to participation 3, 165
return-to-play 18, 64
return-to-sport (RTS) 44
RIAI *see* Re-Injury Anxiety Inventory (RIAI)
ROAQ *see* Rehabilitation Over-adherence Questionnaire (ROAQ)
role clarity 37
rotator cuff tendonitis: AT on 106–8; clarinet professor's perspective 108; cognitive and somatic anxiety 101; description 100–1; ethical considerations 108–9; interprofessional plan of care 104–8; licensed psychologist perspective 104–6; over-adherence 102–3; overview 99–100; re-injury anxiety 101–2; theoretical considerations 103
RTD *see* return-to-duty (RTD)
RTS *see* return-to-sport (RTS)
Ryan, R. E.54, 89,116, 118, 125, 158

Sabo, M. 103
sadness 28–9, 50, 63–4, 67, 72, 140, 154

SDT *see* self-determination theory (SDT)
self-compassion exercise 49, **49**, 50, 56, 120, 133
self-determination theory: autonomy 34, 70–1, 88–9, 102, 118–19, 123–5, 158–9; relatedness 88–9, 118–20, 125, 158–9; competence 22, 89, 91, 109, 118–119, 122, 125, 136, 158–9; *see also* BPNT
self-efficacy theory 108
self-regulation 50, 74, 155; down-regulation 155; up-regulation 155
self-talk 16, 20–2, 49, 125; negative self-talk 74, 101, 120–1; positive self-talk 16; *see also* cognitive restructuring; reframing; thought stopping
Shanmugam, V. 159
simulation training 136
Sisu 162n1
sleep diary 33
sleep patterns 33
SMART *see* specific, measureable, achievable, realistic, and time bound (SMART) goals
smartphone sleep app 33
Smith, B. 134
SOAP notes 29
social support 35; AT's as 70; and athletes' adaptation 152; emotional support 46, 48, 65, 108, 157; informational support 54, 138; limited 45–6; spiritual support 32; tangible support 127; technical support 108, 109
Social Support Survey (SSS) 46
Socratic approach 138, 140
somatic anxiety 101
SP *see* sport psychologist (SP)
Sparkes, A. 135
Sparkes, A. C. 134
SPC *see* sport psychology consultant (SPC)
specific, measureable, achievable, realistic, and time bound (SMART) goals 20, 52, 122
spirituality 27, 30, 36
sport anxiety model 103
sport dietician 166
sport injury rehabilitation *see* specific types of rehabilitation
sport and performance injury: prevention 1, 18, 72, 81, 86, 90, 115; rehabilitation 4–6, 165, 167–8; return to participation process 3, 116, 136, 165
sport psychologist (SP) 115, 132, 136–8, 153–7
sport psychology consultant (SPC) 47, 56, 119; on hamstring strain 137–40; on RTD 119–21; on UCL 48–51